The Economics of Uncertainty and Insurance

Kindle Direct Publishing; 1st edition (February 2019)

ISBN: 9781796685015

Giacomo Bonanno is Professor of Economics at the
University of California, Davis
http://faculty.econ.ucdavis.edu/faculty/bonanno/

Preface

In the last three years I wrote two open access textbooks: one on *Game Theory* (`http://faculty.econ.ucdavis.edu/faculty/bonanno/GT_Book.html`) and the other on *Decision Making* (`http://faculty.econ.ucdavis.edu/faculty/bonanno/DM_Book.html`). Encouraged by the many expressions of appreciation from students and scholars around the world, I decided to write a third textbook: this time on the *Economics of Uncertainty and Insurance*. I have been teaching an upper-division undergraduate class on this topic at the University of California, Davis for 25 years and was not able to find a suitable textbook. Hopefully this book will fill this gap.

I tried to write the book in such a way that it would be accessible to anybody with minimum knowledge of calculus (the ability to calculate the derivative of a function of one variable). The book is appropriate for an upper-division undergraduate class, although some parts of it might be useful also to graduate students.

I have followed the same format as the other two books, by concluding each chapter with a collection of exercises that are grouped according to that chapter's sections. Complete and detailed answers for each exercise are given in the last section of each chapter. The book contains a total of 88 fully solved exercises. It is also richly illustrated with 80 Figures.

I expect that there will be some typos and (hopefully, minor) mistakes. If you come across any typos or mistakes, I would be grateful if you could inform me: I can be reached at `gfbonanno@ucdavis.edu`. I will maintain an updated version of the book on my web page at

`http://www.econ.ucdavis.edu/faculty/bonanno/`

I intend to add, some time in the future, a further collection of exercises with detailed solutions. Details will appear on my web page.

I am very grateful to Elise Tidrick for teaching me how to use spacing and formatting in a (perhaps unconventional) way that makes it easier for the reader to learn the material.

I would like to thank Mathias Legrand for making the latex template used for this book available for free (the template was downloaded from `http://www.latextemplates.com/template/the-legrand-orange-book`).

Contents

1. Introduction

This book offers an introduction to economic analysis under uncertainty, with particular focus on insurance markets.

Life is made up of a never-ending sequence of decisions. Many decisions – such as what to watch on television or what to eat for breakfast – do not have major consequences. Other decisions – such as whether or not to invest all of one's savings in the purchase of a house, or whether to purchase earthquake insurance – can have a significant impact on one's life. We will concern ourselves with decisions that potentially have a considerable impact on the wealth of the individual in question.

Most of the time the outcome of a decision is influenced by external factors that are outside the decision maker's control, such as the side effects of a new drug, or the future price of real estate, or the occurrence of a natural phenomenon (such as a flood, or a fire, or an earthquake). While one is typically aware of the existence of such external factors, as the saying goes "It is difficult to make predictions, especially about the future".[1] Most decisions are shrouded in uncertainty and this book is about how uncertainty affects the actions and decisions of economic agents.

We begin by examining, in **Chapter 2**, what explains the existence and profitability of insurance markets. For this we simply appeal to the definition of risk aversion, without the need for the full power of expected utility theory.

Chapter 3 develops the Theory of Expected Utility, which is central to the rest of the book.

In **Chapter 4** we use the theory of expected utility to re-examine the notion of attitude to risk (risk aversion, risk neutrality and risk love), discuss how to measure the degree of risk aversion of an individual and develop a test for determining when, of two alternative risky prospects, one can unambiguously be labeled as being more risky than the other.

---

[1]This saying is often attributed to the physicist Niels Bohr, but apparently it is an old Danish proverb.

With the help of expected utility theory, in **Chapter 5** study the demand side of insurance markets. We then put together the analysis of the supply side of insurance, developed in Chapter 2, with the analysis of the demand side, to determine the equilibrium of an insurance industry under two opposite scenarios: the case where the industry is a monopoly and the case where there is perfect competition with free entry.

Chapter 6 is devoted to the phenomenon of "moral hazard" in insurance, namely the situation where the probability that the insured individual will face a loss – and thus apply for a reimbursement from the insurance company – is affected by the behavior of the individual, in particular by the effort and care exerted in loss prevention.

Up to Chapter 6 the analysis is focused on the case where the potential customers of an insurance company are essentially identical, that is, face the same circumstances. **Chapter 7** is devoted to the analysis of "adverse selection" in insurance markets. This is the situation where there are different types of individuals, with different propensities to incur losses, and – while each individual knows his or her own type – the insurance company does not. Thus it is a situation of "asymmetric information". We study how asymmetric information affects the decisions of the suppliers of insurance and re-examine the conditions for an equilibrium in the two types of industry structure examined in Chapter 5, namely monopoly and perfect competition.

At the end of each section of each of Chapters 2-7 the reader is invited to test his/her understanding of the concepts introduced in that section by attempting several exercises. In order not to break the flow of the exposition, the exercises are collected in a section at the end of the chapter. Complete and detailed answers for each exercise are given in the last section of each chapter. In total, the book contains 88 fully solved exercises. Attempting to solve the exercises is an integral part of learning the material covered in this book.

The book was written in a way that should be accessible to anyone with minimum knowledge of calculus, in particular the ability to calculate the derivative of a function of one real variable. In order to aid understanding of the concepts, many figures are used throughout the book, for a total of 80.

This book does not necessarily follow conventional formatting standards. Rather, the intention was to break each argument into clearly outlined steps, highlighted by appropriate spacing.

2. Insurance: basic notions

2.1 Uncertainty and lotteries

Most of the important decisions that we make in life are made difficult by the presence of uncertainty: the final outcome is influenced by external factors that we cannot control and we cannot predict with certainty. Because of such external factors, any given decision will typically be associated with different outcomes, depending on what "state of the world" will actually occur. If the decision-maker is able to assign probabilities to these external factors – and thus to the associated outcomes – then one can represent the uncertainty that the decision maker faces as a list of possible outcomes, each with a corresponding probability. We call such lists *lotteries*.

For example, suppose that Ann and Bob are planning their wedding reception. They have a large number of guests and face the choice between two venues: a spacious outdoor area where the guests will be able to roam around or a small indoor area where the guests will feel rather crammed. Ann and Bob want their reception to be a success and their guests to feel comfortable. It seems that the large outdoor area is a better choice; however, there is also an external factor that needs to be taken into account, namely the weather. If it does not rain, then the outdoor area will yield the best outcome (success: denote this outcome by o_1) but if it does rain then the outdoor area will give rise to the worst outcome (failure: denote this outcome by o_3). On the other hand, if Ann and Bob choose the indoor venue, then the corresponding outcome will be a less successful reception but not a failure (call this outcome o_2). Let us denote the possible outcomes as follows:

$$o_1 : \quad \text{successful reception}$$
$$o_2 : \quad \text{mediocre reception}$$
$$o_3 : \quad \text{failed reception.}$$

Clearly they prefer o_1 to o_2 and o_2 to o_3. At the time of deciding which venue to pay for, Ann and Bob do not know what the weather will be like on their wedding day. The most they can do is consult a weather forecast service and obtain probabilistic estimates. Suppose that the forecast service predicts a 30% chance of rain on the day in question. Then we can represent the decision to book the outdoor venue as the following lottery

$$\left(\begin{array}{lcc} \text{outcome:} & o_1 & o_3 \\ \text{probability:} & 0.7 & 0.3 \end{array} \right)$$

On the other hand, the decision to book the indoor venue corresponds to the following degenerate lottery:

$$\left(\begin{array}{lc} \text{outcome:} & o_2 \\ \text{probability:} & 1 \end{array} \right)$$

Throughout this book we will represent the uncertainty facing a decision-maker in terms of lotteries.[1] This assumes that the decision-maker is always able to assign probabilities to the possible outcomes. We interpret these probabilities either as "objective" probabilities, obtained from relevant past data, or as "subjective" estimates by the individual. For example, an individual who is considering whether or not to insure her bicycle against theft, knows that there are two relevant basic outcomes: either the bicycle will be stolen or it will not be stolen. Furthermore, she can look up data on past bicycle thefts in her area and use the proportion of bicycles that were stolen as an objective estimate of the probability that her bicycle will be stolen; alternatively, she can use a more subjective estimate: for example she might use a lower probability of theft than suggested by the data, because she knows herself to be very conscientious and – unlike other people – to always lock her bicycle when left unattended.

In this chapter we will focus on lotteries where the outcomes are sums of money. More general lotteries will be considered in Chapter 3.

2.2 Money lotteries and attitudes to risk

Definition 2.2.1 A *money lottery* is a probability distribution over a list of outcomes, where each outcome consists of a sum of money. Thus, it is an object of the form
$$\left(\begin{array}{cccc} \$x_1 & \$x_2 & ... & \$x_n \\ p_1 & p_2 & ... & p_n \end{array} \right) \text{ with } 0 \le p_i \le 1 \text{ for all } i = 1, 2, ..., n, \text{ and } p_1 + p_2 + ... + p_n = 1.$$

We assume that the individual in question is able to rank any two money lotteries. For example, if asked to choose between getting $400 for sure, which can be viewed as the degenerate lottery $\left(\begin{array}{c} \$400 \\ 1 \end{array} \right)$, and the lottery[2] $\left(\begin{array}{cc} \$900 & \$0 \\ \frac{1}{2} & \frac{1}{2} \end{array} \right)$, she will be able to tell us if she prefers one lottery to the other or is indifferent between the two. In general, there is no "right answer" to this question, as there is no right answer to the question "do you prefer coffee or tea?": it is a matter of individual taste.

---

[1]For some analysis of decision-making in situations where the individual is *not* able to assign probabilities to the outcomes see my book *Decision Making* (http://faculty.econ.ucdavis.edu/faculty/bonanno/DM_Book.html).

[2]We can think of this lottery as tossing a fair coin and then giving the individual $900 if it comes up Heads and nothing if it comes up Tails.

Definition 2.2.2 Given a money lottery $L = \begin{pmatrix} \$x_1 & \$x_2 & ... & \$x_n \\ p_1 & p_2 & ... & p_n \end{pmatrix}$, its *expected value* is the number $\mathbb{E}[L] = x_1 p_1 + x_2 p_2 + ... + x_n p_n$.

For example, the expected value of the money lottery

$$\begin{pmatrix} \$600 & \$180 & \$120 & \$30 \\ \frac{1}{12} & \frac{1}{3} & \frac{5}{12} & \frac{1}{6} \end{pmatrix}$$

is $\frac{1}{12}600 + \frac{1}{3}180 + \frac{5}{12}120 + \frac{1}{6}30 = 165$.

Definition 2.2.3 Let L be a non-degenerate money lottery (that is, a money lottery where at least two different outcomes are assigned positive probability)^a and consider the choice between L and the degenerate lottery

$$\begin{pmatrix} \$\mathbb{E}[L] \\ 1 \end{pmatrix}$$

(that is, the choice between facing the lottery L or getting the expected value of L with certainty).

Then

- An individual who prefers $\$\mathbb{E}[L]$ for certain to L is said to be *risk averse* (relative to L).

- An individual who is indifferent between $\$\mathbb{E}[L]$ for certain and L is said to be *risk neutral* (relative to L).

- An individual who prefers L to $\$\mathbb{E}[L]$ for certain is said to be *risk loving* or *risk seeking* (relative to L).

---

^{a} A money lottery $\begin{pmatrix} \$x_1 & \$x_2 & ... & \$x_n \\ p_1 & p_2 & ... & p_n \end{pmatrix}$ is non-degenerate if, for all $i = 1, 2, ..., n$, $p_i < 1$.

Note that, if an individual

(1) is **risk neutral** relative to *every* money lottery,

(2) has transitive preferences[3] over money lotteries and

(3) prefers more money to less,

then we can tell how that individual ranks any two money lotteries.

For example, how would a risk-neutral individual rank the two lotteries $L_1 = \begin{pmatrix} \$30 & \$45 & \$90 \\ \frac{1}{3} & \frac{5}{9} & \frac{1}{9} \end{pmatrix}$ and $L_2 = \begin{pmatrix} \$5 & \$100 \\ \frac{3}{5} & \frac{2}{5} \end{pmatrix}$? We shall use the symbol $\succ$ to denote strict preference and the symbol $\sim$ to denote indifference.[4] Since $\mathbb{E}[L_1] = 45$ and the

---

[3] That is, if she considers lottery A to be at least as good as lottery B and she considers lottery B to be at least as good as lottery C then she considers A to be at least as good as C.

[4] Thus $A \succ B$ means that the individual prefers A to B and $A \sim B$ means that the individual is indifferent between A and B.

individual is risk neutral, $L_1 \sim \$45$; since $\mathbb{E}[L_2] = 43$ and the individual is risk neutral, $\$43 \sim L_2$; since the individual prefers more money to less, $\$45 \succ \$43$:

$$L_1 \sim \$45 \succ \$43 \sim L_2.$$

Thus, by transitivity, $L_1 \succ L_2$ (see Exercises 2.10-2.13).

On the other hand, knowing that an individual is *risk averse* relative to *every* money lottery, has transitive preferences over money lotteries and prefers more money to less, is not sufficient to predict how she will choose between two arbitrary money lotteries. For example, as we will see in Chapter 3, it is possible that one risk-averse individual will prefer $L_3 = \begin{pmatrix} \$28 \\ 1 \end{pmatrix}$ (whose expected value is 28) to $L_4 = \begin{pmatrix} \$10 & \$50 \\ \frac{1}{2} & \frac{1}{2} \end{pmatrix}$ (whose expected value is 30), while another risk-averse individual will prefer L_4 to L_3.

Similarly, knowing that an individual is *risk loving* relative to *every* money lottery, has transitive preferences over money lotteries and prefers more money to less, is not sufficient to predict how she will choose between two arbitrary money lotteries.

⟨R⟩ Note that "rationality" does not, and should not, dictate whether an individual should be risk neutral, risk averse or risk loving: an individual's attitude to risk is merely a reflection of that individual's preferences. It is a generally accepted principle that *de gustibus non est disputandum* (in matters of taste, there can be no disputes). According to this principle, there is no such thing as an irrational preference and thus there is no such thing as an irrational attitude to risk.

From an empirical point of view, however, most people reveal through their choices (e.g. the decision to buy insurance) that they are risk averse, at least when the stakes are sufficiently high. It is also possible (as we will see in Chapter 4) for an individual to have different attitudes to risk, depending on how high the stakes are (e.g. an individual might display risk aversion, by purchasing home insurance, as well as risk love, by purchasing a lottery ticket).

> Test your understanding of the concepts introduced in this section, by going through the exercises in Section 2.7.1 at the end of this chapter.

2.3 Certainty equivalent and the risk premium

Given a set of money lotteries $\mathscr{L}$, we will assume that the individual under consideration has well-defined preferences over the elements of $\mathscr{L}$. As before, we shall use the symbol $\succ$ to denote *strict preference* ($L_1 \succ L_2$ means that the individual prefers lottery L_1 to lottery L_2) and the symbol $\sim$ to denote *indifference* ($L_1 \sim L_2$ means that the individual is indifferent between L_1 and L_2, that is, she considers L_1 to be just as good as L_2). Finally, we use the symbol $\succsim$ to signify "at least as good as": $L_1 \succsim L_2$ means that the individual considers L_1 to be at least as good as L_2, that is, either she prefers L_1 to L_2 or she is indifferent between L_1 and L_2. The following table summarizes the notation:

notation:	interpretation:
$L_1 \succ L_2$	the individual prefers L_1 to L_2
$L_1 \sim L_2$	the individual is indifferent between L_1 and L_2
$L_1 \succsim L_2$	the individual considers L_1 to be at least as good as L_2, that is, either $L_1 \succ L_2$ or $L_1 \sim L_2$.

We shall assume that the individual is able to rank any two lotteries (her preferences are complete) and her ranking is transitive:

- (completeness) for every L_1 and L_2, either $L_1 \succsim L_2$ or $L_2 \succsim L_1$ or both,

- (transitivity) if $L_1 \succsim L_2$ and $L_2 \succsim L_3$ then $L_1 \succsim L_3$.[5]

We shall also assume throughout that the individual prefers more money to less, that is,

$$\begin{pmatrix} \$x \\ 1 \end{pmatrix} \succ \begin{pmatrix} \$y \\ 1 \end{pmatrix} \text{ if and only if } x > y. \tag{2.1}$$

Suppose that, for every money lottery L there is a sum of money, denoted by C_L, that the individual considers to be just as good as the lottery L; then we call C_L the *certainty equivalent of lottery L* for that individual.

> **Definition 2.3.1** The *certainty equivalent of a money lottery L* is that sum of money C_L such that
> $$ L = \begin{pmatrix} \$x_1 & \dots & \$x_n \\ p_1 & \dots & p_n \end{pmatrix} \sim \begin{pmatrix} \$C_L \\ 1 \end{pmatrix} $$

Typically, the certainty equivalent of a given money lottery will be different for different individuals. However, all risk-neutral individuals will share the same certainty equivalent; in fact, it follows from the definition of risk neutrality (Definition 2.2.3) that

- for a **risk-neutral** individual, the certainty equivalent of a money lottery L coincides with the expected value of L:
  $$ C_L = \mathbb{E}[L]. $$

On the other hand, for a risk-averse individual (who, furthermore, prefers more money to less and whose preferences are complete and transitive) the certainty equivalent of a money lottery will be *less* than the expected value:

- for a **risk-averse** individual, for every money lottery L,

  $$ C_L < \mathbb{E}[L]. $$

---

[5] In Exercises 2.10-2.13 the reader is asked to prove that transitivity of the "at least as good" relation implies transitivity of strict preference and of indifference.

In fact, by definition of risk aversion, $\begin{pmatrix} \$\mathbb{E}[L] \\ 1 \end{pmatrix} \succ L$ and, by definition of certainty equivalent, $L \sim \begin{pmatrix} \$C_L \\ 1 \end{pmatrix}$. Thus, by transitivity, $\begin{pmatrix} \$\mathbb{E}[L] \\ 1 \end{pmatrix} \succ \begin{pmatrix} \$C_L \\ 1 \end{pmatrix}$; hence, by (2.1), $\mathbb{E}[L] > C_L$. Similarly,

- for a **risk-loving** individual, for every money lottery L,

$$C_L > \mathbb{E}[L].$$

From the notion of certainty equivalent we derive another notion which can be used to compare the degree of risk aversion across individuals.

Definition 2.3.2 The *risk premium of a money lottery L*, denoted by R_L, is the amount by which the expected value of L can be reduced to induce indifference between the lottery itself and the reduced amount for certain:

$$L = \begin{pmatrix} \$x_1 & \cdots & \$x_n \\ p_1 & \cdots & p_n \end{pmatrix} \sim \begin{pmatrix} \$(\mathbb{E}[L] - R_L) \\ 1 \end{pmatrix}$$

It follows from Definitions 2.3.1 and 2.3.2 that $C_L = \mathbb{E}[L] - R_L$ or, equivalently,

$$R_L = \mathbb{E}[L] - C_L.$$

Thus, for a risk-neutral individual the risk premium is zero, while for a risk-averse individual the risk premium is positive (and for a risk-loving individual the risk premium is negative). Furthermore, we can label a risk-averse individual as **more risk-averse** (relative to lottery L) than another risk-averse individual if the risk premium for the former is larger than the risk premium for the latter. In fact, the risk premium can be interpreted as the price (relative to the expected value) that the individual is willing to pay to avoid facing lottery L. For example, consider three individuals: Ann, Bob and Carla. They all have the same initial wealth $\$6,000$ and they are facing the lottery L where with probability 50% their wealth is wiped out and with probability 50% their wealth is doubled: $L = \begin{pmatrix} \$0 & \$12,000 \\ \frac{1}{2} & \frac{1}{2} \end{pmatrix}$.

Suppose that Ann's risk premium for this lottery is $R_L^{Ann} = 900$, Bob's is $R_L^{Bob} = 500$ and Carla's is $R_L^{Carla} = 0$. Then Ann and Bob are risk averse and Ann is more risk averse than Bob, while Carla is risk neutral. Ann would be willing to pay up to $\$900$ (thus reducing her wealth from $\$6,000$ to $\$5,100$) in order to avoid the lottery L, while Bob would only be willing to pay up to $\$500$ (thus reducing his wealth from $\$6,000$ to $\$5,500$) in order to avoid the lottery L; on the other hand, Carla would not be willing to pay any amount of money to avoid L, since she is indifferent between keeping her initial wealth of $\$6,000$ and playing lottery L.

Test your understanding of the concepts introduced in this section, by going through the exercises in Section 2.7.2 at the end of this chapter.

2.4 Insurance: basic concepts

Insurance markets are a good example of situations where uncertainty can be represented by means of money lotteries.

Consider an individual who has an initial wealth of $\$W_0 > 0$ and faces the possibility of a loss in the amount of $\$\ell$ $(0 < \ell \leq W_0)$ with probability p $(0 < p < 1)$. For example, it could be an individual who owns a plot of land worth $\$80,000$ and a house built on it worth $\$220,000$ (so that $W_0 = 80,000 + 220,000 = 300,000$). She is worried about the possibility of a fire destroying the house (thus $\ell = 220,000$) and, according to publicly available data, the probability of this happening in her area is 2% (thus $p = 0.02$). An insurance company offers her a contract and she has to decide whether or not to purchase that contract. An insurance contract is typically expressed in terms of two numbers: the *premium*, which we will denote by h, and the *deductible*, which we will denote by d. The premium can be thought of as the price of the contract: it is paid no matter whether the loss is incurred or not. The deductible is the portion of the loss that is *not* covered. If $d = 0$ we say that the contract offers *full insurance*, while if $d > 0$ then we say that the contract offers *partial insurance*:

$$d = 0 \quad \text{full insurance}$$
$$d > 0 \quad \text{partial insurance.}$$

In the above example, if the deductible is $\$40,000$ then, if the loss occurs, the insurance company makes a payment to the insured in the amount of $\$(\ell - d) = \$(220,000 - 40,000) = \$180,000$ (and, of course, if the loss in *not* incurred then the insurance company does not make any payments to the insured). The following table summarizes the notation used in this book in the context of insurance:

W_0	initial wealth
ℓ	potential loss
p	probability of loss
h	premium
d	deductible
$\ell - d$	insured amount
(h,d)	insurance contract.

It will be useful to represent the initial situation and possible insurance contracts graphically. We shall do so by using *wealth diagrams* where, on the horizontal axis, we represent the individual's wealth if a loss occurs, denoted by W_1, and, on the vertical axis, the individual's wealth if there is no loss, denoted by W_2; we shall also refer to the former as *wealth in the bad state* and to the latter as *wealth in the good state*. The no-insurance situation can be represented in the wealth diagram as the point $NI = (W_0 - \ell, W_0)$, as shown in Figure 2.1.

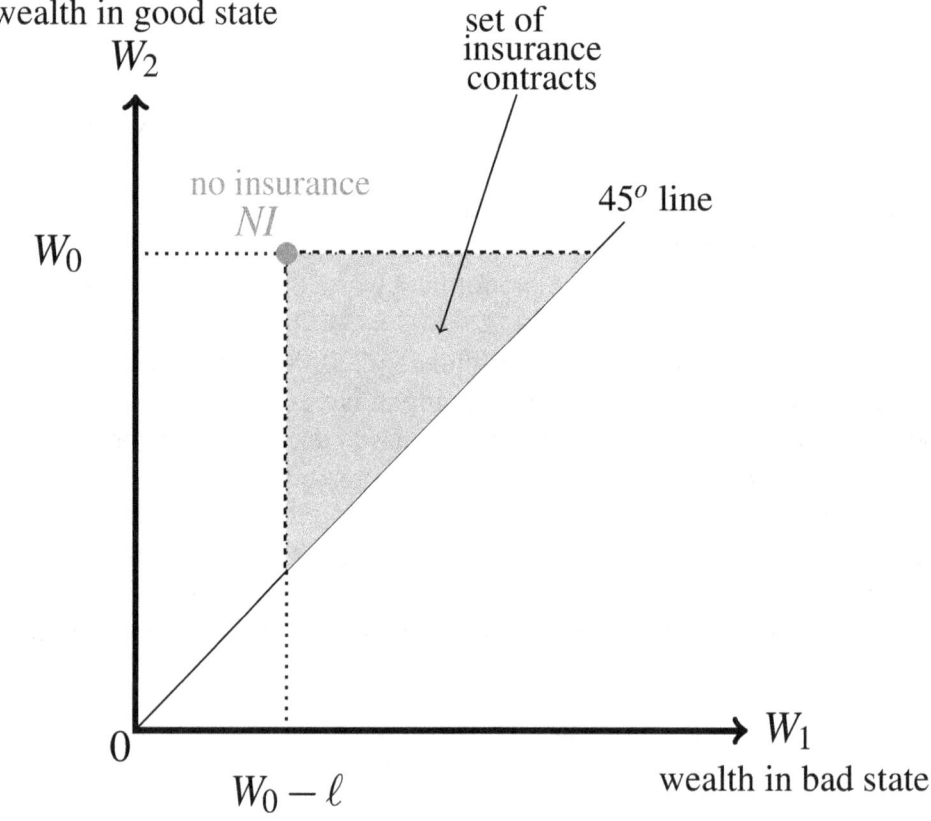

Figure 2.1: The no-insurance point (*NI*) and the set of possible insurance contracts (the shaded triangle).

The purpose of an insurance contract is to protect the individual in case she experiences a loss: thus an insurance contract can be thought of as a point in the diagram where the horizontal coordinate is larger than $W_0 - \ell$ (which is the individual's wealth in the bad state if she does not insure), while the vertical coordinate is smaller than W_0 because of the premium. The set of possible insurance contracts (encoded in terms of the corresponding wealth levels for the individual, in the bad state and in the good state), is shown in Figure 2.1 as a shaded triangle. The "45° line"– which is the line out of the origin with an angle of 45° – is the set of points (W_1, W_2) such that $W_1 = W_2$. As we will see below, the points on the 45° line represent full-insurance contracts.

How do we translate an insurance contract (h, d), expressed in terms of premium h and deductible d, into a point in the (W_1, W_2) diagram? If the individual purchases contract (h, d) then she pays the premium h in any case (that is, whether or not she incurs a loss) and thus her wealth in the good state is equal to $W_2 = W_0 - h$; the premium reduces her wealth also in the bad state, but in this state there is a further reduction due to the deductible, so that $W_1 = W_0 - h - d = W_2 - d$. Conversely, given a contract expressed as a point (W_1, W_2) we can recover the premium and deductible as follows: $h = W_0 - W_2$ and $d = W_2 - W_1$. It is clear from this that $d = 0$ if and only if $W_1 = W_2$, that is, if and only if the point lies on the 45° line.

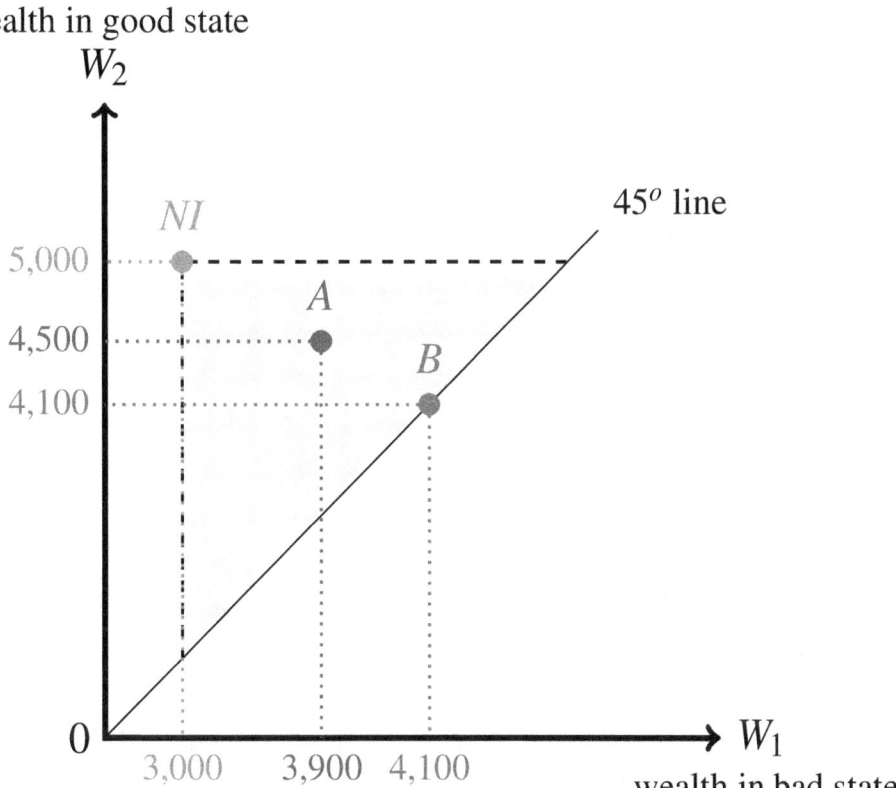

Figure 2.2: The no-insurance point and two insurance contracts.

In Figure 2.2 three points are shown: the no-insurance point $NI = (3,000, 5,000)$ and two possible insurance contracts: $A = (W_1^A = 3,900, \ W_2^A = 4,500)$ and $B = (W_1^B = 4,100, \ W_2^B = 4,100)$. From NI we deduce that

$$W_0 = 5,000 \quad \text{and} \quad \ell = 5,000 - 3,000 = 2,000.$$

Let h_A denote the premium of contract A and d_A the deductible; then

$$h_A = W_0 - W_2^A = 5,000 - 4,500 = 500 \quad \text{and} \quad d_A = W_2^A - W_1^A = 4,500 - 3,900 = 600.$$

Similarly, let h_B denote the premium of contract B and d_B the deductible; then

$$h_B = W_0 - W_2^B = 5,000 - 4,100 = 900 \quad \text{and} \quad d_B = W_2^B - W_1^B = 4,100 - 4,100 = 0.$$

Hence A is a partial-insurance contract, while B is a full-insurance contract.

Figure 2.3 shows how to view the premium and deductible corresponding to a contract $A = (W_1^A, W_2^A)$.

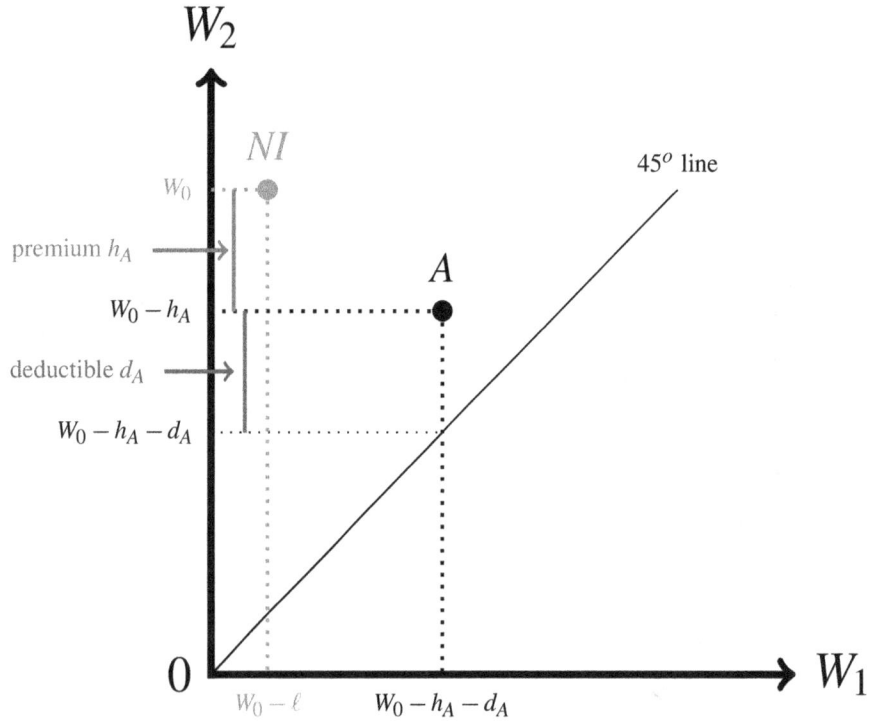

Figure 2.3: The graphical representation of the premium h_A and the deductible d_A corresponding to a contract $A = (W_1^A, W_2^A)$.

As shown in Figure 2.1, there are many potential insurance contracts (the points in the shaded triangle). Will an insurance company be willing to offer any of them? Would an individual be willing to accept any of them? The first question has to do with the incentives of the supplier of contracts (the insurer), while the second question has to do with the incentives of the potential customer (the insured).

We will address the first question in the next sections and postpone a full analysis of the second question to Chapter 4.

Test your understanding of the concepts introduced in this section, by going through the exercises in Section 2.7.3 at the end of this chapter.

2.5 **Isoprofit lines**

Throughout this book we shall assume that insurance companies are *risk neutral* and that their objective is to *maximize expected profits*.[6] Selling a contract (h,d) to a customer corresponds to the following money lottery (in terms of profits) for the insurer:

$$
\begin{pmatrix} \$h & \$[h-(\ell-d)] \\ 1-p & p \end{pmatrix}. \tag{▲}
$$

Given an insurance contract (h,d), we denote by $\pi(h,d)$ the expected value of the corresponding profit lottery (▲), that is, the expected profit from the contract:

$$
\pi(h,d) = (1-p)h + p[h-(\ell-d)] = h - p\ell + pd. \tag{▲▲}
$$

By the assumption of risk neutrality, the insurance company will be indifferent between any two contracts that yield the same expected profit. For example, if $\ell = 4,000$ and $p = \frac{5}{100}$, the two contracts $A = (h_A = 800, \ d_A = 1,000)$ and $B = (h_B = 825, \ d_B = 500)$ yield the same expected profit:

$$
\pi(A) = 800 - \tfrac{5}{100}3,000 = 650 \qquad \text{and} \qquad \pi(B) = 825 - \tfrac{5}{100}3,500 = 650.
$$

Definition 2.5.1 A line in the (W_1, W_2) plane joining all the contracts that give rise to the same expected profit is called an *isoprofit line*.

We want to show that an isoprofit line is a downward-sloping straight line with slope $-\frac{p}{1-p}$.

Let $A = \left(W_1^A, W_2^A\right)$ and $B = \left(W_1^B, W_2^B\right)$ be two contracts that yield the same expected profit, that is,

$$
\underbrace{W_0 - W_2^A}_{=h_A} - p\ell + p\underbrace{(W_2^A - W_1^A)}_{=d_A} = \underbrace{W_0 - W_2^B}_{=h_B} - p\ell + p\underbrace{(W_2^B - W_1^B)}_{=d_B}.
$$

Deleting $W_0 - p\ell$ from both sides of the equation and rearranging the terms we get

$$
-(1-p)W_2^A - pW_1^A = -(1-p)W_2^B - pW_1^B
$$

or, equivalently,

$$
\frac{rise}{run} = \frac{W_2^A - W_2^B}{W_1^A - W_1^B} = -\frac{p}{1-p}
$$

which gives the slope of the line segment joining points A and B. Note that the slope is a constant, that is, it does not vary with the points A and B that are chosen.

---

[6] The assumption of risk neutrality is not needed if the insurance company sells the same contract to a large number of individuals. Let n be a large number of customers insured by the insurance company with contract (h,d). Let n_0 be the number of customers who do not suffer a loss and n_1 be the number of customers who suffer a loss (thus $n_0 + n_1 = n$). Then the insurer's *total* profits will be $(n_0 + n_1)h - n_1(\ell - d)$, so that profit *per customer*, or profit *per contract*, is $\frac{nh - n_1(\ell-d)}{n} = h - \frac{n_1}{n}(\ell - d)$. By the Law of Large Numbers in probability theory, $\frac{n_1}{n}$ will be approximately equal to p (the probability of loss), so that the profit per customer will be approximately equal to $\pi(h,d) = h - p\ell + pd$ as defined above.

Figure 2.4 shows an isoprofit line and two contracts, A and B, on this line.

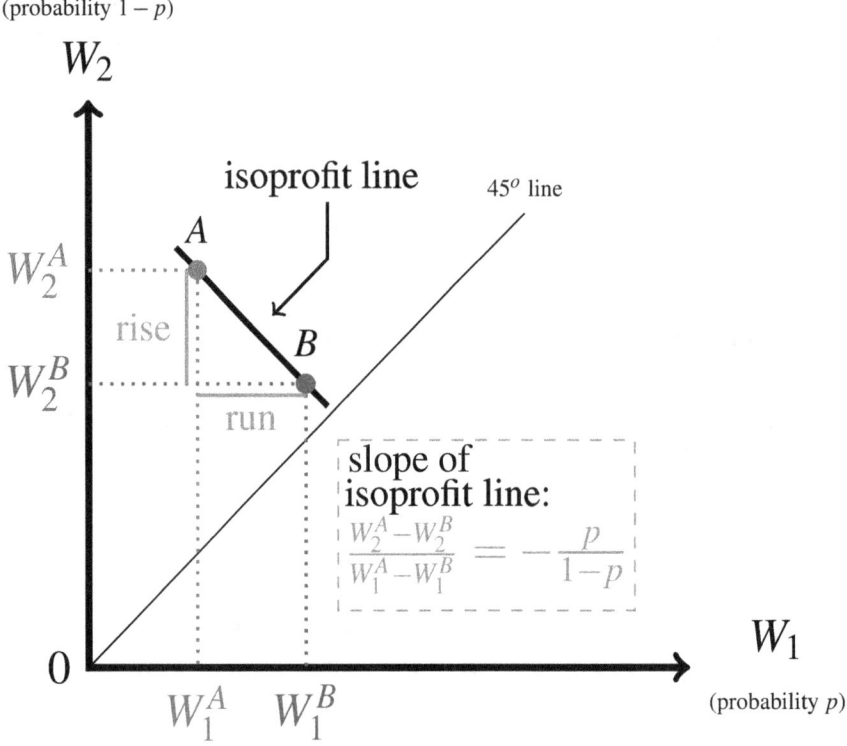

Figure 2.4: The slope of an isoprofit line.

Thus

- isoprofit lines are straight lines,

- isoprofit lines are downward-sloping or decreasing, since the slope is negative: $-\frac{p}{1-p} < 0$ because $0 < p < 1$.

For each point in the (W_1, W_2) plane there is an isoprofit line that goes through that point. Hence the plane is filled with parallel isoprofit lines (each with slope $-\frac{p}{1-p}$).

Let $A = \left(W_1^A, W_2^A\right)$ and $C = \left(W_1^C, W_2^C\right)$ be two insurance contracts and suppose that

$$\pi(A) = (W_0 - W_2^A) - p[\ell - (W_2^A - W_1^A)] \neq \pi(C) = (W_0 - W_2^C) - p[\ell - (W_2^C - W_1^C)].$$

What is the relative position of the isoprofit line that goes through A and the isoprofit line that goes through C? In other words, if the isoprofit line through one contract is below the isoprofit line through another contract, which of the two lines corresponds to a higher level of profit?

To answer this question, start from a point $A = \left(W_1^A, W_2^A\right)$ and draw a point $B = \left(W_1^B, W_2^B\right)$ vertically below it, as shown in Figure 2.5.

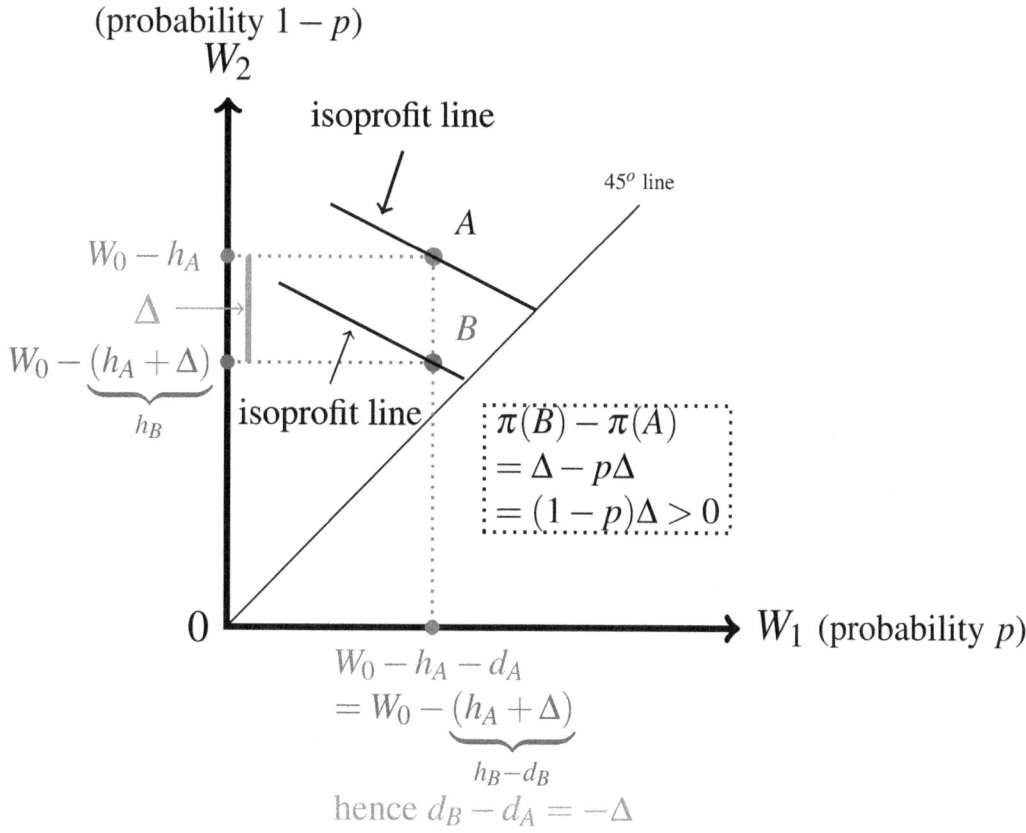

Figure 2.5: A lower isoprofit line corresponds to a higher level of profit.

Since point B is vertically below point A, the horizontal coordinate of B coincides with the horizontal coordinate of A: $W_1^B = W_1^A$; furthermore, the vertical coordinate of B is less than the vertical coordinate of A: $W_2^B < W_2^A$. From the latter fact we deduce that the premium of contract B is higher than the premium of contract A. Let $\Delta = W_2^A - W_2^B > 0$ be the amount by which B's premium exceeds A's premium. From the fact that $W_1^B = W_1^A$ we calculate the difference between the deductible of contract B and the deductible of contract A as follows:

$$\underbrace{\overbrace{W_2^B}^{= W_2^A - \Delta} - \overbrace{W_1^B}^{= W_1^A}}_{d_B} = \underbrace{W_2^A - W_1^A}_{d_A} - \Delta,$$

so that

$$d_B - d_A = -\Delta.$$

Thus, when contract B is vertically below contract A, then h_B is greater than h_A and, letting Δ be the amount by which h_B exceeds h_A ($\Delta = h_B - h_A$), $d_B - d_A = -\Delta$, that is, the deductible of contract B is *less than* the deductible of contract A by an amount equal to

Δ. From this we deduce that contract B yields higher profits that contract A, because it yields an extra $\$\Delta$ for sure (the premium is received with probability 1) and involves an extra payment of $\$\Delta$ to the insured only with probability p (the payment is made with probability $p < 1$), that is,[7]

$$\pi(B) - \pi(A) = \Delta - p\Delta = (1-p)\Delta > 0.$$

Thus we have shown that moving from an isoprofit line to a lower one corresponds to moving from lower profits to higher profits. This is illustrated in Figure 2.6.

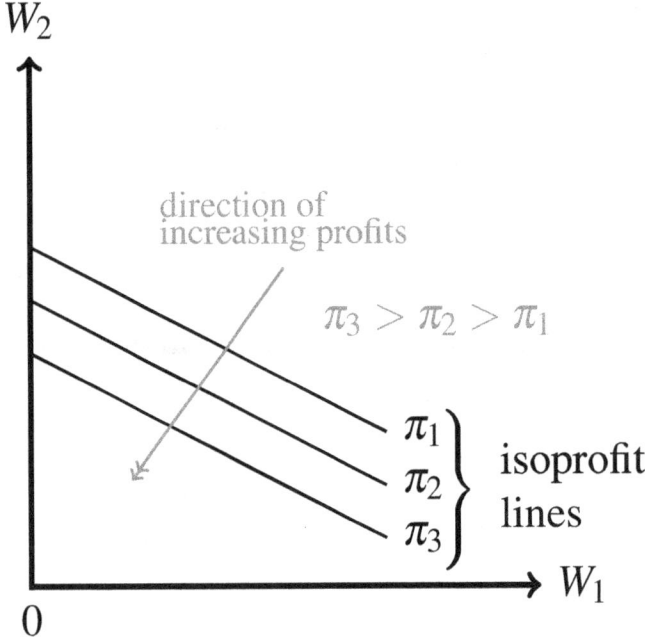

Figure 2.6: The direction of increasing profits.

Among the isoprofit lines there is one which is of particular interest, namely the *zero-profit line*, that is, the line that joins all the contracts that yield zero profits. Like all the other isoprofit lines, this is a straight line with slope $-\frac{p}{1-p}$. Furthermore, it goes through the no-insurance point *NI*; in fact, *NI* can be thought of as a trivial contract with zero premium and full deductible: such a contract obviously involves zero profits because the insurance company receives no payment ($h_{NI} = 0$) and makes no payment ($d_{NI} = \ell$ so that $\ell - d_{NI} = 0$).

Ⓡ   The zero-profit line is also called the *fair odds line*.

---

[7]This conclusion can be verified directly, as follows: $\pi(B) = W_0 - W_2^B - p\ell + p(W_2^B - W_1^B)$ and $\pi(A) = W_0 - W_2^A - p\ell + p(W_2^A - W_1^A)$ so that (recall that $W_1^B = W_1^A$ and thus $pW_1^B = pW_1^A$)

$$\pi(B) - \pi(A) = (W_2^A - W_2^B) - p(W_2^A - W_2^B) = (1-p)\underbrace{(W_2^A - W_2^B)}_{\Delta}.$$

The zero-profit line is shown in Figure 2.7. Points above the line represent contracts that yield negative profits and points below the line represent contracts that yield positive profits.

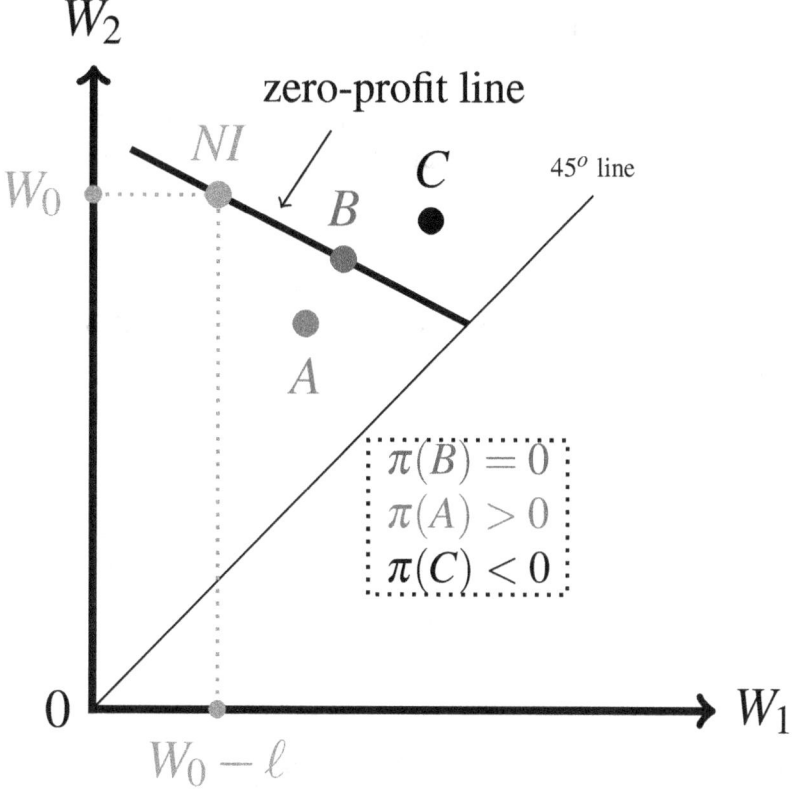

Figure 2.7: The zero-profit line.

Test your understanding of the concepts introduced in this section, by going through the exercises in Section 2.7.4 at the end of this chapter.

2.6 Profitable insurance requires risk aversion

2.6.1 Insuring a risk-neutral individual

Recall that the no-insurance option corresponds to the wealth lottery

$$NI = \begin{pmatrix} W_0 & W_0 - \ell \\ 1-p & p \end{pmatrix} \quad \text{whose expected value is} \quad \mathbb{E}[NI] = W_0 - p\ell \qquad (2.2)$$

where, as usual, W_0 is the initial wealth, ℓ the potential loss and p the probability of loss. Now suppose that the individual is **risk neutral** and is offered an insurance contract (h,d) that yields positive profits, that is,

$$h - p\ell + pd > 0 \quad \text{or, equivalently} \quad h + pd > p\ell. \qquad (2.3)$$

For the potential customer, such a contract corresponds to the wealth lottery

$$A = \begin{pmatrix} W_0 - h & W_0 - h - d \\ 1-p & p \end{pmatrix}$$

whose expected value is

$$\mathbb{E}[A] = W_0 - h - pd = W_0 - (h + pd) \qquad (2.4)$$

Using the fact that, by (2.3), $h + pd > p\ell$, we get that

$$\mathbb{E}[A] < W_0 - p\ell = \mathbb{E}[NI]. \qquad (2.5)$$

By risk neutrality, the individual is indifferent between NI and $\mathbb{E}[NI]$ for sure and is also indifferent between A and $\mathbb{E}[A]$ for sure. Assuming that the individual prefers more money to less, by (2.5) she prefers $\mathbb{E}[NI]$ for sure to $\mathbb{E}[A]$ for sure: denoting, as before, indifference by $\sim$ and strict preference by $\succ$, we can write this as

$$NI \sim \mathbb{E}[NI] \succ \mathbb{E}[A] \sim A.$$

Assuming that the individual's preferences are transitive, it follows that

$$NI \succ A,$$

that is, the individual strictly prefers not insuring to purchasing contract A. Hence *it is not possible for an insurance company to make positive profits by selling insurance contracts to risk-neutral individuals*: the individuals will simply not buy the offered insurance contracts.

Although it is intuitively clear that also a risk-loving individual would reject any insurance contract that would yield non-negative profits to the insurer, the proof requires more tools than we have developed so far.[8]

Thus we are left with the case of a risk-averse individual, to which we now turn.

---

[8] In Exercise 2.22 (at the end of this chapter) the reader is asked to show that a risk-loving individual would reject a full-insurance contract that yields zero profits to the insurance company.

2.6.2 Insuring a risk-averse individual

In this section we show that, if an individual is risk averse, it is possible for an insurance company to make positive profits by offering a contract that will be accepted by the individual.

The argument assumes that the individual's preferences are **continuous**, in the sense that if she prefers contract B to contract A then contracts that are sufficiently close to B are still better than A. This is shown in Figure 2.8. Suppose that contract B is preferred to contract A; then continuity of preferences says that, if we take some other contract C in a "sufficiently small disk" around B, then it will be true also for C that it is better than A.[9]

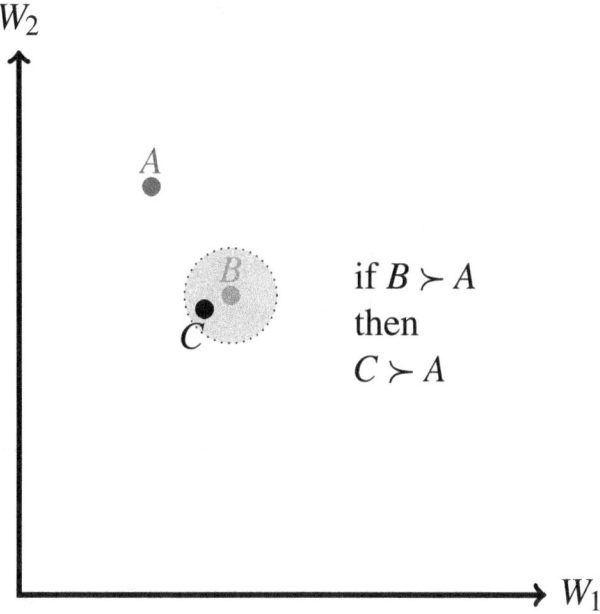

Figure 2.8: Continuity of preferences.

Now consider a risk-averse individual. By definition of risk aversion, she will strictly prefer the full-insurance contract B with premium $h = p\ell$ to not insuring, since such contract leaves her with a wealth of $W_0 - p\ell$ for sure and $W_0 - p\ell$ is the expected value of the no-insurance lottery NI:

$$B \succ NI. \tag{2.6}$$

Contract B yields zero profits for the insurer:[10]

$$\pi(B) = 0. \tag{2.7}$$

By continuity of preferences and (2.6), any contract C sufficiently close to B will also be such that

$$C \succ NI. \tag{2.8}$$

---

[9] This is similar to the property of real numbers that, if $b > a$ then any number c in a sufficiently small interval around b will also be greater than a.

[10] In fact, contract B lies at the intersection of the zero-profit line and the 45° line.

If we choose such a contract C which is *below* the zero-profit line, then – as we saw in Section 2.5 – $\pi(C) > \pi(B)$ and thus, by (2.7), $\pi(C) > 0$ and, by (2.8), the individual will purchase contract C, since it makes her better off relative to not insuring. Hence it is possible to sell a profitable contract to a risk-averse individual.

The above argument is illustrated graphically in Figure 2.9.

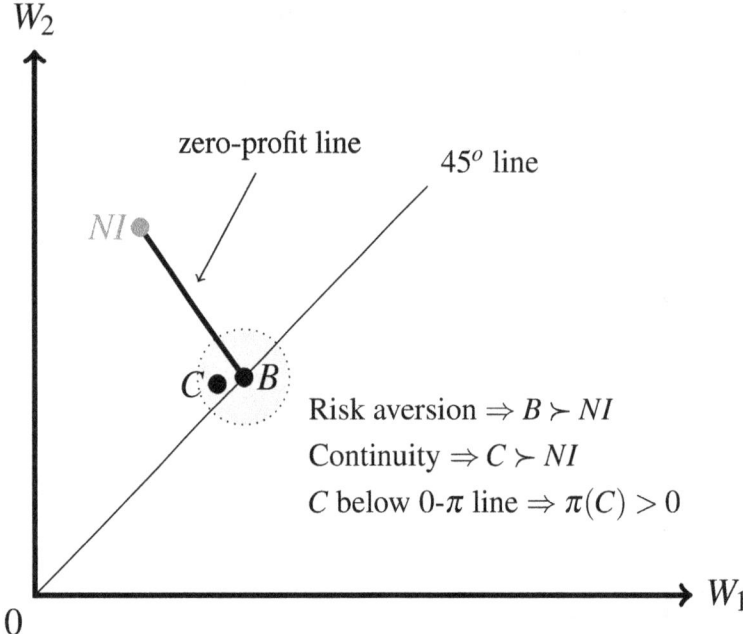

Figure 2.9: Contract C yields positive profits and is better than no insurance.

2.6.3 The profit-maximizing contract for a monopolist

Suppose that the insurance industry is a monopoly, that is, there is only one firm in the industry. Would a profit-maximizing monopolist want to offer a full insurance contract or a partial insurance contract to a risk-averse individual? Extending the argument of the previous section, we can show that for the monopolist *the profit-maximizing choice is to offer full insurance.*

Consider any *partial* insurance contract $B = (h_B, d_B)$ (thus $d_B > 0$) that the potential customer is willing to purchase (thus $B \succ NI$); note that the monopolist's profit from this contract is

$$\pi(B) = h_B - p\ell + pd_B.$$

We want to show that there is a full-insurance contract $C = (h_C, 0)$ which the potential customer is willing to purchase ($C \succ NI$) and is such that $\pi(C) > \pi(B)$, so that it cannot be profit-maximizing to offer contract B.

Let A be the following full-insurance contract: $A = (h_B + pd_B, 0)$. The monopolist's profit from this contract would be

$$\pi(A) = h_B + pd_B - p\ell = \pi(B),$$

that is, A and B lie on the same isoprofit line and hence the monopolist is indifferent between these two contracts. The customer, however, would strictly prefer contract A to contract B: $A \succ B$. In fact, purchasing contract $B = (h_B, d_B)$ can be viewed as playing the lottery $\begin{pmatrix} W_0 - h_B & W_0 - h_B - d_B \\ 1 - p & p \end{pmatrix}$ whose expected value is $W_0 - h_B - pd_B$ and the full-insurance contract A guarantees this amount with certainty; thus, by the assumed risk-aversion of the customer, $A \succ B$. By continuity of preferences, any contract C sufficiently close to A would still be such that $C \succ B$ and thus, by transitivity (since, by hypothesis, $B \succ NI$) $C \succ NI$. Choosing such a contract below the isoprofit line going through contracts A and B ensures that $\pi(C) > \pi(B)$. Hence if the monopolist were to switch from contract B to contract C the customer would still purchase insurance and the monopolist's profits would increase. The argument is illustrated in Figure 2.10.

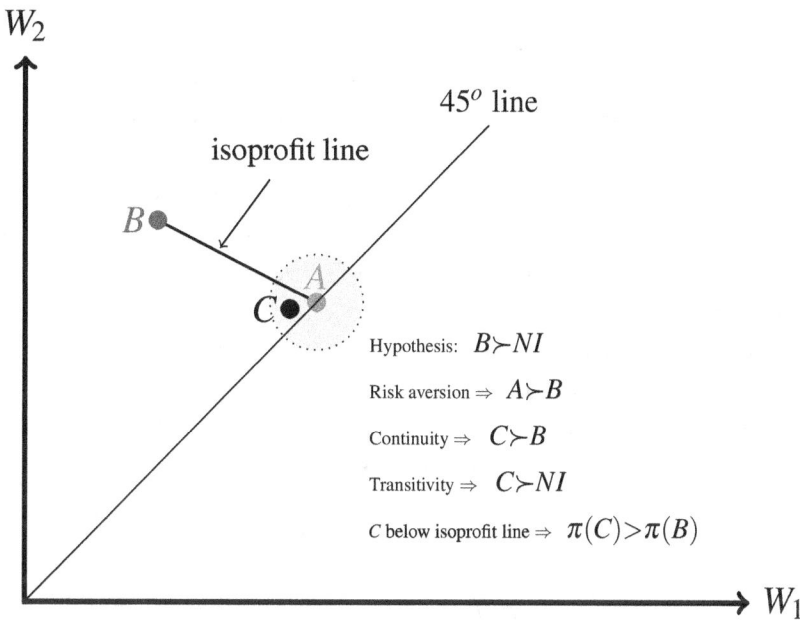

Figure 2.10: Contract C yields higher profits than contract B and is still better than NI.

Thus a monopolist would offer a full-insurance contract to the potential customer. What is the maximum premium that the monopolist would be able to charge for full-insurance without turning the customer away? We can answer this question by appealing to the notion of risk premium (Definition 2.3.2): the monopolist can set the premium up to the amount

$$h_{max} = p\ell + R_{NI}$$

where R_{NI} is the customer's risk premium for the no-insurance lottery $NI = \begin{pmatrix} W_0 & W_0 - \ell \\ 1 - p & p \end{pmatrix}$; that is, the maximum premium the customer would be willing to pay for full insurance is equal to the expected loss, $p\ell$, augmented by the risk premium, R_{NI}. In fact, $\mathbb{E}[NI] = W_0 - p\ell$ and thus, by definition of risk premium,

$$NI \sim \begin{pmatrix} W_0 - p\ell - R_{NI} \\ 1 \end{pmatrix}.$$

In other words, if the customer purchases insurance at premium $h_{max} = p\ell + R_{NI}$ then she is guaranteed the certainty equivalent of the no-insurance lottery. If offered full insurance at this premium, the potential customer would be indifferent between insuring and not insuring; thus the monopolist might want to offer full insurance at a slightly lower premium in order to provide the customer with an incentive to purchase insurance.

2.6.4 Perfectly competitive industry with free entry

In the previous section we considered the extreme case of complete absence of competition, that is, the case where the insurance industry is a monopoly. In this section we consider the opposite extreme, namely an insurance industry where competition is so intense that profits are driven down to zero. The story that is often told for such a mythical industry is that there is free entry into the industry and thus, if firms in the industry are making positive profits, then some new entrepreneur will enter seeking to share in these profits; entry of new firms intensifies competition and drives profits down. We shall assume that all the potential customers in the industry are identical, in the sense that they have the same preferences, the same initial wealth and face the same potential loss with the same probability (the case where potential customers are not identical will be analysed in Chapter 7). Furthermore, we assume that if a new contract is introduced that the insured customers prefer to their current contract, then they will switch to the new contract.

Define a *free-entry competitive equilibrium* as a situation where

1. each firm in the industry makes zero profits, and

2. there is no unexploited profit opportunity in the industry, that is, there is no currently not offered contract that would yield positive profits to a (existing or new) firm that offered that contract.

By adopting a simple extension of the argument used in the previous section, we now show that at a competitive free-entry equilibrium all the active firms, that is, all the firms that are actually selling insurance,[11] offer the same contract, namely the "fair" full-insurance contract with premium $h = p\ell$.

---

[11] There could be inactive firms whose contracts nobody purchases: these firms are also trivially making zero profits.

The first step in the argument is that – by the zero-profit condition – any actually purchased contract must lie on the zero-profit line. Suppose that there is a contract, call it A, that is currently being purchased by some customers (thus $A \succsim NI$) and is different from the "fair" full-insurance contract with premium $h = p\ell$; call the latter contract B: see Figure 2.11. By definition of risk aversion, it must be that $B \succ A$ and, by continuity of preferences, any contract sufficiently close to B must also be better than A (thus, since $A \succsim NI$, by transitivity of preferences such a contract is better than no insurance). Pick a contract C sufficiently close to B and below the zero-profit line (see Figure 2.11). Then $\pi(C) > 0$ and thus a firm that offered this contract would attract all the customers who are currently purchasing contract A and would make positive profit, so that the initial situation cannot be a free-entry competitive equilibrium.

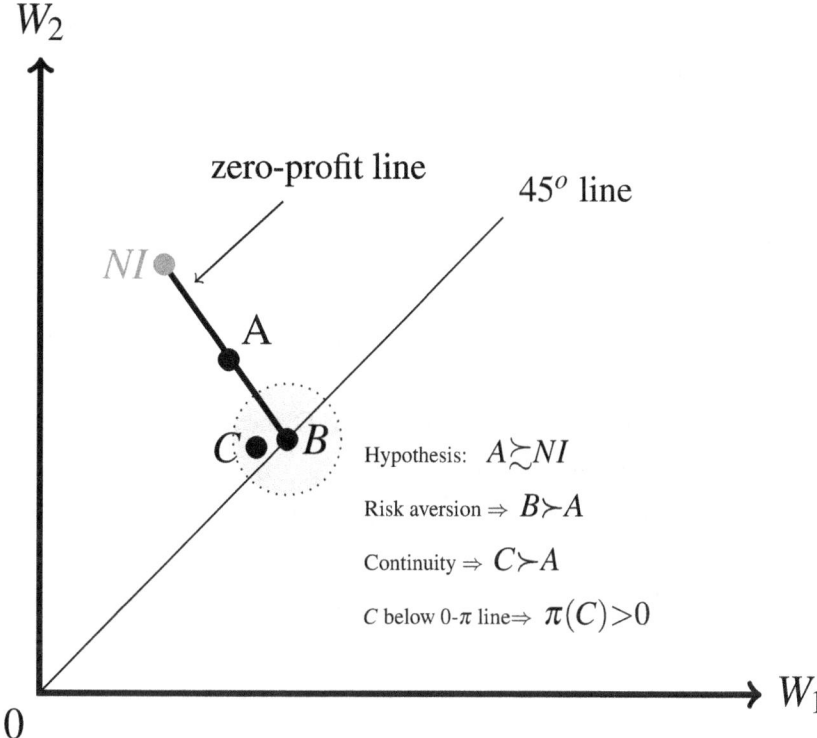

Figure 2.11: Contract C yields positive profits and is better than NI.

We have seen that, no matter whether the insurance industry is a monopoly or a perfectly competitive industry, the outcome is qualitatively the same, namely that potential customers are offered full insurance (and only full insurance). There is an important difference, however: in a perfectly competitive industry the premium of the full-insurance contract is the "fair" premium $h = p\ell$, while the premium that the monopolist charges for full insurance is higher, namely $h = p\ell + R_{NI}$ (recall that R_{NI} is the risk premium of the no-insurance lottery).

> Test your understanding of the concepts introduced in this section, by going through the exercises in Section 2.7.5 at the end of this chapter.

2.7 Exercises

The solutions to the following exercises are given in Section 2.8 at the end of this chapter.

2.7.1 Exercises for Section 2.2: Money lotteries and attitudes to risk

Exercise 2.1 Consider the following money lottery:

$$\begin{pmatrix} \$10 & \$15 & \$18 & \$20 & \$25 & \$30 & \$36 \\ \frac{3}{12} & \frac{1}{12} & 0 & \frac{3}{12} & \frac{2}{12} & 0 & \frac{3}{12} \end{pmatrix}$$

(a) What is its expected value?

(b) If a risk-neutral individual is given a choice between the above lottery and $23 for sure, what will she choose?

Exercise 2.2 Consider the lottery $\begin{pmatrix} o_1 & o_2 & o_3 \\ \frac{3}{10} & \frac{5}{10} & \frac{2}{10} \end{pmatrix}$ where

- o_1 is the outcome where you get $100 and an A in the class on the Economics of Uncertainty and Information,
- o_2 is the outcome where you get a free trip to Disneyland (which would normally cost $500) and a C in the class and
- o_3 is the outcome where you get a $150 gift certificate at Amazon.com and a B in the class.

If you are risk neutral, what sum of money would you consider to be just as good as the lottery?

Exercise 2.3 Given the choice between getting $18 for sure or playing the lottery

$$\begin{pmatrix} \$10 & \$20 & \$30 \\ \frac{3}{10} & \frac{5}{10} & \frac{2}{10} \end{pmatrix}$$

James – who likes money (that is, prefers more money to less) – chooses to get $18 for sure. Is he risk neutral?

Exercise 2.4 Find the expected value of the following lottery

$$\begin{pmatrix} 24 & 12 & 48 & 6 \\ \frac{1}{6} & \frac{2}{6} & \frac{1}{6} & \frac{2}{6} \end{pmatrix}.$$

Exercise 2.5 Consider the lottery $\begin{pmatrix} o_1 & o_2 & o_3 \\ \frac{1}{4} & \frac{1}{2} & \frac{1}{4} \end{pmatrix}$ where

- o_1 = you get an invitation to have dinner at the White House,
- o_2 = you get (for free) a puppy of your choice,
- o_3 = you get \$600.

What is the expected value of this lottery?

Exercise 2.6 Consider the following money lottery

$$L = \begin{pmatrix} \$10 & \$15 & \$18 & \$20 & \$25 & \$30 & \$36 \\ \frac{3}{12} & \frac{1}{12} & 0 & \frac{3}{12} & \frac{2}{12} & 0 & \frac{3}{12} \end{pmatrix}$$

(a) What is the expected value of the lottery?

(b) Ann prefers more money to less and has transitive preferences. She says that, between getting \$20 for certain and playing the above lottery, she would prefer \$20 for certain. What is her attitude to risk?

(c) Bob prefers more money to less and has transitive preferences. He says that, given the same choice as Ann, he would prefer playing the lottery. What is his attitude to risk?

Exercise 2.7 Sam has a debilitating illness and has been offered two mutually exclusive courses of action:

(1) take some well-known drugs which have been tested for a long time, or

(2) take a new experimental drug.

If he chooses (1) then for certain his pain will be reduced to a bearable level. If he chooses (2) then he has a 50% chance of being completely cured and a 50% chance of no benefits from the drug and possibly some harmful side effects. He chose (1). What is his attitude to risk?

Exercise 2.8 Shirley owns a house worth \$200,000. The value of the building is \$75,000 and the value of the land is \$125,000. In the area where she lives there is a 10% probability that a fire will completely destroy the building in a given year (on the other hand, the land would not be affected by a fire). An insurance company offers a policy that covers the full replacement cost of the building in the event of fire (that is, there is no deductible). The premium for this policy is \$7,500 per year. What attitude to risk must Shirley have in order to purchase the insurance policy? [Hint: think in terms of wealth levels.]

Exercise 2.9 Bill's entire wealth consists of the money in his bank account: $12,000$. Bill's friend Bob claims to have discovered a great investment opportunity, which would require an investment of $10,000$. Bob does not have any money and asks Bill to provide the $10,000$. According to Bob, the investment could yield a return of $150,000$, in which case Bob will return the initial $10,000$ to Bill and then give him 50% of the remaining $140,000$. According to Bob the probability that the investment will be successful is 12% and the probability that the initial investment of $10,000$ will be completely lost is 88%. Bill decides to go ahead with the investment and gives $10,000$ to Bob. What is Bill's attitude to risk?

2.7.2 Exercises for Section 2.3: Certainty equivalent and risk premium

Exercise 2.10 In Section 2.3 we defined three relations over money lotteries: the strict preference relation (denoted by $\succ$), the indifference relation (denoted by $\sim$) and the 'at least as good' relation (denoted by $\succsim$). As a matter of fact, one can simply postulate just one relation, the 'at least as good' relation $\succsim$, and derive the other two from it as follows:

- $L_1 \succ L_2$ if and only if $L_1 \succsim L_2$ and it is **not** the case that $L_2 \succsim L_1$,
- $L_1 \sim L_2$ if and only if $L_1 \succsim L_2$ and also $L_2 \succsim L_1$.

Recall that a relation $\succsim$ over a set $\mathscr{L}$ of money lotteries is *complete* if, for every two lotteries $L_1, L_2 \in \mathscr{L}$, either $L_1 \succsim L_2$ or $L_2 \succsim L_1$ (or both) and is *transitive* if, for every three lotteries $L_1, L_2, L_3 \in \mathscr{L}$, if $L_1 \succsim L_2$ and $L_2 \succsim L_3$ then $L_1 \succsim L_3$.

Prove that if the 'at least as good' relation $\succsim$ is complete and transitive then the derived 'strict preference' relation $\succ$ is also transitive, that is, if $L_1 \succ L_2$ and $L_2 \succ L_3$ then $L_1 \succ L_3$.

Exercise 2.11 As in Exercise 2.10 take the 'at least as good' relation $\succsim$ as primitive and derive from it the indifference relation $\sim$. Prove that if the 'at least as good' relation $\succsim$ is transitive then the derived indifference relation $\sim$ is also transitive, that is, if $L_1 \sim L_2$ and $L_2 \sim L_3$ then $L_1 \sim L_3$.

Exercise 2.12 As in Exercise 2.10 take the 'at least as good' relation $\succsim$ as primitive and derive from it the 'strict preference' relation $\succ$ and the indifference relation $\sim$. Prove that if the 'at least as good' relation $\succsim$ is transitive then if $L_1 \succ L_2$ and $L_2 \sim L_3$ then $L_1 \succ L_3$.

Exercise 2.13 As in Exercise 2.10 take the 'at least as good' relation $\succsim$ as primitive and derive from it the 'strict preference' relation $\succ$ and the indifference relation $\sim$. Prove that if the 'at least as good' relation $\succsim$ is transitive then if $L_1 \sim L_2$ and $L_2 \succ L_3$ then $L_1 \succ L_3$.

2.7.3 Exercises for Section 2.4: Insurance: basic concepts

Exercise 2.14 Tom's entire wealth consists of a boat which is worth $38,000. He is worried about the possibility of a hurricane damaging the boat. Typically, restoring a damaged boat costs $25,000. Unfortunately, because of global warming, the probability of a hurricane hitting his area is not negligible: it is 12%. The diagrams requested below should all be drawn, as usual, in the cartesian plane where on the horizontal axis you measure wealth in the bad state (W_1) and on the vertical axis wealth in the good state (W_2). Call such a diagram a "wealth diagram".

    (a) Represent the no-insurance option (*NI*) as a point in a wealth diagram.

    (b) Suppose that an insurance company offers the following insurance contract, call it *B*: the premium is $2,000 and the deductible is $9,000. Represent contract *B* in the wealth diagram of Part (a).

    (c) Suppose that another insurance company offers the following full-insurance contract, call it *C*: the premium is $3,000. Represent contract *C* in the wealth diagram of Part (a).

    (d) If Tom is risk neutral, how will he rank the three options: *NI*, *B* and *C*?

    (e) If Tom is risk averse, has transitive preferences and prefers more money to less, how will he rank the three options: *NI*, *B* and *C*?

Exercise 2.15 Refer to the diagram shown in Figure 2.12.

    (a) Calculate the potential loss ℓ.

    (b) Calculate the premium h_A and the deductible d_A of contract *A*.

    (c) Calculate the premium h_B and the deductible d_B of contract *B*.

    (d) For each of the two contracts state whether it is a partial-insurance contract or a full-insurance contract.

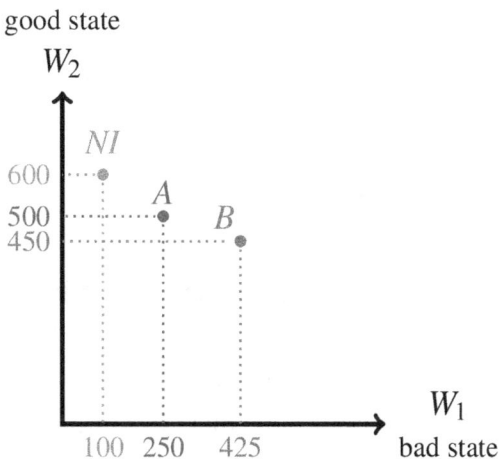

Figure 2.12: The diagram for Exercise 2.15

2.7.4   **Exercises for Section 2.5: Isoprofit lines**

Exercise 2.16 Consider again the information given in Exercise 2.14: Tom's entire wealth consists of a boat which is worth $38,000$; he is worried about the possibility of a hurricane damaging the boat, in which case it would cost him $25,000$ to repair the boat; the probability of a hurricane hitting his area is 12%. He is considering two insurance contracts: contract B, with premium $2,000$ and deductible $9,000$, and contract C, with premium $3,000$ and zero deductible.

(a) If Tom were to purchase contract B, what would the expected profit be for the insurance company?

(b) If Tom were to purchase contract C, what would the expected profit be for the insurance company?

(c) What is the slope of an isoprofit line?

(d) Find the equation of the isoprofit line that goes through contract B and draw it in a wealth diagram.

(e) Find the equation of the isoprofit line that goes through contract C and draw it in a wealth diagram.

Exercise 2.17 Consider again the information given in Exercise 2.15 (shown in Figure 2.12). Assume that the probability of loss is 20%.

(a) Calculate the expected profit from contract A.

(b) Calculate the expected profit from contract B.

(c) Draw the zero-profit line.

(d) Draw the isoprofit line that goes through contract A.

(e) Draw the isoprofit line that goes through contract B.

Exercise 2.18 The equation of the zero-profit line is $W_2 = 8,100 - \frac{1}{9}W_1$. The individual's initial wealth is $7,600$.

(a) What is the probability of loss?

(b) Calculate the potential loss ℓ.

(c) Find a full-insurance contract, call it A, that yields a profit of 40.

(d) Find a contract, call it B, that lies on the isoprofit line through A and has a deductible of $1,500$.

(e) Find a contract, call it C, with deductible $d = 2,000$ that yields a profit of 25.

(f) Write the equation of the isoprofit line that goes through contract A (in the wealth diagram).

(g) Write the equation of the isoprofit line that goes through contract C (in the wealth diagram).

Exercise 2.19 Consider the wealth diagram shown in Figure 2.13. Let $p = 0.2$.

(a) Interpret each point (including NI) as an insurance contract and express it in terms of premium and deductible.

(b) Calculate the expected profit from each contract.

(c) Find the equation of the isoprofit line that goes through each contract (including the one that goes through point NI).

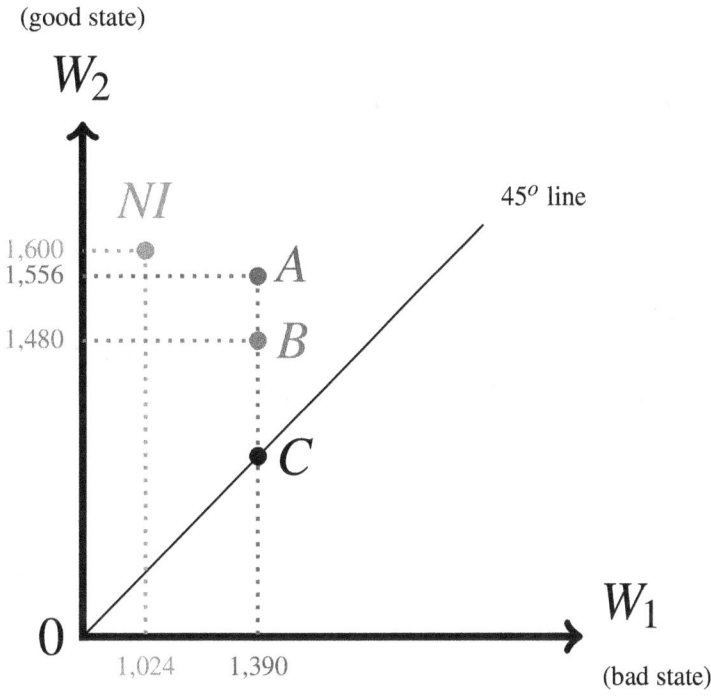

Figure 2.13: The wealth diagram for Exercise 2.19

Exercise 2.20 In a wealth diagram

(a) show the subset of the set of insurance contracts that contains the contracts that yield non-negative profits to the insurer (recall that the set of insurance contracts is the shaded triangle shown in Figure 2.1 on page 16),

(b) of all the contracts that yield non-negative profits to the insurer, find the one that is most preferred by a risk-averse individual and explain why there is only one such contract,

(c) of all the contracts that yield non-negative profits to the insurer, find the ones that are most preferred by a risk-neutral individual.

2.7.5   **Exercises for Section 2.6: Profitable insurance requires risk aversion**

> **Exercise 2.21** Prove that a risk-neutral individual is indifferent between no insurance and a full-insurance contract that yields zero profits to the insurance company.

> **Exercise 2.22** Prove that a risk-loving individual strictly prefers no insurance to a "fair" full-insurance contract (that is, a full-insurance contract that yields zero profits to the insurance company).

> **Exercise 2.23** Ann has an initial wealth of $24,000$ and faces a potential loss of $15,000$ with probability 20%. The risk premium of the no-insurance lottery for Ann is $2,000$. If Ann is offered full insurance for a premium of $4,920$ will she take it?

> **Exercise 2.24** Bob has an initial wealth of $18,000$ and faces a potential loss of $10,000$. The risk premium of the no-insurance lottery for Bob is 900. The maximum premium that he is willing to pay for full insurance is $4,000$. What is the probability of loss?

2.8   Solutions to Exercises

Solution to Exercise 2.1.
(a) The expected value is

$$\frac{3}{12}10+\frac{1}{12}15+0\,(18)+\frac{3}{12}20+\frac{2}{12}25+0\,(30)+\frac{3}{12}36=\frac{263}{12}=\$21.92.$$

(b) A risk-neutral person is indifferent between the lottery and $21.92 for sure. Assuming that she prefers more money to less, she will prefer $23 to $21.92. Thus, if her preferences are transitive, she will prefer $23 to the lottery. □

Solution to Exercise 2.2. One might be tempted to compute the "expected value" $\frac{3}{10}100+\frac{5}{10}500+\frac{2}{10}150=310$ and answer: $310. However, this answer would be wrong, because the given lottery is not a money lottery: the outcomes are not just sums of money (they do involve sums of money but also what grade you get in the class). The definition of risk neutrality can only be applied to money lotteries. □

Solution to Exercise 2.3. The expected value of the lottery is $\frac{3}{10}10+\frac{5}{10}20+\frac{2}{10}30=19$. If James were risk-neutral he would consider the lottery to be just as good as getting $19 for sure and would therefore choose the lottery (since getting $19 is better than getting $18). Hence, he is *not* risk neutral. □

Solution to Exercise 2.4 The expected value of the lottery $\begin{pmatrix} 24 & 12 & 48 & 6 \\ \frac{1}{6} & \frac{2}{6} & \frac{1}{6} & \frac{2}{6} \end{pmatrix}$ is
$\frac{1}{6}24 + \frac{2}{6}12 + \frac{1}{6}48 + \frac{2}{6}6 = 18.$ □

Solution to Exercise 2.5 This was a trick question! There is no expected value because the outcomes are not numbers. □

Solution to Exercise 2.6

(a) As already computed in Exercise 2.1, the expected value of the lottery

$$L = \begin{pmatrix} \$10 & \$15 & \$18 & \$20 & \$25 & \$30 & \$36 \\ \frac{3}{12} & \frac{1}{12} & 0 & \frac{3}{12} & \frac{2}{12} & 0 & \frac{3}{12} \end{pmatrix}$$

is $\mathbb{E}[L] = \frac{3}{12}10 + \frac{1}{12}15 + 0\,(18) + \frac{3}{12}20 + \frac{2}{12}25 + 0\,(30) + \frac{3}{12}36 = \frac{263}{12} = \$21.92.$

(b) Since Ann prefers more money to less, she prefers $21.92 to $20 ($21.92 ≻ $20). She said that she prefers $20 to lottery L ($20 ≻ L). Thus, since her preferences are transitive, she prefers $21.92 to lottery L ($21.92 ≻ L). Hence, she is risk averse.

(c) The answer is: we cannot tell. First of all, since Bob prefers more money to less, he prefers $21.92 to $20 ($21.92 ≻ $20). Bob could be risk neutral, because a risk neutral person would be indifferent between L and $21.92 ($L \sim $21.92); since Bob prefers $21.92 to $20 and has transitive preferences, if risk neutral he would prefer L to $20. However, Bob could also be risk loving: a risk-loving person prefers L to $21.92 ($L \succ $21.92) and we know that he prefers $21.92 to $20; thus, by transitivity, he would prefer L to $20. But Bob could also be risk averse: he could consistently prefer $21.92 to L and L to $20 (for example, he could consider L to be just as good as $20.50). □

Solution to Exercise 2.7 Just like Exercise 2.5, this was a trick question! Here the basic outcomes are not sums of money but states of health. Since the described choice is not one between money lotteries, the definitions of risk aversion/neutrality/love are not applicable. □

Solution to Exercise 2.8 The decision not to buy insurance is the decision to face the following lottery: with probability 0.9 Shirley's wealth will be $200,000, with probability 0.1 it will be $125,000. The expected value of this lottery is: $0.9(200,000) + 0.1(125,000) = \$192,500$. The insurance policy guarantees a wealth of $200,000 - 7,500 = 192,500$. Hence Shirley will buy the insurance policy if she is risk-averse, will be indifferent between buying and not buying if she is risk-neutral and will prefer not to buy if she is risk-loving. □

Solution to Exercise 2.9 If Bill refuses to invest, his wealth is $12,000 for sure. If Bill gives $10,000 to Bob to invest then he faces the following lottery: $L = \begin{pmatrix} \$2,000 & \$82,000 \\ 0.88 & 0.12 \end{pmatrix}$. The expected value of L is $\mathbb{E}[L] = \frac{88}{100}2,000 + \frac{12}{100}82,000 = \$11,600$. If Bill were risk averse he would prefer \$11,600 for sure to the investment (lottery L) and obviously he will prefer \$12,000 to \$11,600; thus he would prefer \$12,000 for sure to the investment; since he decides to go ahead with the investment he is not risk averse. If Bill were risk neutral he would be indifferent between \$11,600 for sure and the investment (lottery L) and obviously he will prefer \$12,000 to \$11,600; thus he would prefer \$12,000 for sure to the investment; since he decides to go ahead with the investment he is not risk neutral either. Hence Bill is risk-loving.   □

Solution to Exercise 2.10 Let $L_1, L_2, L_3 \in \mathscr{L}$ be such that $L_1 \succ L_2$ and $L_2 \succ L_3$. We need to show that $L_1 \succ L_3$. Since $L_1 \succ L_2$, $L_1 \succsim L_2$ and since $L_2 \succ L_3$, $L_2 \succsim L_3$. Thus, by transitivity of $\succsim$, $L_1 \succsim L_3$. It remains to prove that it is not the case that $L_3 \succsim L_1$. Suppose that $L_3 \succsim L_1$; then, since $L_1 \succsim L_2$ it would follow from transitivity of $\succsim$ that $L_3 \succsim L_2$, contradicting the hypothesis that $L_2 \succ L_3$.   □

Solution to Exercise 2.11 Let $L_1, L_2, L_3 \in \mathscr{L}$ be such that $L_1 \sim L_2$ and $L_2 \sim L_3$. We need to show that $L_1 \sim L_3$. Since $L_1 \sim L_2$, $L_1 \succsim L_2$ and since $L_2 \sim L_3$, $L_2 \succsim L_3$; thus, by transitivity of $\succsim$, $L_1 \succsim L_3$. Similarly, since $L_1 \sim L_2$, $L_2 \succsim L_1$ and since $L_2 \sim L_3$, $L_3 \succsim L_2$; thus, by transitivity of $\succsim$, $L_3 \succsim L_1$. It follows from $L_1 \succsim L_3$ and $L_3 \succsim L_1$ that $L_1 \sim L_3$.   □

Solution to Exercise 2.12 Let $L_1, L_2, L_3 \in \mathscr{L}$ be such that $L_1 \succ L_2$ and $L_2 \sim L_3$. We need to show that $L_1 \succ L_3$. Since $L_1 \succ L_2$, $L_1 \succsim L_2$ and since $L_2 \sim L_3$, $L_2 \succsim L_3$; thus, by transitivity of $\succsim$, $L_1 \succsim L_3$. It remains to show that it is not the case that $L_3 \succsim L_1$. Suppose that $L_3 \succsim L_1$; then, in conjunction with $L_1 \succsim L_3$, we get that $L_3 \sim L_1$; since, by hypothesis, $L_2 \sim L_3$, it would follow from transitivity of $\sim$ (proved in Exercise 2.11) that $L_1 \sim L_2$ contradicting the hypothesis that $L_1 \succ L_2$.   □

Solution to Exercise 2.13 Let $L_1, L_2, L_3 \in \mathscr{L}$ be such that $L_1 \sim L_2$ and $L_2 \succ L_3$. We need to show that $L_1 \succ L_3$. Since $L_1 \sim L_2$, $L_1 \succsim L_2$ and since $L_2 \succ L_3$, $L_2 \succsim L_3$; thus, by transitivity of $\succsim$, $L_1 \succsim L_3$. It remains to show that it is not the case that $L_3 \succsim L_1$. Suppose that $L_3 \succsim L_1$; then, in conjunction with $L_1 \succsim L_3$, we get that $L_3 \sim L_1$; since, by hypothesis, $L_2 \sim L_1$, it would follow from transitivity of $\sim$ (proved in Exercise 2.11) that $L_2 \sim L_3$ contradicting the hypothesis that $L_2 \succ L_3$.   □

Solution to Exercise 2.14

(a) See Figure 2.14.

(b) $W_1^B = 38,000 - 2,000 - 9,000 = 27,000$ and $W_2^B = 38,000 - 2,000 = 36,000$. Contract B is shown in Figure 2.14.

(c) $W_1^C = 38,000 - 3,000 = 35,000 = W_2^C$. Contract C is shown in Figure 2.12.

(d) NI represents the lottery $\begin{pmatrix} 13,000 & 38,000 \\ \frac{12}{100} & \frac{88}{100} \end{pmatrix}$ whose expected value is $\frac{12}{100}13,000 +$ $\frac{88}{100}38,000 = 35,000$. Contract B represents the lottery $\begin{pmatrix} 27,000 & 36,000 \\ \frac{12}{100} & \frac{88}{100} \end{pmatrix}$ whose expected value is $\frac{12}{100}27,000 + \frac{88}{100}36,000 = 34,920$. Contract C represents the lottery $\begin{pmatrix} 35,000 \\ 1 \end{pmatrix}$ whose expected value is $35,000$. Thus if Tom is risk neutral then he is indifferent between NI and C and prefers either of them to B.

(e) By risk aversion, Tom strictly prefers C to NI. He also strictly prefers C to B: since he prefers more money to less, he prefers \$35,000 to \$34,920 and, by risk aversion, he prefers \$34,920 for sure to B; hence, by transitivity, he prefers C to B. On the other hand, we cannot tell how he ranks NI relative to B. □

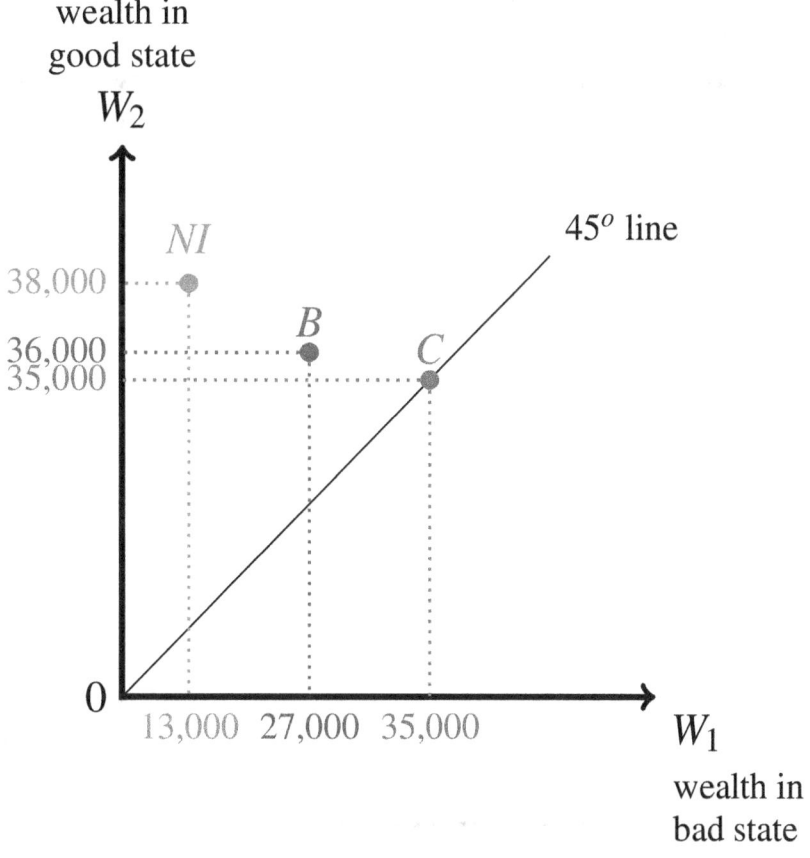

Figure 2.14: The diagram for Exercise 2.14

Solution to Exercise 2.15

  (a) $\ell = 600 - 100 = 500$.

  (b) $h_A = 600 - 500 = 100$, $d_A = 500 - 250 = 250$.

  (c) $h_B = 600 - 450 = 150$, $d_B = 450 - 425 = 25$.

  (d) Both contracts are partial-insurance contracts (neither of them lies on the 45° line).   □

Solution to Exercise 2.16

  (a) $\pi(B) = h_B - p\ell + p\, d_B = 2{,}000 - \frac{12}{100}25{,}000 + \frac{12}{100}9{,}000 = 80$.

  (b) $\pi(C) = h_C - p\ell = 3{,}000 - \frac{12}{100}25{,}000 = 0$.

  (c) The slope of each isoprofit line is $-\frac{p}{1-p} = -\frac{\frac{12}{100}}{\frac{88}{100}} = -\frac{3}{22} = -0.136$.

  (d) Since isoprofit lines are straight lines with slope $-\frac{3}{22}$, they are of the form $W_2 = a - \frac{3}{22}W_1$. To find the value of a replace W_2 with $36{,}000$ and W_1 with $27{,}000$ and solve for a to get $a = \frac{436{,}500}{11} = 39{,}681.82$. The isoprofit line is shown in Figure 2.15.

  (e) This is the zero-profit line and thus it goes through the no-insurance point NI. Again, it is of the form $W_2 = a - \frac{3}{22}W_1$. To find the value of a replace both W_1 and W_2 with $35{,}000$ and solve for a to get $a = \frac{437{,}500}{11} = 39{,}772.73$. The isoprofit line is shown in Figure 2.15.   □

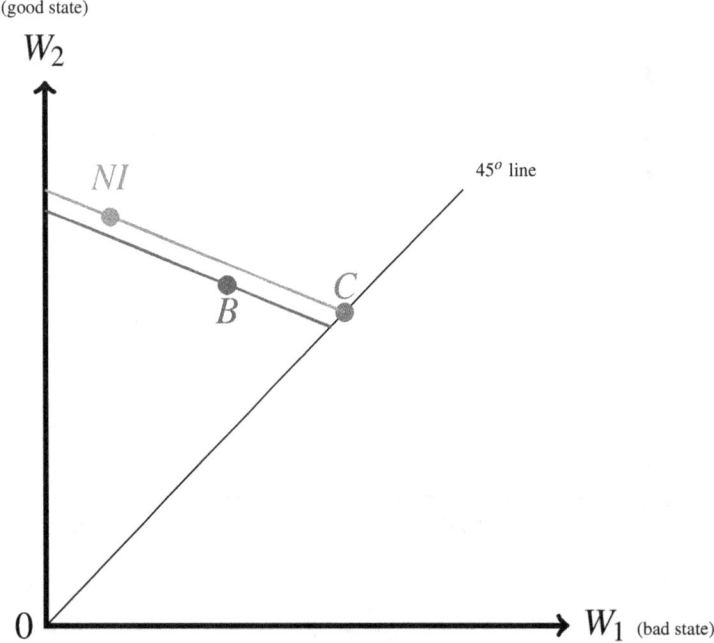

Figure 2.15: The diagram for Exercise 2.16

Solution to Exercise 2.17

(a) $\pi(A) = h_A - p(\ell - d_A) = 100 - \frac{1}{5}(500 - 250) = 50.$

(b) $\pi(B) = h_B - p(\ell - d_B) = 150 - \frac{1}{5}(500 - 25) = 55.$

(c) See Figure 2.16. All three profit lines have a slope of $-\frac{0.2}{0.8} = -\frac{1}{4}$. The equation of the zero-profit line is $W_2 = 625 - \frac{1}{4}W_1$.

(d) See Figure 2.16. The equation of the line is $W_2 = 562.5 - \frac{1}{4}W_1$.

(e) See Figure 2.16. The equation of the line is $W_2 = 556.25 - \frac{1}{4}W_1$. □

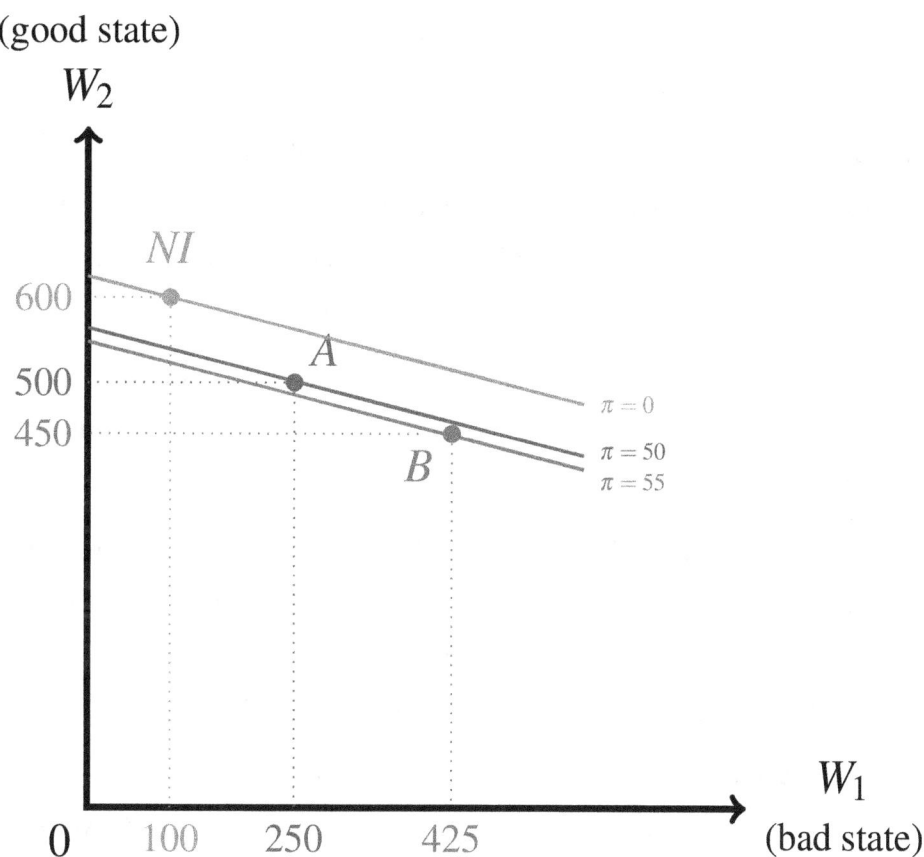

Figure 2.16: The diagram for Exercise 2.17

Solution to Exercise 2.18

(a) Let p be the probability of loss. We know that the slope of any isoprofit line is $-\frac{p}{1-p}$. Thus, since the slope of the zero-profit line is $-\frac{1}{9}$, it must be that $\frac{p}{1-p} = \frac{1}{9}$. Solving for p we get that $p = \frac{1}{10}$.

(b) The no-insurance point is on the zero-profit line. We know that the vertical coordinate of the no-insurance point is $W_0 = 7,600$. Thus, to find the horizontal coordinate, which is equal to $W_0 - \ell$, we must solve the equation $7,600 = 8,100 - \frac{1}{9}W_1$ which gives $W_1 = 4,500$. Thus $\ell = 7,600 - 4,500 = 3,100$.

(c) A full-insurance contract with premium h yields a profit of $h - p\ell = h - \frac{1}{10}3,100 = h - 310$. Thus we want h to solve the equation $h - 310 = 40$. Hence contract A has a premium of 350 (and, of course, zero deductible).

(d) A contract with premium h and deductible $1,500$ yields a profit of $h - p\ell + 1,500p = h - 310 + 150 = h - 160$. Hence, since B is on the same isoprofit line as A, it must be that $h - 160 = 40$, that is, $h = 200$. Thus contract B has a premium of 200 and a deductible of $1,500$.

(e) Similar reasoning as in Part (d): we need $h - p\ell + 2,000p$ to be equal to 25. Hence we must solve $h - 310 + 200 = 25$, which gives $h = 135$. Thus contract C has a premium of 135 and a deductible of $2,000$.

(f) The equation of an isoprofit line is of the form $W_2 = a - \frac{1}{9}W_1$. To find the value of a for the isoprofit line that goes through contract A we must solve $7,600 - 350 = a - \frac{1}{9}(7,600 - 350)$ to get $a = \frac{72,500}{9} = 8,055.56$. Thus the equation of the isoprofit line that goes through contract A is $W_2 = 8,055.56 - \frac{1}{9}W_1$.

(g) Again, the equation of an isoprofit line is of the form $W_2 = a - \frac{1}{9}W_1$. To find the value of a for the isoprofit line that goes through contract C we must solve $7,600 - 135 = a - \frac{1}{9}(7,600 - 135 - 2,000)$ to get $a = \frac{72,650}{9} = 8,072.22$. Thus the equation the isoprofit line that goes through contract C is $W_2 = 8,072.22 - \frac{1}{9}W_1$.

Solution to Exercise 2.19

(a) First of all, note that the initial wealth is $W_0 = 1,600$ and the potential loss is $\ell = 1,600 - 1,024 = 576$. Let us write each point as a pair (h,d) where $h = W_0 - W_2$ is the premium and $d = W_2 - W_1$ is the deductible. Thus

$NI = (0,576),$

$A = (1600 - 1556,\ 1556 - 1390) = (44,166),$

$B = (1600 - 1480,\ 1480 - 1390) = (120,90),$

$C = (1600 - 1390,\ 0) = (210,0).$

(b) The expected profit from contract (h,d) is $\pi = h - p(\ell - d)$. Thus $\pi(NI) = 0$, $\pi(A) = -38$, $\pi(B) = 22.8$ and $\pi(C) = 94.8$.

(c) All the isoprofit lines are straight lines and all have the same slope given by $-\frac{p}{1-p} = -\frac{\frac{1}{5}}{\frac{4}{5}} = -\frac{1}{4}$. Thus starting at a point (W_1, W_2), if you reduce W_1 to 0 then the vertical coordinate changes to $W_2 + \frac{1}{4}W_1$, yielding the vertical intercept. Applying this to point NI we get that by reducing the horizontal coordinate by 1,024, the vertical coordinate increases by $\frac{1,024}{4} = 256$ to $1,600 + 256 = 1,856$. Hence the equation of the isoprofit line that goes through point NI (which is the zero-profit line) is $W_2 = 1,856 - \frac{1}{4}W_1$. Applying the same procedure we get that

Equation of isoprofit line through A: $W_2 = 1,903.5 - \frac{1}{4}W_1$

Equation of isoprofit line through B: $W_2 = 1,827.5 - \frac{1}{4}W_1$

Equation of isoprofit line through C: $W_2 = 1,737.5 - \frac{1}{4}W_1$

Solution to Exercise 2.20

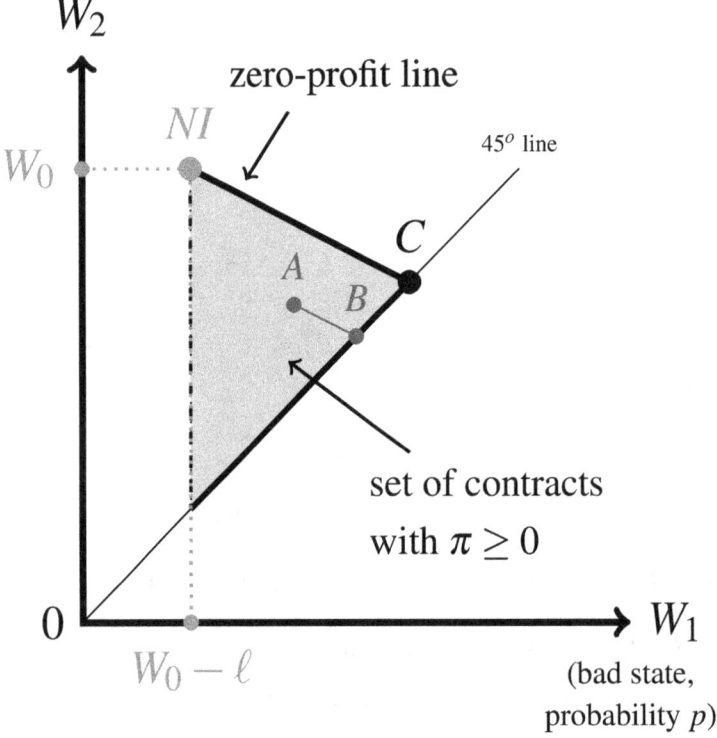

(good state,
probability $1 - p$)

Figure 2.17: The diagram for Exercise 2.20

(a) The set of contracts that yield non-negative profits is shown as a shaded triangle in Figure 2.17.

(b) Contract C shown in Figure 2.17 is the contract that is most preferred by a risk-averse individual among the contracts in the shaded triangle. C is a full-insurance contract with premium $h = p\ell$ guaranteeing a wealth of $W_0 - p\ell$. Any other contract on the zero-profit line is worse than contract C because it gives rise to a non-degenerate lottery with expected value $W_0 - p\ell$. Any other contract on the thick part of the 45° line is worse than contract C because it has a higher premium (while still being a full-insurance contract). Finally, any contract, say A, inside the shaded area lies on **an isoprofit line that goes through a contract which is on the thick part of the 45°** line below point C, call this point B (see Figure 2.17); then B is better than A (since it guarantees the expected value of A) but is worse than C, so that C is better than A.

(c) The contracts on the thick line from NI to C: the individual is indifferent among all these contracts, because they correspond to lotteries that have the same expected value as the NI lottery. On the other hand, contracts below this line have an expected value which is less than the expected value of the NI lottery and thus are worse than NI.

Solution to Exercise 2.21 The no-insurance option corresponds to the wealth lottery $NI = \begin{pmatrix} W_0 & W_0 - \ell \\ 1 - p & p \end{pmatrix}$ whose expected value is

$$\mathbb{E}[NI] = W_0 - p\ell. \tag{2.9}$$

Suppose that the individual is **risk neutral** and is offered a full-insurance contract $(h, 0)$ which yields zero profits, that is,

$$h - p\ell = 0 \quad \text{or, equivalently,} \quad h = p\ell. \tag{2.10}$$

For the potential customer, such a contract corresponds to the wealth lottery $C = \begin{pmatrix} W_0 - h \\ 1 \end{pmatrix}$ whose expected value is

$$\mathbb{E}[C] = W_0 - h \underbrace{=}_{\text{using (2.9) and (2.10)}} \mathbb{E}[NI]. \tag{2.11}$$

By risk neutrality, the individual is indifferent between NI and $\mathbb{E}[NI]$ for sure ($NI \sim \mathbb{E}[NI]$) and is also indifferent between C and $\mathbb{E}[NI]$ for sure (since – by (2.11) – C and $\mathbb{E}[NI]$ for sure are the same contract):

$$NI \sim \mathbb{E}[NI] \sim C.$$

Assuming that the individual's preferences are transitive, it follows that

$$NI \sim C.$$

Solution to Exercise 2.22 The proof is a simple modification of the proof for Exercise

2.21: the no-insurance option corresponds to the wealth lottery $NI = \begin{pmatrix} W_0 & W_0 - \ell \\ 1 - p & p \end{pmatrix}$ whose expected value is

$$\mathbb{E}[NI] = W_0 - p\ell. \tag{2.12}$$

Suppose that the individual is **risk loving** and is offered a full-insurance contract $(h, 0)$ that yields zero profits, that is,

$$h = p\ell. \tag{2.13}$$

For the potential customer, such a contract corresponds to the wealth lottery $C = \begin{pmatrix} W_0 - h \\ 1 \end{pmatrix}$ which is the same as $\begin{pmatrix} \mathbb{E}[C] \\ 1 \end{pmatrix} = \mathbb{E}[C] = W_0 - h \underbrace{=}_{\text{by (2.13)}} \mathbb{E}[NI]$. Since the individual is risk loving, he prefers NI to $\mathbb{E}[NI]$ for sure ($NI \succ \mathbb{E}[NI]$) and is indifferent between C and $\mathbb{E}[NI]$ for sure, since it is the same lottery ($C \sim \mathbb{E}[NI]$); thus $NI \succ \mathbb{E}[NI] \sim C$. Assuming that the individual's preferences are transitive, it follows that $NI \succ C$.

Solution to Exercise 2.23 The maximum premium that Ann is willing to pay for full insurance is $h_{max} = p\ell + R_{NI} = \frac{1}{3}15,000 + 2,000 = 5,000$. Since she is offered full insurance at a lower premium, namely $4,920$, she will take it (she is better off with full insurance at this premium than with no insurance).

Solution to Exercise 2.24 The maximum premium that Bob is willing to pay for full insurance is $h_{max} = p\ell + R_{NI} = p10,000 + 900$. We are told that this is equal to $4,000$. Thus, to find p we solve the equation $p10,000 + 900 = 4,000$ whose solution is $p = \frac{3,100}{10,000} = 0.31$.

3. Expected Utility Theory

3.1 Expected utility: theorems

As noted in the previous chapter, with the exception of risk-neutral individuals, even if we restrict attention to money lotteries we are not able to say much – in general – about how an individual would choose among lotteries. What we need is a theory of "rational" preferences over lotteries that

(1) is general enough to cover lotteries whose outcomes are not necessarily sums of money and

(2) is capable of accounting for different attitudes to risk in the case of money lotteries.

One such theory is the theory of expected utility, to which we now turn.

The theory of expected utility was developed by the founders of Game Theory, namely John von Neumann and Oskar Morgenstern, in their 1944 book *Theory of Games and Economic Behavior*. In a rather unconventional way, we shall first (in this section) state the main result of the theory (which we split into two theorems) and then (in the following section) explain the assumptions (or axioms) behind that result. The reader who is not interested in understanding the conceptual foundations of expected utility theory, but wants to understand what the theory says and how it can be used, can study this section and skip the next.

Let O be a set of *basic outcomes*. Note that a basic outcome need not be a sum of money: it could be the state of an individual's health, or whether the individual under consideration receives an award, or whether it will rain on the day of a planned outdoor party, etc. Let $\mathscr{L}(O)$ be the set of *simple lotteries* (or probability distributions) over O.

We will assume throughout this chapter that O is a finite set: $O = \{o_1, o_2, ..., o_m\}$ ($m \geq 1$).

Thus, an element of $\mathcal{L}(O)$ is of the form $\begin{pmatrix} o_1 & o_2 & \cdots & o_m \\ p_1 & p_2 & \cdots & p_m \end{pmatrix}$ with $0 \leq p_i \leq 1$, for all

$i = 1, 2, ..., m$, and $p_1 + p_2 + ... + p_m = 1$. We will use the symbol L (with or without subscript) to denote an element of $\mathcal{L}(O)$, that is, a simple lottery. Lotteries are used to represent situations of uncertainty. For example, if $m = 4$ and the individual faces the

lottery $L = \begin{pmatrix} o_1 & o_2 & o_3 & o_4 \\ \frac{2}{5} & 0 & \frac{1}{5} & \frac{2}{5} \end{pmatrix}$ then she knows that, eventually, the outcome will be

one and only one of o_1, o_2, o_3, o_4, but does not know which one; furthermore, she is able to quantify her uncertainty by assigning probabilities to these outcomes. We interpret these probabilities either as objectively obtained from relevant (past) data or as subjective estimates by the individual, as explained in Chapter 2 (Section 2.1).

The assignment of *zero probability* to a particular basic outcome is taken to be an expression of *belief, not impossibility*: the individual is confident that the outcome will not arise, but she cannot rule out that outcome on logical grounds or by appealing to the laws of nature.

Among the elements of $\mathcal{L}(O)$ there are the degenerate lotteries that assign probability 1

to one basic outcome: for example, if $m = 4$ one degenerate lottery is $\begin{pmatrix} o_1 & o_2 & o_3 & o_4 \\ 0 & 0 & 1 & 0 \end{pmatrix}$.

To simplify the notation we will often denote degenerate lotteries as basic outcomes, that

is, instead of writing $\begin{pmatrix} o_1 & o_2 & o_3 & o_4 \\ 0 & 0 & 1 & 0 \end{pmatrix}$ we will simply write o_3. Thus, in general,

the degenerate lottery $\begin{pmatrix} o_1 & \cdots & o_{i-1} & o_i & o_{i+1} & \cdots & o_m \\ 0 & 0 & 0 & 1 & 0 & 0 & 0 \end{pmatrix}$ will be denoted by o_i. As

another simplification, we will often omit those outcomes that are assigned zero probability.

For example, if $m = 4$, the lottery $\begin{pmatrix} o_1 & o_2 & o_3 & o_4 \\ \frac{1}{3} & 0 & \frac{2}{3} & 0 \end{pmatrix}$ will be written more simply as

$\begin{pmatrix} o_1 & o_3 \\ \frac{1}{3} & \frac{2}{3} \end{pmatrix}$.

Throughout this chapter we shall call the individual under consideration the Decision-Maker, or *DM* for short. The theory of expected utility assumes that the *DM* has a complete and transitive ranking $\succsim$ of the elements of $\mathcal{L}(O)$ (indeed, this is one of the axioms listed in the next section). As in Chapter 2, the interpretation of $L \succsim L'$ is that the *DM* considers L to be at least as good as L'. By completeness, given any two lotteries L and L', either $L \succ L'$ (the *DM* prefers L to L') or $L' \succ L$ (the *DM* prefers L' to L) or $L \sim L'$ (the *DM* is indifferent between L and L'). Furthermore, by transitivity, for any three lotteries L_1, L_2 and L_3, if $L_1 \succsim L_2$ and $L_2 \succsim L_3$, then $L_1 \succsim L_3$. Besides completeness and transitivity, a number of other "rationality" constraints are postulated on the ranking $\succsim$ of the elements of $\mathcal{L}(O)$; these constraints are the so-called Expected Utility Axioms and are discussed in the next section.

> **Definition 3.1.1** A ranking $\succsim$ of the elements of $\mathscr{L}(O)$ that satisfies the Expected
> Utility Axioms (listed in the next section) is called a *von Neumann-Morgenstern ranking*.

The two theorems in this section are the key results in the theory of expected utility.

Theorem 3.1.1 [von Neumann-Morgenstern, 1944].

Let $O = \{o_1, o_2, ..., o_m\}$ be a set of basic outcomes and $\mathscr{L}(O)$ the set of simple lotteries over O. If $\succsim$ is a von Neumann-Morgenstern ranking of the elements of $\mathscr{L}(O)$ then there exists a function $U : O \to \mathbb{R}$, called a *von Neumann-Morgenstern utility function*, that assigns a number (called *utility*) to every basic outcome and is such that, for any

two lotteries $L = \begin{pmatrix} o_1 & o_2 & ... & o_m \\ p_1 & p_2 & ... & p_m \end{pmatrix}$ and $L' = \begin{pmatrix} o_1 & o_2 & ... & o_m \\ q_1 & q_2 & ... & q_m \end{pmatrix}$,

$$L \succ L' \text{ if and only if } \mathbb{E}[U(L)] > \mathbb{E}[U(L')], \quad \text{and}$$

$$L \sim L' \text{ if and only if } \mathbb{E}[U(L)] = \mathbb{E}[U(L')]$$

where

$$U(L) = \begin{pmatrix} U(o_1) & U(o_2) & ... & U(o_m) \\ p_1 & p_2 & ... & p_m \end{pmatrix}, \ U(L') = \begin{pmatrix} U(o_1) & U(o_2) & ... & U(o_m) \\ q_1 & q_2 & ... & q_m \end{pmatrix},$$

$\mathbb{E}[U(L)]$ is the expected value of the lottery $U(L)$ and $\mathbb{E}[U(L')]$ is the expected value of the lottery $U(L')$, that is,

$$\mathbb{E}[U(L)] = p_1 U(o_1) + p_2 U(o_2) + ... + p_m U(o_m), \text{ and}$$

$$\mathbb{E}[U(L')] = q_1 U(o_1) + q_2 U(o_2) + ... + q_m U(o_m).$$

$\mathbb{E}[U(L)]$ is called the *expected utility* of lottery L (and $\mathbb{E}[U(L')]$ the expected utility of lottery L').

We say that any function $U : O \to \mathbb{R}$ that satisfies the property that, for any two lotteries L and L', $L \succsim L'$ if and only if $\mathbb{E}[U(L)] \geq \mathbb{E}[U(L')]$ *represents the preferences* (or ranking) $\succsim$.

Before we comment on Theorem 3.1.1 we give an example of how one can use it. Theorem 3.1.1 sometimes allows us to predict an individual's choice between two lotteries C and D if we know how that individual ranks two different lotteries A and B.

For example, suppose we observe that Susan is faced with the choice between lotteries A and B below and she says that she prefers A to B:

$$A = \begin{pmatrix} o_1 & o_2 & o_3 \\ 0 & 0.25 & 0.75 \end{pmatrix} \qquad B = \begin{pmatrix} o_1 & o_2 & o_3 \\ 0.2 & 0 & 0.8 \end{pmatrix}$$

With this information we can predict which of the following two lotteries C and D she will choose, if she has von Neumann-Morgenstern preferences:

$$C = \begin{pmatrix} o_1 & o_2 & o_3 \\ 0.8 & 0 & 0.2 \end{pmatrix} \qquad D = \begin{pmatrix} o_1 & o_2 & o_3 \\ 0 & 1 & 0 \end{pmatrix} = o_2.$$

Let U be a von Neumann-Morgenstern utility function whose existence is guaranteed by Theorem 3.1.1. Let $U(o_1) = a$, $U(o_2) = b$ and $U(o_3) = c$ (where a, b and c are numbers). Then, since Susan prefers A to B, the expected utility of A must be greater than the expected utility of B: $0.25b + 0.75c > 0.2a + 0.8c$. This inequality is equivalent to $0.25b > 0.2a + 0.05c$ or, dividing both sides by 0.25, $b > 0.8a + 0.2c$. It follows from this and Theorem 3.1.1 that Susan prefers D to C, because the expected utility of D is b and the expected utility of C is $0.8a + 0.2c$. Note that, in this example, we merely used the fact that a von Neumann-Morgenstern utility function *exists*, even though we do not know what the values of this function are.

Theorem 3.1.1 is an example of a "representation theorem" and is a generalization of a similar result for the case of the ranking of a finite set of basic outcomes O. It is not difficult to prove that if $\succsim$ is a complete and transitive ranking of O then there exists a function $U : O \to \mathbb{R}$, called a utility function, such that, for any two basic outcomes $o, o' \in O$, $U(o) \geq U(o')$ if and only if $o \succsim o'$. Now, it is quite possible that an individual has a complete and transitive ranking of O, is fully aware of her ranking and yet she is not able to answer the question "what is your utility function?", perhaps because she has never heard about utility functions. A utility function is a *tool* that we can use to represent her ranking, nothing more than that. The same applies to von Neumann-Morgenstern rankings: Theorem 3.1.1 tells us that if an individual has a von Neumann-Morgenstern ranking of the set of lotteries $\mathscr{L}(O)$ then there exists a von Neumann-Morgenstern utility function that we can use to represent her preferences, but it would not make sense for us to ask the individual "what is your von Neumann-Morgenstern utility function?" (indeed this was a question that could not even be conceived before von Neumann and Morgenstern stated and proved Theorem 3.1.1 in 1944!).

Theorem 3.1.1 tells us that a von Neumann-Morgenstern utility function exists; the next theorem can be used to actually construct such a function, by asking the individual to answer a few questions, formulated in a way that is fully comprehensible to her (that is, without using the word 'utility'). The theorem says that, although there are many utility functions that represent a given von Neumann-Morgenstern ranking, once you know one function you "know them all", in the sense that there is a simple operation that transforms one function into the other.

Theorem 3.1.2 [von Neumann-Morgenstern, 1944].

Let $\succsim$ be a von Neumann-Morgenstern ranking of the set of basic lotteries $\mathscr{L}(O)$, where $O = \{o_1, o_2, ..., o_m\}$. Then the following are true.

(A) If $U : O \to \mathbb{R}$ is a von Neumann-Morgenstern utility function that represents $\succsim$, then, for any two real numbers a and b, with $a > 0$, the function $V : O \to \mathbb{R}$ defined by $V(o_i) = aU(o_i) + b$ (for every $i = 1, ..., m$) is also a von Neumann-Morgenstern utility function that represents $\succsim$.

(B) If $U : O \to \mathbb{R}$ and $V : O \to \mathbb{R}$ are two von Neumann-Morgenstern utility functions that represent $\succsim$, then there exist two real numbers a and b, with $a > 0$, such that $V(o_i) = aU(o_i) + b$ (for every $i = 1, ..., m$).

Proof. The proof of Part A of Theorem 3.1.2 is very simple. Let a and b be two numbers, with $a > 0$. The hypothesis is that $U : O \to \mathbb{R}$ is a von Neumann-Morgenstern utility function that represents $\succsim$, that is, that, for any two lotteries $L = \begin{pmatrix} o_1 & \cdots & o_m \\ p_1 & \cdots & p_m \end{pmatrix}$ and

$$L' = \begin{pmatrix} o_1 & \cdots & o_m \\ q_1 & \cdots & q_m \end{pmatrix},$$

$$L \succsim L' \text{ if and only if } p_1 U(o_1) + ... + p_m U(o_m) \geq q_1 U(o_1) + ... + q_m U(o_m) \quad (3.1)$$

Multiplying both sides of inequality (3.1) by $a > 0$ and adding $(p_1 + \cdots + p_m)b$ to the left-hand side and $(q_1 + \cdots + q_m)b$ to the right-hand side[1] we obtain

$$p_1 [aU(o_1) + b] + ... + p_m [aU(o_m) + b] \geq q_1 [aU(o_1) + b] + ... + q_m [aU(o_m) + b] \quad (3.2)$$

Defining $V(o_i) = aU(o_i) + b$, it follows from (3.1) and (3.2) that

$$L \succsim L' \text{ if and only if } p_1 V(o_1) + ... + p_m V(o_m) \geq q_1 V(o_1) + ... + q_m V(o_m),$$

that is, the function V is a von Neumann-Morgenstern utility function that represents the ranking $\succsim$. The proof of Part B will be given later, after introducing more notation and some observations. ∎

---

[1] Note that $(p_1 + \cdots + p_m) = (q_1 + \cdots + q_m) = 1$.

Suppose that the *DM* has a von Neumann-Morgenstern ranking of the set of lotteries $\mathscr{L}(O)$. Since among the lotteries there are the degenerate ones that assign probability 1 to a single basic outcome, it follows that the *DM* has a complete and transitive ranking of the basic outcomes. We shall write o_{best} for a best basic outcome, that is, a basic outcome which is at least as good as any other basic outcome ($o_{best} \succsim o$, for every $o \in O$) and o_{worst} for a worst basic outcome, that is, a basic outcome such that every other outcome is at least as good as it ($o \succsim o_{worst}$, for every $o \in O$). Note that there may be several best outcomes (then the *DM* would be indifferent among them) and several worst outcomes; then o_{best} will denote an arbitrary best outcome and o_{worst} an arbitrary worst outcome. We shall assume throughout that the *DM* is not indifferent among all the outcomes, that is, we shall assume that $o_{best} \succ o_{worst}$.

We now show that, in virtue of Theorem 3.1.2, among the von Neumann-Morgenstern utility functions that represent a given von Neumann-Morgenstern ranking $\succsim$ of $\mathscr{L}(O)$, there is one that assigns the value 1 to the best basic outcome(s) and the value 0 to the worst basic outcome(s). To see this, consider an arbitrary von Neumann-Morgenstern utility function $F : O \to \mathbb{R}$ that represents $\succsim$ and define $G : O \to \mathbb{R}$ as follows: for every $o \in O$, $G(o) = F(o) - F(o_{worst})$. Then, by Theorem 3.1.2 (with $a = 1$ and $b = -F(o_{worst})$), G is also a utility function that represents $\succsim$ and, by construction, $G(o_{worst}) = F(o_{worst}) - F(o_{worst}) = 0$; note also that, since $o_{best} \succ o_{worst}$, it follows that $G(o_{best}) > 0$. Finally, define $U : O \to \mathbb{R}$ as follows: for every $o \in O$, $U(o) = \frac{G(o)}{G(o_{best})}$. Then, by Theorem 3.1.2 (with $a = \frac{1}{G(o_{best})}$ and $b = 0$), U is a utility function that represents $\succsim$ and, by construction, $U(o_{worst}) = 0$ and $U(o_{best}) = 1$. For example, if there are six basic outcomes and the ranking of the basic outcomes is $o_3 \sim o_6 \succ o_1 \succ o_4 \succ o_2 \sim o_5$, then one can take as o_{best} either o_3 or o_6 and as o_{worst} either o_2 or o_5; furthermore, if F is given by

o_1	o_2	o_3	o_4	o_5	o_6
2	−2	8	0	−2	8

then G is the function

o_1	o_2	o_3	o_4	o_5	o_6
4	0	10	2	0	10

and U is the function

o_1	o_2	o_3	o_4	o_5	o_6
0.4	0	1	0.2	0	1

.

Definition 3.1.2 Let $U : O \to \mathbb{R}$ be a utility function that represents a given von Neumann-Morgenstern ranking $\succsim$ of the set of lotteries $\mathscr{L}(O)$. We say that U is *normalized* if $U(o_{worst}) = 0$ and $U(o_{best}) = 1$.

The transformations described above show how to normalize any given utility function. Armed with the notion of a normalized utility function we can now complete the proof of Theorem 3.1.2.

Proof of Part B of Theorem 3.1.2. Let $F : O \rightarrow \mathbb{R}$ and $G : O \rightarrow \mathbb{R}$ be two von Neumann-Morgenstern utility functions that represent a given von Neumann-Morgenstern ranking of $\mathscr{L}(O)$. Let $U : O \rightarrow \mathbb{R}$ be the normalization of F and $V : O \rightarrow \mathbb{R}$ be the normalization of G. First we show that it must be that $U = V$, that is, $U(o) = V(o)$ for every $o \in O$. Suppose, by contradiction, that there is an $\hat{o} \in O$ such that $U(\hat{o}) \neq V(\hat{o})$. Without loss of generality we can assume that $U(\hat{o}) > V(\hat{o})$. Construct the following lottery: $L = \begin{pmatrix} o_{best} & o_{worst} \\ \hat{p} & 1 - \hat{p} \end{pmatrix}$ with $\hat{p} = U(\hat{o})$ (recall that U is normalized and thus takes on values in the interval from 0 to 1). Then $\mathbb{E}[U(L)] = \mathbb{E}[V(L)] = U(\hat{o})$. Hence, according to U it must be that $\hat{o} \sim L$ (this follows from Theorem 3.1.1), while according to V it must be (again, by Theorem 3.1.1) that $L \succ \hat{o}$ (since $\mathbb{E}[V(L)] = U(\hat{o}) > V(\hat{o})$). Then U and V cannot be two representations of the same ranking. Now let $a_1 = \frac{1}{F(o_{best}) - F(o_{worst})}$ and $b_1 = -\frac{F(o_{worst})}{F(o_{best}) - F(o_{worst})}$. Note that $a_1 > 0$. Then it is easy to verify that, for every $o \in O$, $U(o) = a_1 F(o) + b_1$. Similarly let $a_2 = \frac{1}{G(o_{best}) - G(o_{worst})}$ and $b_2 = -\frac{G(o_{worst})}{G(o_{best}) - G(o_{worst})}$; again, $a_2 > 0$ and, for every $o \in O$, $V(o) = a_2 G(o) + b_2$. We can invert the latter transformation and obtain that, for every $o \in O$, $G(o) = \frac{V(o)}{a_2} - \frac{b_2}{a_2}$. Thus, we can transform F into U, which – as proved above – is the same as V, and then transform V into G thus obtaining the following transformation of F into G:

$$G(o) = aF(o) + b \text{ where } a = \frac{a_1}{a_2} > 0 \text{ and } b = \frac{b_1 - b_2}{a_2}.$$

∎

Theorem 3.1.2 is often stated as follows: a utility function that represents a von Neumann-Morgenstern ranking $\succsim$ of $\mathscr{L}(O)$ is *unique up to a positive affine transformation*. An affine transformation is a function $f : \mathbb{R} \rightarrow \mathbb{R}$ of the form $f(x) = ax + b$ with $a, b \in \mathbb{R}$. The affine transformation is positive if $a > 0$.
Because of Theorem 3.1.2, a von Neumann-Morgenstern utility function is usually referred to as a *cardinal* utility function.

Theorem 3.1.1 guarantees the existence of a utility function that represents a given von Neumann-Morgenstern ranking $\succsim$ of $\mathscr{L}(O)$ and Theorem 3.1.2 characterizes the set of such functions. Can one actually construct a utility function that represents a given ranking? The answer is affirmative: if there are m basic outcomes one can construct an individual's von Neumann-Morgenstern utility function by asking her at most $(m - 1)$ questions. The first question is "what is your ranking of the basic outcomes?". Then we can construct the normalized utility function by first assigning the value 1 to the best outcome(s) and the value 0 to the worst outcome(s). This leaves us with at most

$(m-2)$ values to determine. For this we appeal to one of the axioms discussed in the next section, namely the Continuity Axiom, which says that, for every basic outcome o_i there is a probability $p_i \in [0,1]$ such that the *DM* is indifferent between o_i for certain and the lottery that gives a best outcome with probability p_i and a worst outcome with probability $(1-p_i)$: $o_i \sim \begin{pmatrix} o_{best} & o_{worst} \\ p_i & 1-p_i \end{pmatrix}$. Thus, for each basic outcome o_i for which a utility has not been determined yet, we should ask the individual to tell us the value of p_i such that $o_i \sim \begin{pmatrix} o_{best} & o_{worst} \\ p_i & 1-p_i \end{pmatrix}$; then we can set $U_i(o_i) = p_i$, because the expected utility of the lottery $\begin{pmatrix} o_{best} & o_{worst} \\ p_i & 1-p_i \end{pmatrix}$ is $p_i U_i(o_{best}) + (1-p_i) U_i(o_{worst}) = p_i(1) + (1-p_i)0 = p_i$.

■ **Example 3.1** Suppose that there are five basic outcomes, that is, $O = \{o_1, o_2, o_3, o_4, o_5\}$ and the *DM*, who has von Neumann-Morgenstern preferences, tells us that her ranking of the basic outcomes is as follows: $o_2 \succ o_1 \sim o_5 \succ o_3 \sim o_4$. Then we can begin by assigning utility 1 to the best outcome o_2 and utility 0 to the worst outcomes o_3 and o_4: $\begin{pmatrix} \text{outcome:} & o_1 & o_2 & o_3 & o_4 & o_5 \\ \text{utility:} & ? & 1 & 0 & 0 & ? \end{pmatrix}$. There is only one value left to be determined, namely the utility of o_1 (which is also the utility of o_5, since $o_1 \sim o_5$). To find this value, we ask the *DM* to tell us what value of p makes her indifferent between the lottery $L = \begin{pmatrix} o_2 & o_3 \\ p & 1-p \end{pmatrix}$ and outcome o_1 with certainty. Suppose that her answer is: 0.4. Then her normalized von Neumann-Morgenstern utility function is

$$\begin{pmatrix} \text{outcome:} & o_1 & o_2 & o_3 & o_4 & o_5 \\ \text{utility:} & 0.4 & 1 & 0 & 0 & 0.4 \end{pmatrix}.$$

Knowing this, we can predict her choice among any set of lotteries over these five basic outcomes.   ■

Test your understanding of the concepts introduced in this section, by going through the exercises in Section 3.3.2 at the end of this chapter.

3.2 Expected utility: the axioms

We can now turn to the list of rationality axioms proposed by von Neumann and Morgenstern. This section makes heavy use of mathematical notation and, as mentioned in the previous section, if the reader is not interested in understanding in what sense the theory of expected utility captures the notion of rationality, he/she can skip it without affecting his/her ability to understand the rest of this book.

Let $O = \{o_1, o_2, \ldots, o_m\}$ be the set of basic outcomes and $\mathscr{L}(O)$ the set of simple lotteries, that is, the set of probability distributions over O. Let $\succsim$ be a binary relation on $\mathscr{L}(O)$. We say that $\succsim$ is a *von Neumann-Morgenstern ranking* of $\mathscr{L}(O)$ if it satisfies the following four axioms or properties.

Axiom 1 [Completeness and transitivity]. $\succsim$ is complete (for every two lotteries L and L' either $L \succsim L'$ or $L' \succsim L$ or both) and transitive (for any three lotteries L_1, L_2 and L_3, if $L_1 \succsim L_2$ and $L_2 \succsim L_3$ then $L_1 \succsim L_3$).

As noted in the previous section, Axiom 1 implies that there is a complete and transitive ranking of the basic outcomes. Recall that o_{best} denotes a best basic outcome and o_{worst} denotes a worst basic outcome and that we are assuming that $o_{best} \succ o_{worst}$, that is, that the *DM* is not indifferent among all the basic outcomes.

Axiom 2 [Monotonicity]. $\begin{pmatrix} o_{best} & o_{worst} \\ p & 1-p \end{pmatrix} \succsim \begin{pmatrix} o_{best} & o_{worst} \\ q & 1-q \end{pmatrix}$ if and only if $p \geq q$.

Axiom 3 [Continuity]. For every basic outcome o_i there is a $p_i \in [0,1]$ such that

$$o_i \sim \begin{pmatrix} o_{best} & o_{worst} \\ p_i & 1-p_i \end{pmatrix}.$$

Before we introduce the last axiom we need to define a compound lottery.

Definition 3.2.1 A *compound lottery* is a lottery of the form $\begin{pmatrix} x_1 & x_2 & \ldots & x_r \\ p_1 & p_2 & \ldots & p_r \end{pmatrix}$ where each x_i is either an element of O or an element of $\mathscr{L}(O)$.

For example, let $m = 4$. Then $L = \begin{pmatrix} o_1 & o_2 & o_3 & o_4 \\ \frac{2}{5} & 0 & \frac{1}{5} & \frac{2}{5} \end{pmatrix}$ is a simple lottery (an element of

$\mathscr{L}(O)$), while

$$
C = \left(\begin{array}{ccc}
\left(\begin{array}{cccc} o_1 & o_2 & o_3 & o_4 \\ \frac{1}{3} & \frac{1}{6} & \frac{1}{3} & \frac{1}{6} \end{array} \right) & o_1 & \left(\begin{array}{cccc} o_1 & o_2 & o_3 & o_4 \\ \frac{1}{5} & 0 & \frac{1}{5} & \frac{3}{5} \end{array} \right) \\
\frac{1}{2} & \frac{1}{4} & \frac{1}{4}
\end{array} \right)
$$

is a compound lottery.[2] The compound lottery C can be viewed graphically as a tree, as shown in Figure 3.1.

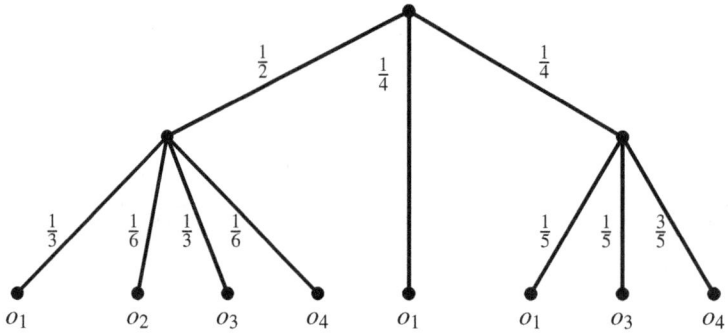

Figure 3.1: A compound lottery

Next we define the simple lottery $L(C)$ corresponding to a compound lottery C. Before introducing the formal definition, we shall explain in an example how to construct such a simple lottery. Continuing with the example of the compound lottery C given above and illustrated in Figure 3.1, first we replace a sequence of edges with a single edge and associate with it the product of the probabilities along the sequence of edges, as shown in Figure 3.2.

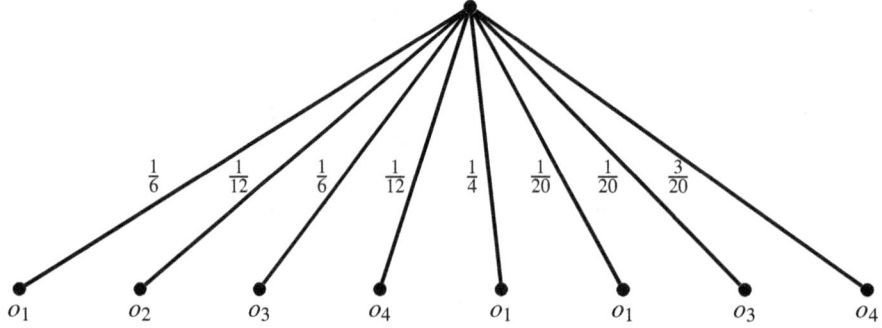

Figure 3.2: Simplification of Figure 3.1 obtained by merging paths into simple edges and associating with the simple edges the products of the probabilities along the path.

---

[2]With $r = 3$, $x_1 = \left(\begin{array}{cccc} o_1 & o_2 & o_3 & o_4 \\ \frac{1}{3} & \frac{1}{6} & \frac{1}{3} & \frac{1}{6} \end{array} \right)$, $x_2 = o_1$, $x_3 = \left(\begin{array}{cccc} o_1 & o_2 & o_3 & o_4 \\ \frac{1}{5} & 0 & \frac{1}{5} & \frac{3}{5} \end{array} \right)$, $p_1 = \frac{1}{2}, p_2 = \frac{1}{4}$ and $p_3 = \frac{1}{4}$.

Then we add up the probabilities of each outcome, as shown in Figure 3.3. Thus, the simple lottery $L(C)$ that corresponds to C is $L(C) = \begin{pmatrix} o_1 & o_2 & o_3 & o_4 \\ \frac{28}{60} & \frac{5}{60} & \frac{13}{60} & \frac{14}{60} \end{pmatrix}$, namely the lottery shown in Figure 3.3.

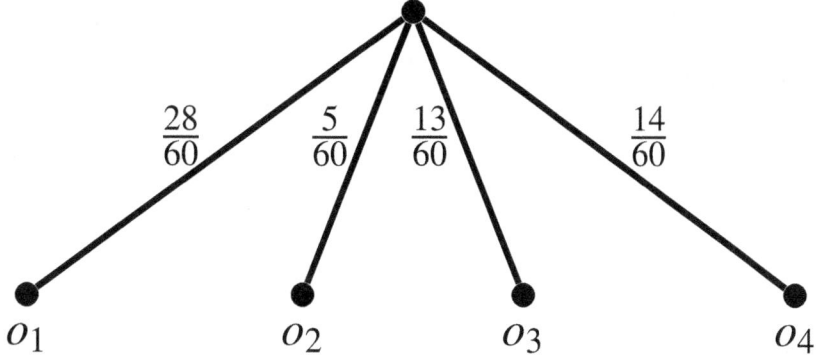

Figure 3.3: Simplification of Figure 3.2 obtained by adding, for each outcome, the probabilities of that outcome.

Definition 3.2.2 Given a compound lottery $C = \begin{pmatrix} x_1 & x_2 & \dots & x_r \\ p_1 & p_2 & \dots & p_r \end{pmatrix}$ the *correspond-*

ing simple lottery $L(C) = \begin{pmatrix} o_1 & o_2 & \dots & o_m \\ q_1 & q_2 & \dots & q_m \end{pmatrix}$ is defined as follows. First of all, for

$i = 1, \dots, m$ and $j = 1, \dots, r$, define

$$o_i(x_j) = \begin{cases} 1 & \text{if } x_j = o_i \\ 0 & \text{if } x_j = o_k \text{ with } k \neq i \\ s_i & \text{if } x_j = \begin{pmatrix} o_1 & \dots & o_{i-1} & o_i & o_{i+1} & \dots & o_m \\ s_1 & \dots & s_{i-1} & s_i & s_{i+1} & \dots & s_m \end{pmatrix} \end{cases}$$

Then $q_i = \sum\limits_{j=1}^{r} p_j o_i(x_j)$.

Continuing the above example where

$$C = \left(\begin{array}{ccc} \begin{pmatrix} o_1 & o_2 & o_3 & o_4 \\ \frac{1}{3} & \frac{1}{6} & \frac{1}{3} & \frac{1}{6} \end{pmatrix} & o_1 & \begin{pmatrix} o_1 & o_2 & o_3 & o_4 \\ \frac{1}{5} & 0 & \frac{1}{5} & \frac{3}{5} \end{pmatrix} \\ \frac{1}{2} & \frac{1}{4} & \frac{1}{4} \end{array} \right)$$

we have that

$$r = 3, \quad x_1 = \begin{pmatrix} o_1 & o_2 & o_3 & o_4 \\ \frac{1}{3} & \frac{1}{6} & \frac{1}{3} & \frac{1}{6} \end{pmatrix}, \quad x_2 = o_1 \quad \text{and} \quad x_3 = \begin{pmatrix} o_1 & o_2 & o_3 & o_4 \\ \frac{1}{5} & 0 & \frac{1}{5} & \frac{3}{5} \end{pmatrix},$$

so that

$$o_1(x_1) = \tfrac{1}{3}, \quad o_1(x_2) = 1, \quad \text{and} \quad o_1(x_3) = \tfrac{1}{5}$$

and thus $q_1 = \frac{1}{2}\left(\frac{1}{3}\right) + \frac{1}{4}(1) + \frac{1}{4}\left(\frac{1}{5}\right) = \frac{28}{60}$. Similarly, $q_2 = \frac{1}{2}\left(\frac{1}{6}\right) + \frac{1}{4}(0) + \frac{1}{4}(0) = \frac{1}{12} = \frac{5}{60}$, $q_3 = \frac{1}{2}\left(\frac{1}{3}\right) + \frac{1}{4}(0) + \frac{1}{4}\left(\frac{1}{5}\right) = \frac{13}{60}$ and $q_4 = \frac{1}{2}\left(\frac{1}{6}\right) + \frac{1}{4}(0) + \frac{1}{4}\left(\frac{3}{5}\right) = \frac{14}{60}$.

Axiom 4 [Independence or substitutability]. Consider an arbitrary basic outcome o_i and an arbitrary simple lottery $L = \begin{pmatrix} o_1 & \cdots & o_{i-1} & o_i & o_{i+1} & \cdots & o_m \\ p_1 & \cdots & p_{i-1} & p_i & p_{i+1} & \cdots & p_m \end{pmatrix}$. If $\hat{L}$ is a simple lottery such that $o_i \sim \hat{L}$, then $L \sim M$ where M is the simple lottery corresponding to the compound lottery $C = \begin{pmatrix} o_1 & \cdots & o_{i-1} & \hat{L} & o_{i+1} & \cdots & o_m \\ p_1 & \cdots & p_{i-1} & p_i & p_{i+1} & \cdots & p_m \end{pmatrix}$ obtained by replacing o_i with $\hat{L}$ in L.

We can now prove the first theorem of the previous section.

Proof of Theorem 3.1.1. To simplify the notation, throughout this proof we will assume that we have renumbered the basic outcomes in such a way that $o_{best} = o_1$ and $o_{worst} = o_m$. First of all, for every basic outcome o_i, let $u_i \in [0,1]$ be such that $o_i \sim \begin{pmatrix} o_1 & o_m \\ u_i & 1-u_i \end{pmatrix}$. The existence of such a value u_i is guaranteed by the Continuity Axiom (Axiom 3); clearly $u_1 = 1$ and $u_m = 0$. Now consider an arbitrary lottery

$$L_1 = \begin{pmatrix} o_1 & \cdots & o_m \\ p_1 & \cdots & p_m \end{pmatrix}.$$

First we show that

$$L_1 \sim \begin{pmatrix} o_1 & o_m \\ \sum_{i=1}^{m} p_i u_i & 1 - \sum_{i=1}^{m} p_i u_i \end{pmatrix} \tag{3.3}$$

This is done through a repeated application of the Independence Axiom (Axiom 4), as follows. Consider the compound lottery

$$\mathscr{C}_2 = \begin{pmatrix} o_1 & \begin{pmatrix} o_1 & o_m \\ u_2 & 1-u_2 \end{pmatrix} & o_3 & \cdots & o_m \\ p_1 & p_2 & p_3 & \cdots & p_m \end{pmatrix}$$

obtained by replacing o_2 in lottery L_1 with the lottery $\begin{pmatrix} o_1 & o_m \\ u_2 & 1-u_2 \end{pmatrix}$ that the *DM* considers to be just as good as o_2. The simple lottery corresponding to $\mathscr{C}_2$ is

$$L_2 = \begin{pmatrix} o_1 & o_3 & \cdots & o_{m-1} & o_m \\ p_1 + p_2 u_2 & p_3 & \cdots & p_{m-1} & p_m + p_2(1-u_2) \end{pmatrix}.$$

Note that o_2 is assigned probability 0 in L_2 and thus we have omitted it. By Axiom 4, $L_1 \sim L_2$. Now apply the same argument to L_2: let

$$\mathscr{C}_3 = \begin{pmatrix} o_1 & \begin{pmatrix} o_1 & o_m \\ u_3 & 1-u_3 \end{pmatrix} & \cdots & o_{m-1} & o_m \\ p_1 + p_2 u_2 & p_3 & \cdots & p_{m-1} & p_m + p_2(1-u_2) \end{pmatrix}$$

whose corresponding simple lottery is

$$L_3 = \begin{pmatrix} o_1 & \cdots & o_m \\ p_1 + p_2 u_2 + p_3 u_3 & \cdots & p_m + p_2(1-u_2) + p_3(1-u_3) \end{pmatrix}.$$

Note, again, that o_3 is assigned probability zero in L_3. By Axiom 4, $L_2 \sim L_3$; thus, by transitivity (since $L_1 \sim L_2$ and $L_2 \sim L_3$) we have that $L_1 \sim L_3$. Repeating this argument we get that $L_1 \sim L_{m-1}$, where

$$L_{m-1} = \begin{pmatrix} o_1 & o_m \\ p_1 + p_2 u_2 + \ldots + p_{m-1} u_{m-1} & p_m + p_2(1-u_2) + \ldots + p_{m-1}(1-u_{m-1}) \end{pmatrix}.$$

Since $u_1 = 1$ (so that $p_1 u_1 = p_1$) and $u_m = 0$ (so that $p_m u_m = 0$),

$$p_1 + p_2 u_2 + \ldots + p_{m-1} u_{m-1} = \sum_{i=1}^{m} p_i u_i$$

and

$$p_2(1-u_2) + \ldots + p_{m-1}(1-u_{m-1}) + p_m = \sum_{i=2}^{m} p_i - \sum_{i=2}^{m-1} p_i u_i = p_1 + \sum_{i=2}^{m} p_i - \sum_{i=2}^{m-1} p_i u_i - p_1$$

$$= \text{(since } u_1=1 \text{ and } u_m=0\text{)} \sum_{i=1}^{m} p_i - \sum_{i=2}^{m-1} p_i u_i - p_1 u_1 - p_m u_m = \left(\text{since } \sum_{i=1}^{m} p_i = 1\right) 1 - \sum_{i=1}^{m} p_i u_i.$$

Thus, $L_{m-1} = \begin{pmatrix} o_1 & & o_m \\ & & \\ \sum_{i=1}^{m} p_i u_i & & 1 - \sum_{i=1}^{m} p_i u_i \end{pmatrix}$, which proves (3.3). Now define the following

utility function $U : \{o_1,...,o_m\} \to [0,1]$: $U(o_i) = u_i$, where, as before, for every basic

outcome o_i, $u_i \in [0,1]$ is such that $o_i \sim \begin{pmatrix} o_1 & o_m \\ & \\ u_i & 1-u_i \end{pmatrix}$. Consider two arbitrary lotteries

$L = \begin{pmatrix} o_1 & \cdots & o_m \\ & & \\ p_1 & \cdots & p_m \end{pmatrix}$ and $L' = \begin{pmatrix} o_1 & \cdots & o_m \\ & & \\ q_1 & \cdots & q_m \end{pmatrix}$. We want to show that $L \succsim L'$ if and only

if $\mathbb{E}[U(L)] \geq \mathbb{E}[U(L')]$, that is, if and only if $\sum_{i=1}^{m} p_i u_i \geq \sum_{i=1}^{m} q_i u_i$. By (3.3), $L \sim M$, where

$M = \begin{pmatrix} o_1 & & o_m \\ & & \\ \sum_{i=1}^{m} p_i u_i & & 1 - \sum_{i=1}^{m} p_i u_i \end{pmatrix}$ and also $L' \sim M'$, where $M' = \begin{pmatrix} o_1 & & o_m \\ & & \\ \sum_{i=1}^{m} q_i u_i & & 1 - \sum_{i=1}^{m} q_i u_i \end{pmatrix}$.

Thus, by transitivity of $\succsim$, $L \succsim L'$ if and only if $M \succsim M'$; by the Monotonicity Axiom

(Axiom 2), $M \succsim M'$ if and only if $\sum_{i=1}^{m} p_i u_i \geq \sum_{i=1}^{m} q_i u_i$. ∎

The following example, known as the *Allais paradox*, suggests that one should view expected utility theory as a "prescriptive" or "normative" theory (that is, as a theory about how rational people *should* choose) rather than as a descriptive theory (that is, as a theory about the *actual* behavior of individuals). In 1953 the French economist Maurice Allais published a paper regarding a survey he had conducted in 1952 concerning a hypothetical decision problem. Subjects "with good training in and knowledge of the theory of probability, so that they could be considered to behave rationally" were asked to rank the following pairs of lotteries:

$$A = \begin{pmatrix} \$5 \text{ Million} & \$0 \\ \frac{89}{100} & \frac{11}{100} \end{pmatrix} \quad versus \quad B = \begin{pmatrix} \$1 \text{ Million} & \$0 \\ \frac{90}{100} & \frac{10}{100} \end{pmatrix}$$

and

$$C = \begin{pmatrix} \$5 \text{ Million} & \$1 \text{ Million} & \$0 \\ \frac{89}{100} & \frac{10}{100} & \frac{1}{100} \end{pmatrix} \quad versus \quad D = \begin{pmatrix} \$1 \text{ Million} \\ 1 \end{pmatrix}.$$

Most subjects reported the following ranking: $A \succ B$ and $D \succ C$. Such ranking violates the axioms of expected utility. To see this, let $O = \{o_1, o_2, o_3\}$ with $o_1 = \$5$ Million, $o_2 = \$1$ Million and $o_3 = \$0$. Let us assume that the individual in question prefers more money to less, so that $o_1 \succ o_2 \succ o_3$ and has a von Neumann-Morgenstern ranking of the lotteries over $\mathscr{L}(O)$. Let $u_2 \in (0, 1)$ be such that $D \sim \begin{pmatrix} \$5 \text{ Million} & \$0 \\ u_2 & 1 - u_2 \end{pmatrix}$ (the existence of such u_2 is guaranteed by the Continuity Axiom). Then, since $D \succ C$, by transitivity

$$\begin{pmatrix} \$5 \text{ Million} & \$0 \\ u_2 & 1 - u_2 \end{pmatrix} \succ C. \tag{3.4}$$

Let C' be the simple lottery corresponding to the compound lottery

$$\begin{pmatrix} \$5 \text{ Million} & \begin{pmatrix} \$5 \text{ Million} & \$0 \\ u_2 & 1 - u_2 \end{pmatrix} & \$0 \\ \frac{89}{100} & \frac{10}{100} & \frac{1}{100} \end{pmatrix}.$$

Then $C' = \begin{pmatrix} \$5 \text{ Million} & \$0 \\ \frac{89}{100} + \frac{10}{100}u_2 & 1 - \left(\frac{89}{100} + \frac{10}{100}u_2\right) \end{pmatrix}.$

By the Independence Axiom, $C \sim C'$ and thus, by (3.4) and transitivity,

$$\begin{pmatrix} \$5 \text{ Million} & \$0 \\ u_2 & 1 - u_2 \end{pmatrix} \succ \begin{pmatrix} \$5 \text{ Million} & \$0 \\ \frac{89}{100} + \frac{10}{100}u_2 & 1 - \left(\frac{89}{100} + \frac{10}{100}u_2\right) \end{pmatrix}.$$

Hence, by the Monotonicity Axiom, $u_2 > \frac{89}{100} + \frac{10}{100}u_2$, that is,

$$u_2 > \frac{89}{90}. \tag{3.5}$$

Let B' be the simple lottery corresponding to the following compound lottery, constructed from B by replacing the basic outcome '$\$1$ Million' with $\begin{pmatrix} \$5 \text{ Million} & \$0 \\ u_2 & 1 - u_2 \end{pmatrix}$:

$$\begin{pmatrix} \begin{pmatrix} \$5 \text{ Million} & \$0 \\ u_2 & 1 - u_2 \end{pmatrix} & \$0 \\ \frac{90}{100} & \frac{10}{100} \end{pmatrix}.$$

Then

$$B' = \begin{pmatrix} \$5 \text{ Million} & \$0 \\ \frac{90}{100}u_2 & 1 - \frac{90}{100}u_2 \end{pmatrix}.$$

By the Independence Axiom, $B \sim B'$; thus, since $A \succ B$, by transitivity, $A \succ B'$ and therefore, by the Monotonicity Axiom, $\frac{89}{100} > \frac{90}{100} u_2$, that is, $u_2 < \frac{89}{90}$, contradicting (3.5).

Thus, if one finds the expected utility axioms compelling as axioms of rationality, then one cannot consistently express a preference for A over B and also a preference for D over C.

Another well-known paradox is the *Ellsberg paradox*. Suppose that you are told that an urn contains 30 red balls and 60 more balls that are either blue or yellow. You don't know how many blue or how many yellow balls there are, but the number of blue balls plus the number of yellow ball equals 60 (they could be all blue or all yellow or any combination of the two). The balls are well mixed so that each individual ball is as likely to be drawn as any other. You are given a choice between bets A and B, where

A = you get \$100 if you pick a red ball and nothing otherwise,

B = you get \$100 if you pick a blue ball and nothing otherwise.

Many subjects in experiments state a strict preference for A over B: $A \succ B$. Consider now the following bets:

C = you get \$100 if you pick a red or yellow ball and nothing otherwise,

D = you get \$100 if you pick a blue or yellow ball and nothing otherwise.

Do the axioms of expected utility constrain your ranking of C and D? Many subjects in experiments state the following ranking: $A \succ B$ and $D \succsim C$. All such people violate the axioms of expected utility. The fraction of red balls in the urn is $\frac{30}{90} = \frac{1}{3}$. Let p_2 be the fraction of blue balls and p_3 the fraction of yellow balls (either of these can be zero: all we know is that $p_2 + p_3 = \frac{60}{90} = \frac{2}{3}$). Then A, B, C and D can be viewed as the following lotteries:

$$A = \begin{pmatrix} \$100 & \$0 \\ \frac{1}{3} & p_2 + p_3 \end{pmatrix}, \quad B = \begin{pmatrix} \$100 & \$0 \\ p_2 & \frac{1}{3} + p_3 \end{pmatrix}$$

$$C = \begin{pmatrix} \$100 & \$0 \\ \frac{1}{3} + p_3 & p_2 \end{pmatrix}, \quad D = \begin{pmatrix} \$100 & \$0 \\ p_2 + p_3 = \frac{2}{3} & \frac{1}{3} \end{pmatrix}$$

Let U be the normalized von Neumann-Morgenstern utility function that represents the individual's ranking; then $U(\$100) = 1$ and $U(0) = 0$. Thus,

$$\mathbb{E}[U(A)] = \tfrac{1}{3}, \quad \mathbb{E}[U(B)] = p_2, \quad \mathbb{E}[U(C)] = \tfrac{1}{3} + p_3, \quad \text{and} \quad \mathbb{E}[U(D)] = p_2 + p_3 = \tfrac{2}{3}.$$

Hence, $A \succ B$ if and only if $\tfrac{1}{3} > p_2$, which implies that $p_3 > \tfrac{1}{3}$, so that $\mathbb{E}[U(C)] = \tfrac{1}{3} + p_3 > \mathbb{E}[U(D)] = \tfrac{2}{3}$ and thus $C \succ D$ (similarly, $B \succ A$ if and only if $\tfrac{1}{3} < p_2$, which implies that $\mathbb{E}[U(C)] < \mathbb{E}[U(D)]$ and thus $D \succ C$).

> Test your understanding of the concepts introduced in this section, by going through the exercises in Section 3.3.2 at the end of this chapter.

3.3 Exercises

The solutions to the following exercises are given in Section 3.4 at the end of this chapter.

3.3.1 Exercises for Section 3.1: Expected utility: theorems

Exercise 3.1 Ben is offered a choice between the following two money lotteries:

$$A = \begin{pmatrix} \$4,000 & \$0 \\ 0.8 & 0.2 \end{pmatrix} \quad \text{and} \quad B = \begin{pmatrix} \$3,000 \\ 1 \end{pmatrix}.$$

He says he strictly prefers B to A. Which of the following two lotteries, C and D, will Ben choose if he satisfies the axioms of expected utility and prefers more money to less?

$$C = \begin{pmatrix} \$4,000 & \$0 \\ 0.2 & 0.8 \end{pmatrix}, \quad D = \begin{pmatrix} \$3,000 & \$0 \\ 0.25 & 0.75 \end{pmatrix}.$$

Exercise 3.2 There are three basic outcomes, o_1, o_2 and o_3. Ann satisfies the axioms of expected utility theory and her preferences over lotteries involving these three outcomes can be represented by the following von Neumann-Morgenstern utility function:

$$V(o_2) = a > V(o_1) = b > V(o_3) = c.$$

Normalize the utility function.

Exercise 3.3 Consider the following lotteries:

$$L_1 = \begin{pmatrix} \$3000 & \$500 \\ \frac{5}{6} & \frac{1}{6} \end{pmatrix}, \quad L_2 = \begin{pmatrix} \$3000 & \$500 \\ \frac{2}{3} & \frac{1}{3} \end{pmatrix},$$

$$L_3 = \begin{pmatrix} \$3000 & \$2000 & \$1000 & \$500 \\ \frac{1}{4} & \frac{1}{4} & \frac{1}{4} & \frac{1}{4} \end{pmatrix}, \quad L_4 = \begin{pmatrix} \$2000 & \$1000 \\ \frac{1}{2} & \frac{1}{2} \end{pmatrix}.$$

Jennifer says that she is indifferent between lottery L_1 and getting \$2,000 for certain. She is also indifferent between lottery L_2 and getting \$1,000 for certain. Finally, she says that between L_3 and L_4 she would chose L_3. Is she rational according to the theory of expected utility? [Assume that she prefers more money to less.]

Exercise 3.4 Consider the following basic outcomes:

- o_1 = a Summer internship at the White House,
- o_2 = a free one-week vacation in Europe,
- o_3 = \$800,
- o_4 = a free ticket to a concert.

Rachel says that her ranking of these outcomes is $o_1 \succ o_2 \succ o_3 \succ o_4$. She also says that (1) she is indifferent between $\begin{pmatrix} o_2 \\ 1 \end{pmatrix}$ and $\begin{pmatrix} o_1 & o_4 \\ \frac{4}{5} & \frac{1}{5} \end{pmatrix}$ and (2) she is indifferent between $\begin{pmatrix} o_3 \\ 1 \end{pmatrix}$ and $\begin{pmatrix} o_1 & o_4 \\ \frac{1}{2} & \frac{1}{2} \end{pmatrix}$. If she satisfies the axioms of expected utility theory, which of the two lotteries $L_1 = \begin{pmatrix} o_1 & o_2 & o_3 & o_4 \\ \frac{1}{8} & \frac{2}{8} & \frac{3}{8} & \frac{2}{8} \end{pmatrix}$ and $L_2 = \begin{pmatrix} o_1 & o_2 & o_3 \\ \frac{1}{5} & \frac{3}{5} & \frac{1}{5} \end{pmatrix}$ will she choose?

Exercise 3.5 Consider the following lotteries:

$$L_1 = \begin{pmatrix} \$30 & \$28 & \$24 & \$18 & \$8 \\ \frac{2}{10} & \frac{1}{10} & \frac{1}{10} & \frac{2}{10} & \frac{4}{10} \end{pmatrix} \quad \text{and} \quad L_2 = \begin{pmatrix} \$30 & \$28 & \$8 \\ \frac{1}{10} & \frac{4}{10} & \frac{5}{10} \end{pmatrix}.$$

(a) Which lottery would a risk neutral person choose?

(b) Paul's von Neumann-Morgenstern utility-of-money function is $U(\$m) = ln(m)$, where ln denotes the natural logarithm. Which lottery would Paul choose?

Exercise 3.6 There are five basic outcomes. Jane has a von Neumann-Morgenstern ranking of the set of lotteries over basic outcomes that can be represented by either of the following utility functions U and V:
$$\begin{pmatrix} & o_1 & o_2 & o_3 & o_4 & o_5 \\ U: & 44 & 170 & -10 & 26 & 98 \\ V: & 32 & 95 & 5 & 23 & 59 \end{pmatrix}.$$

(a) Show how to normalize each of U and V and verify that you get the same normalized utility function.

(b) Show how to transform U into V with a positive affine transformation of the form $x \mapsto ax + b$ with $a, b \in \mathbb{R}$ and $a > 0$.

Exercise 3.7 Consider the following lotteries: $L_3 = \begin{pmatrix} \$28 \\ 1 \end{pmatrix}$, $L_4 = \begin{pmatrix} \$10 & \$50 \\ \frac{1}{2} & \frac{1}{2} \end{pmatrix}$.

(a) Ann has the following von Neumann-Morgenstern utility function: $U_{Ann}(\$m) = \sqrt{m}$. How does she rank the two lotteries?

(b) Bob has the following von Neumann-Morgenstern utility function: $U_{Bob}(\$m) = 2m - \frac{m^4}{100^3}$. How does he rank the two lotteries?

(c) Verify that both Ann and Bob are risk averse, by determining what they would choose between lottery L_4 and its expected value for certain.

3.3.2 Exercises for Section 3.2: Expected utility: the axioms

Exercise 3.8 Let $O = \{o_1, o_2, o_3, o_4\}$. Find the simple lottery corresponding to the following compound lottery

$$\left(\begin{pmatrix} o_1 & o_2 & o_3 & o_4 \\ \frac{2}{5} & \frac{1}{10} & \frac{3}{10} & \frac{1}{5} \end{pmatrix} \quad \begin{pmatrix} o_2 \\ 1 \end{pmatrix} \quad \begin{pmatrix} o_1 & o_3 & o_4 \\ \frac{1}{5} & \frac{1}{5} & \frac{3}{5} \end{pmatrix} \quad \begin{pmatrix} o_2 & o_3 \\ \frac{1}{3} & \frac{2}{3} \end{pmatrix} \\ \frac{1}{8} \quad\quad \frac{1}{4} \quad\quad \frac{1}{8} \quad\quad \frac{1}{2} \right)$$

Exercise 3.9 Let $O = \{o_1, o_2, o_3, o_4\}$. Suppose that the *DM* has a von Neumann-Morgenstern ranking of $\mathscr{L}(O)$ and states the following indifference:

$$o_1 \sim \begin{pmatrix} o_2 & o_4 \\ \frac{1}{4} & \frac{3}{4} \end{pmatrix} \quad \text{and} \quad o_2 \sim \begin{pmatrix} o_3 & o_4 \\ \frac{3}{5} & \frac{2}{5} \end{pmatrix}.$$

Find a lottery that the *DM* considers just as good as

$$L = \begin{pmatrix} o_1 & o_2 & o_3 & o_4 \\ \frac{1}{3} & \frac{2}{9} & \frac{1}{9} & \frac{1}{3} \end{pmatrix}.$$

Do not add any information to what is given above (in particular, do not make any assumptions about which outcome is best and which is worst).

Exercise 3.10 — **More difficult.** Would you be willing to pay more in order to reduce the probability of dying within the next hour from one sixth to zero or from four sixths to three sixths? Unfortunately, this is not a hypothetical question: you accidentally entered the office of a mad scientist and have been overpowered and tied to a chair. The mad scientist has put six glasses in front of you, numbered 1 to 6, and tells you that one of them contains a deadly poison and the other five contain a harmless liquid. He says that he is going to roll a die and make you drink from the glass whose number matches the number that shows up from the rolling of the die. You beg to be exempted and he asks you "what is the largest amount of money that you would be willing to pay to replace the glass containing the poison with one containing a harmless liquid?". Interpret this question as "what sum of money x makes you indifferent between

(1) leaving the poison in whichever glass contains it and rolling the die, and

(2) reducing your wealth by $\$x$ and rolling the die after the poison has been replaced by a harmless liquid". Your answer is: $\$X$.

Then he asks you "suppose that instead of one glass with poison there had been four glasses with poison (and two with a harmless liquid); what is the largest amount of money that you would be willing to pay to replace one glass with poison with a glass containing a harmless liquid (and thus roll the die with 3 glasses with poison and 3 with a harmless liquid)?". Your answer is: $\$Y$.

Show that if $X > Y$ then you do not satisfy the axioms of Expected Utility Theory.

[Hint: think about what the basic outcomes are; assume that you do not care about how much money is left in your estate if you die and that, when alive, you prefer more money to less.]

3.4   Solutions to Exercises

Solution to Exercise 3.1 Since Ben prefers B to A, he must prefer D to C.

Proof. Let U be a von Neumann-Morgenstern utility function that represents Ben's preferences. Let $U(\$4,000) = a, U(\$3,000) = b$ and $U(\$0) = c$. Since Ben prefers more money to less, $a > b > c$. Then $\mathbb{E}[U(A)] = 0.8\,U(\$4,000) + 0.2\,U(\$0) = 0.8a + 0.2c$ and $\mathbb{E}[U(B)] = U(\$3,000) = b$. Since Ben prefers B to A, it must be that $b > 0.8a + 0.2c$. Let us now compare C and D: $\mathbb{E}[U(C)] = 0.2a + 0.8c$ and $\mathbb{E}[U(D)] = 0.25b + 0.75c$. Since $b > 0.8a + 0.2c$, $0.25b > 0.25(0.8a + 0.2c) = 0.2a + 0.05c$ and thus, adding $0.75c$ to both sides, we get that $0.25b + 0.75c > 0.2a + 0.8c$, that is, $\mathbb{E}[U(D)] > \mathbb{E}[U(C)]$, so that $D \succ C$. Note that the proof would have been somewhat easier if we had taken the normalized utility function, so that $a = 1$ and $c = 0$. $\square$

Solution to Exercise 3.2 Define the function U as follows: $U(x) = \frac{1}{a-c}V(x) - \frac{c}{a-c} = \frac{V(x)-c}{a-c}$ (note that, by hypothesis, $a > c$ and thus $\frac{1}{a-c} > 0$). Then U represents the same preferences as V. Then $U(o_2) = \frac{V(o_2)-c}{a-c} = \frac{a-c}{a-c} = 1$, $U(o_1) = \frac{V(o_1)-c}{a-c} = \frac{b-c}{a-c}$, and $U(o_3) = \frac{V(o_3)-c}{a-c} = \frac{c-c}{a-c} = 0$. Note that, since $a > b > c$, $0 < \frac{b-c}{a-c} < 1$. $\qquad\square$

Solution to Exercise 3.3 We can take the set of basic outcomes to be $\{\$3000, \$2000, \$1000, \$500\}$. Suppose that there is a von Neumann-Morgenstern utility function U that represents Jennifer's preferences. We can normalize it so that $U(\$3000) = 1$ and $U(\$500) = 0$. Since Jennifer is indifferent between L_1 and $\$2000$, $U(\$2000) = \frac{5}{6}$ (since the expected utility of L_1 is $\frac{5}{6}(1) + \frac{1}{6}(0) = \frac{5}{6}$). Since she is indifferent between L_2 and $\$1000$, $U(\$1000) = \frac{2}{3}$ (since the expected utility of L_2 is $\frac{2}{3}(1) + \frac{1}{3}(0) = \frac{2}{3}$). Thus, $\mathbb{E}[U(L_3)] = \frac{1}{4}(1) + \frac{1}{4}\left(\frac{5}{6}\right) + \frac{1}{4}\left(\frac{2}{3}\right) + \frac{1}{4}(0) = \frac{5}{8}$ and $\mathbb{E}[U(L_4)] = \frac{1}{2}\left(\frac{5}{6}\right) + \frac{1}{2}\left(\frac{2}{3}\right) = \frac{3}{4}$. Since $\frac{3}{4} > \frac{5}{8}$, Jennifer should prefer L_4 to L_3. Hence, she is not rational according to the theory of expected utility. $\qquad\square$

Solution to Exercise 3.4 Normalize her utility function so that $U(o_1) = 1$ and $U(o_4) = 0$. Then, since Rachel is indifferent between $\begin{pmatrix} o_2 \\ 1 \end{pmatrix}$ and $\begin{pmatrix} o_1 & o_4 \\ \frac{4}{5} & \frac{1}{5} \end{pmatrix}$, we have that $U(o_2) = \frac{4}{5}$. Similarly, since she is indifferent between $\begin{pmatrix} o_3 \\ 1 \end{pmatrix}$ and $\begin{pmatrix} o_1 & o_4 \\ \frac{1}{2} & \frac{1}{2} \end{pmatrix}$, $U(o_3) = \frac{1}{2}$. Then the expected utility of $L_1 = \begin{pmatrix} o_1 & o_2 & o_3 & o_4 \\ \frac{1}{8} & \frac{2}{8} & \frac{3}{8} & \frac{2}{8} \end{pmatrix}$ is $\frac{1}{8}(1) + \frac{2}{8}\left(\frac{4}{5}\right) + \frac{3}{8}\left(\frac{1}{2}\right) + \frac{2}{8}(0) = \frac{41}{80} = 0.5125$, while the expected utility of $L_2 = \begin{pmatrix} o_1 & o_2 & o_3 \\ \frac{1}{5} & \frac{3}{5} & \frac{1}{5} \end{pmatrix}$ is $\frac{1}{5}(1) + \frac{3}{5}\left(\frac{4}{5}\right) + \frac{1}{5}\left(\frac{1}{2}\right) = \frac{39}{50} = 0.78$. Hence, she prefers L_2 to L_1. $\qquad\square$

Solution to Exercise 3.5

(a) The expected value of L_1 is $\frac{2}{10}(30) + \frac{1}{10}(28) + \frac{1}{10}(24) + \frac{2}{10}(18) + \frac{4}{10}(8) = 18$ and the expected value of L_2 is $\frac{1}{10}(30) + \frac{4}{10}(28) + \frac{5}{10}8 = 18.2$. Hence, a risk-neutral person would prefer L_2 to L_1.

(b) The expected utility of L_1 is $\frac{1}{5}\ln(30) + \frac{1}{10}\ln(28) + \frac{1}{10}\ln(24) + \frac{1}{5}\ln(18) + \frac{2}{5}\ln(8) = 2.741$ while the expected utility of L_2 is $\frac{1}{10}\ln(30) + \frac{2}{5}\ln(28) + \frac{1}{2}\ln(8) = 2.713$. Thus, Paul would choose L_1 (since he prefers L_1 to L_2). $\qquad\square$

Solution to Exercise 3.6

(a) To normalize U first add 10 to each value and then divide by 180. Denote the normalization of U by $\bar{U}$. Then

$$
\begin{array}{cccccc}
 & o_1 & o_2 & o_3 & o_4 & o_5 \\
\bar{U}: & \frac{54}{180}=0.3 & \frac{180}{180}=1 & \frac{0}{180}=0 & \frac{36}{180}=0.2 & \frac{108}{180}=0.6
\end{array}
$$

To normalize V first subtract 5 from each value and then divide by 90. Denote the normalization of V by $\bar{V}$. Then

$$
\begin{array}{cccccc}
 & o_1 & o_2 & o_3 & o_4 & o_5 \\
\bar{V}: & \frac{27}{90}=0.3 & \frac{90}{90}=1 & \frac{0}{90}=0 & \frac{18}{90}=0.2 & \frac{54}{90}=0.6
\end{array}
$$

(b) The transformation is of the form $V(o)=aU(o)+b$. To find the values of a and b plug in two sets of values and solve the system of equations $\begin{cases} 44a+b=32 \\ 170a+b=95 \end{cases}$.
The solution is $a=\frac{1}{2}$, $b=10$. Thus, $V(o)=\frac{1}{2}U(o)+10$. $\qquad\square$

Solution to Exercise 3.7

(a) Ann prefers L_3 to L_4 ($L_3 \succ_{Ann} L_4$). In fact, $\mathbb{E}[U_{Ann}(L_3)]=\sqrt{28}=5.2915$ while $\mathbb{E}[U_{Ann}(L_4)]=\frac{1}{2}\sqrt{10}+\frac{1}{2}\sqrt{50}=5.1167$.

(b) Bob prefers L_4 to L_3 ($L_4 \succ_{Bob} L_3$). In fact, $\mathbb{E}[U_{Bob}(L_3)]=2(28)-\frac{28^4}{100^3}=55.3853$ while $\mathbb{E}[U_{Bob}(L_4)]=\frac{1}{2}\left[2(10)-\frac{10^4}{100^3}\right]+\frac{1}{2}\left[2(50)-\frac{50^4}{100^3}\right]=56.87$.

(c) The expected value of lottery L_4 is $\frac{1}{2}10+\frac{1}{2}50=30$; thus, a risk-averse person would strictly prefer \$30 with certainty to lottery L_4. We saw in Part (a) that for Ann the expected utility of lottery L_4 is 5.1167; the utility of \$30 is $\sqrt{30}=5.4772$. Thus, Ann would indeed choose \$30 for certain over the lottery L_4. We saw in Part (b) that for Bob the expected utility of lottery L_4 is 56.87; the utility of \$30 is $2(30)-\frac{30^4}{100^3}=59.19$. Thus, Bob would indeed choose \$30 for certain over the lottery L_4. $\qquad\square$

Solution to Exercise 3.8 The simple lottery is $\begin{pmatrix} o_1 & o_2 & o_3 & o_4 \\ \frac{18}{240} & \frac{103}{240} & \frac{95}{240} & \frac{24}{240} \end{pmatrix}$. For example, the

probability of o_2 is computed as follows: $\frac{1}{8}\left(\frac{1}{10}\right)+\frac{1}{4}(1)+\frac{1}{8}(0)+\frac{1}{2}\left(\frac{1}{3}\right)=\frac{103}{240}$. $\qquad\square$

Solution to Exercise 3.9 Using the stated indifference, use lottery L to construct the compound lottery

$$\left(\left(\begin{array}{cc} o_2 & o_4 \\ \frac{1}{4} & \frac{3}{4} \end{array} \right) \quad \left(\begin{array}{cc} o_3 & o_4 \\ \frac{3}{5} & \frac{2}{5} \end{array} \right) \quad o_3 \quad o_4 \\ \frac{1}{3} \qquad \frac{2}{9} \qquad \frac{1}{9} \quad \frac{1}{3} \right),$$

whose corresponding simple lottery is $L' = \left(\begin{array}{cccc} o_1 & o_2 & o_3 & o_4 \\ 0 & \frac{1}{12} & \frac{11}{45} & \frac{121}{180} \end{array} \right)$. Then, by the Independence Axiom, $L \sim L'$. $\qquad\square$

Solution to Exercise 3.10 Let W be your initial wealth. The basic outcomes are:

1. you do not pay any money, do not die and live to enjoy your wealth W (denote this outcome by A_0),

2. you pay \$$Y$, do not die and live to enjoy your remaining wealth $W - Y$ (call this outcome A_Y),

3. you pay \$$X$, do not die and live to enjoy your remaining wealth $W - X$ (call this outcome A_X),

4. you die (call this outcome D); this could happen because (a) you do not pay any money, roll the die and drink the poison or (b) you pay \$$Y$, roll the die and drink the poison; we assume that you are indifferent between these two outcomes.

Since, by hypothesis, $X > Y$, your ranking of these outcomes must be $A_0 \succ A_Y \succ A_X \succ D$. If you satisfy the von Neumann-Morgenstern axioms, then your preferences can be represented by a von Neumann-Morgenstern utility function U defined on the set of basic outcomes. We can normalize your utility function by setting $U(A_0) = 1$ and $U(D) = 0$. Furthermore, it must be that

$$U(A_Y) > U(A_X). \tag{3.6}$$

The maximum amount \$$P$ that you are willing to pay is that amount that makes you indifferent between (1) rolling the die with the initial number of poisoned glasses and (2) giving up \$$P$ and rolling the die with one less poisoned glass.

Thus – based on your answers – you are indifferent between the two lotteries

$$\left(\begin{array}{cc} D & A_0 \\ \frac{1}{6} & \frac{5}{6} \end{array} \right) \quad \text{and} \quad \left(\begin{array}{c} A_X \\ 1 \end{array} \right)$$

and you are indifferent between the two lotteries:

$$\begin{pmatrix} D & A_0 \\ \frac{4}{6} & \frac{2}{6} \end{pmatrix} \text{ and } \begin{pmatrix} D & A_Y \\ \frac{3}{6} & \frac{3}{6} \end{pmatrix}.$$

Thus,

$$\underbrace{\tfrac{1}{6}U(D) + \tfrac{5}{6}U(A_0)}_{=\tfrac{1}{6}0+\tfrac{5}{6}1=\tfrac{5}{6}} = U(A_X) \qquad \text{and} \qquad \underbrace{\tfrac{4}{6}U(D) + \tfrac{2}{6}U(A_0)}_{=\tfrac{4}{6}0+\tfrac{2}{6}1=\tfrac{2}{6}} = \underbrace{\tfrac{3}{6}U(D) + \tfrac{3}{6}U(A_Y)}_{=\tfrac{3}{6}0+\tfrac{3}{6}U(A_Y)}.$$

Hence, $U(A_X) = \tfrac{5}{6}$ and $U(A_Y) = \tfrac{2}{3} = \tfrac{4}{6}$, so that $U(A_X) > U(A_Y)$, contradicting (3.6). $\square$

4. Money lotteries revisited

4.1 von Neumann Morgenstern preferences over money lotteries

In this section we revisit the notions of risk aversion/neutrality/love in the context of von Neumann-Morgenstern preferences. From now on we will use the abbreviation "vNM" for "von Neumann Morgenstern" and, unless explicitly stated otherwise, we will assume that the individual in question has vNM preferences.

4.1.1 The vNM utility-of-money function of a risk-neutral agent

Recall from Chapter 2 (Section 2.2) that, given a money lottery $L = \begin{pmatrix} \$m_1 & \$m_2 & ... & \$m_n \\ p_1 & p_2 & ... & p_n \end{pmatrix}$, an individual is said to be risk neutral relative to L if she is indifferent between L and the expected value of L for sure: $L \sim \begin{pmatrix} \$\mathbb{E}[L] \\ 1 \end{pmatrix}$. If the individual has vNM preferences over money lotteries then, by Theorem 3.1.1 (Chapter 3), there exists a utility function U (that assigns a real number to each sums of money) such that

$$\underbrace{L \sim \begin{pmatrix} \$\mathbb{E}[L] \\ 1 \end{pmatrix}}_{L \text{ is as good as } \mathbb{E}[L]} \quad \text{if and only if} \quad \mathbb{E}[U(L)] = U(\mathbb{E}[L]), \text{that is, if and only if,}$$

$$(4.1)$$

$$\underbrace{p_1 U(m_1) + ... + p_n U(m_n)}_{\mathbb{E}[U(L)]} = U \left(\underbrace{p_1 m_1 + ... + p_n m_n}_{\mathbb{E}[L]} \right).$$

It is clear that one utility function that satisfies (4.1) is the identity function $U(m) = m$. In fact, when U is the identity function

$$p_1 U(m_1) + ... + p_n U(m_n) = p_1 m_1 + ... + p_n m_n = U(p_1 m_1 + ... + p_n m_n). \quad (4.2)$$

(R) The utility-of-money function $U(m) = m$ represents the vNM preferences of an
individual who is risk neutral relative to all money lotteries, or risk neutral for short.
Hence, by Theorem 3.1.1 (Chapter 3), any function of the form $U(m) = am + b$
with $a > 0$ is an alternative vNM utility function representing the preferences of a
risk-neutral person.

In Chapter 3 we assumed that the set of possible monetary outcomes (over which lotteries
were defined) was finite. If we allow for any non-negative amount of money then the vNM
utility-of-money function of a risk-neutral individual is represented by the 45° line, as
shown in Figure 4.1.

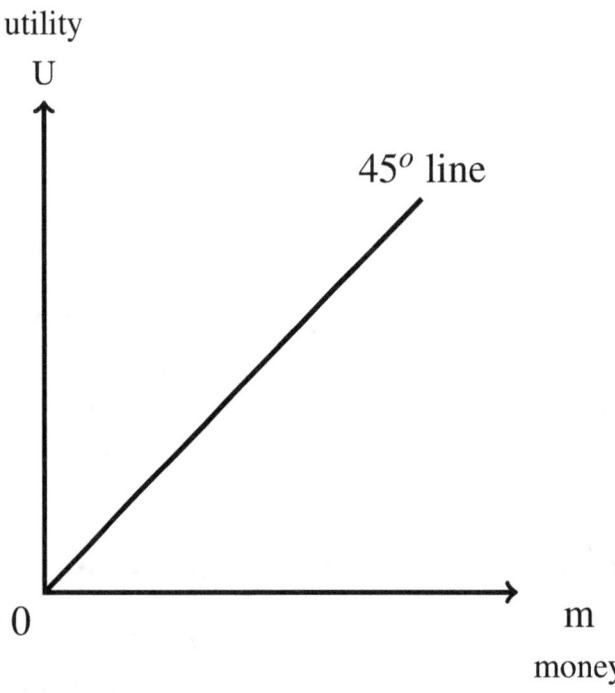

Figure 4.1: The identity function $U(m) = m$ represents the vNM preferences of a risk-
neutral individual.

4.1.2 Concavity and risk aversion

In Chapter 2 we said that, given a non-degenerate money lottery $L = \begin{pmatrix} \$m_1 & \$m_2 & ... & \$m_n \\ p_1 & p_2 & ... & p_n \end{pmatrix}$,
an individual is defined to be **risk averse** relative to L if she prefers the expected value of
L for sure to the lottery: $\mathbb{E}[L] \succ L$.[1] If the individual has vNM preferences over money
lotteries then, by Theorem 3.1.1 (Chapter 3), there exists a utility-of-money function U

---

[1] It would be more precise to write $\begin{pmatrix} \$\mathbb{E}[L] \\ 1 \end{pmatrix} \succ L$ instead of $\mathbb{E}[L] \succ L$, but from now on we shall use
the latter, simpler, notation.

such that

$$\mathbb{E}[L] \succ L \quad \text{if and only if} \quad U\left(\mathbb{E}[L]\right) > \mathbb{E}[U(L)], \text{that is, if and only if,}$$

$$U\left(\underbrace{p_1 m_1 + \ldots + p_n m_n}_{\mathbb{E}[L]}\right) \quad > \quad \underbrace{p_1 U(m_1) + \ldots + p_n U(m_n)}_{\mathbb{E}[U(L)]}. \tag{4.3}$$

The inequality in (4.3) is shown graphically in Figure 4.2 when $n = 2$, that is, with reference to the lottery $L = \begin{pmatrix} \$m_1 & \$m_2 \\ p & 1-p \end{pmatrix}$ with $m_1 < m_2$ and $0 < p < 1$.

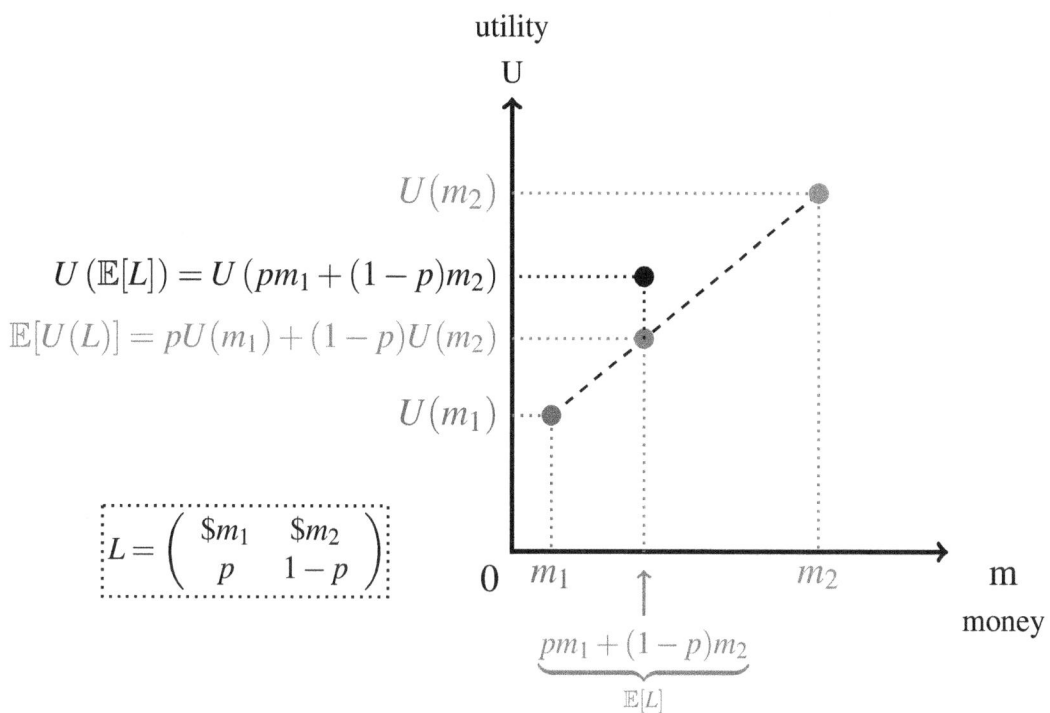

Figure 4.2: A graphical representation of the inequality $U\left(\mathbb{E}[L]\right) > \mathbb{E}[U(L)]$, that is $U(pm_1 + (1-p)m_2) > pU(m_1) + (1-p)U(m_2)$.

In Figure 4.2, the point $pm_1 + (1-p)m_2$ is a point on the horizontal axis between m_1 and m_2 (the closer to m_1, the closer p is to 1). Since the individual is assumed to prefer more money to less, $U(m_1) < U(m_2)$. The point $pU(m_1) + (1-p)U(m_2)$ is a point on the vertical axis between $U(m_1)$ and $U(m_2)$. To find that point, draw a straight-line segment from the point $(m_1, U(m_1))$ to the point $(m_2, U(m_2))$ (the dashed line in Figure 4.2) and go vertically up from the point $pm_1 + (1-p)m_2$ on the horizontal axis to the dashed line and from there horizontally to the vertical axis. By (4.3) this point must be below the point $U(pm_1 + (1-p)m_2)$.

It follows from the above discussion that, if we draw a continuous vNM utility-of-money function for a risk-averse individual, the corresponding curve must lie *above* the straight-line segment joining any two points on the graph, as shown in Figure 4.3. This property is know as *strict concavity*.

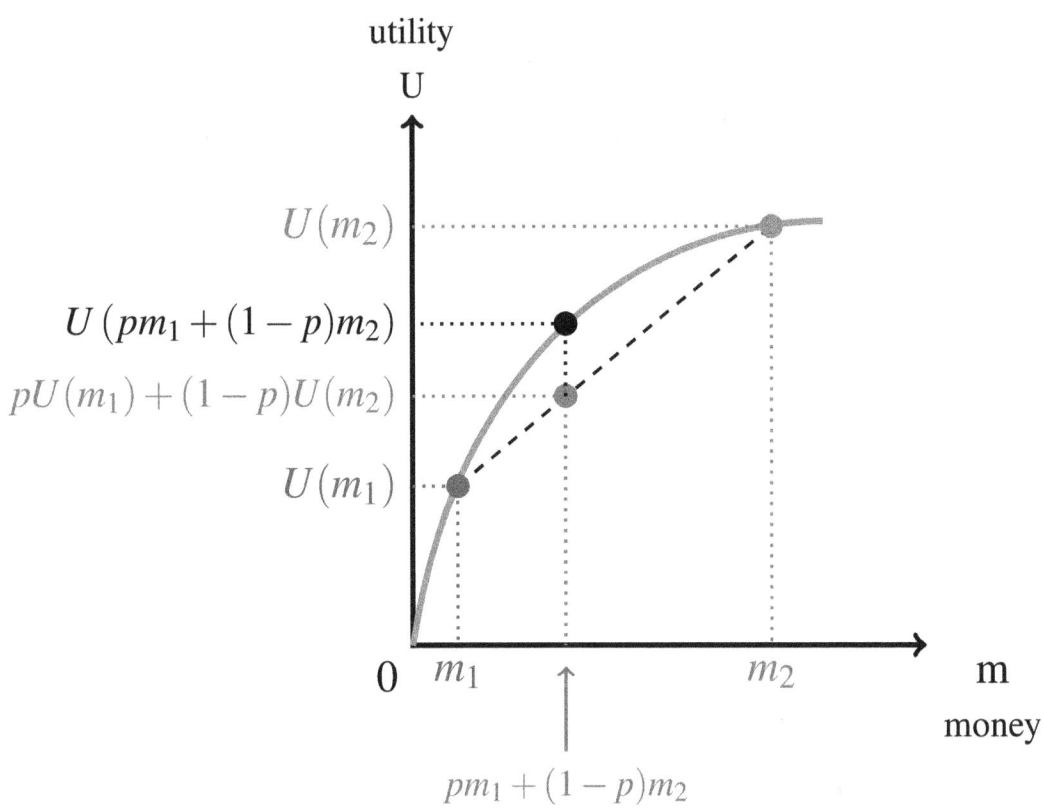

Figure 4.3: The utility function of a risk-averse individual is strictly concave.

Definition 4.1.1 A function $f : \mathbb{R}^+ \to \mathbb{R}$ (where $\mathbb{R}^+$ denotes the set of non-negative real numbers) is *stricly concave* if, for every $x, y \in \mathbb{R}$ and for every $p \in (0,1)$,

$$f(px + (1-p)y) > pf(x) + (1-p)f(y).$$

Ⓡ   The vNM utility-of-money function of a risk-averse individual (that is, of an individual who is risk averse relative to every non-degenerate money lottery) is strictly concave.

4.1.3 Convexity and risk loving

Given a non-degenerate money lottery $L = \begin{pmatrix} \$m_1 & \$m_2 & ... & \$m_n \\ p_1 & p_2 & ... & p_n \end{pmatrix}$, a risk-loving individual prefers the lottery L to its expected value for sure: $L \succ \mathbb{E}[L]$. If the individual has vNM preferences over money lotteries then, by Theorem 3.1.1 (Chapter 3), there exists a utility-of-money function U such that

$$L \succ \mathbb{E}[L] \quad \text{if and only if} \quad \mathbb{E}[U(L)] > U(\mathbb{E}[L]), \quad \text{that is, if and only if,}$$

$$\underbrace{p_1 U(m_1) + ... + p_n U(m_n)}_{\mathbb{E}[U(L)]} \quad > \quad U\left(\underbrace{p_1 m_1 + ... + p_n m_n}_{\mathbb{E}[L]}\right). \tag{4.4}$$

An argument similar to the one used in the previous section leads to the conclusion that, if we draw a continuous vNM utility-of-money function for a risk-loving individual, the graph must lie *below* the straight-line segment joining any two points on the graph, as shown in Figure 4.4. This property is know as *strict convexity*.

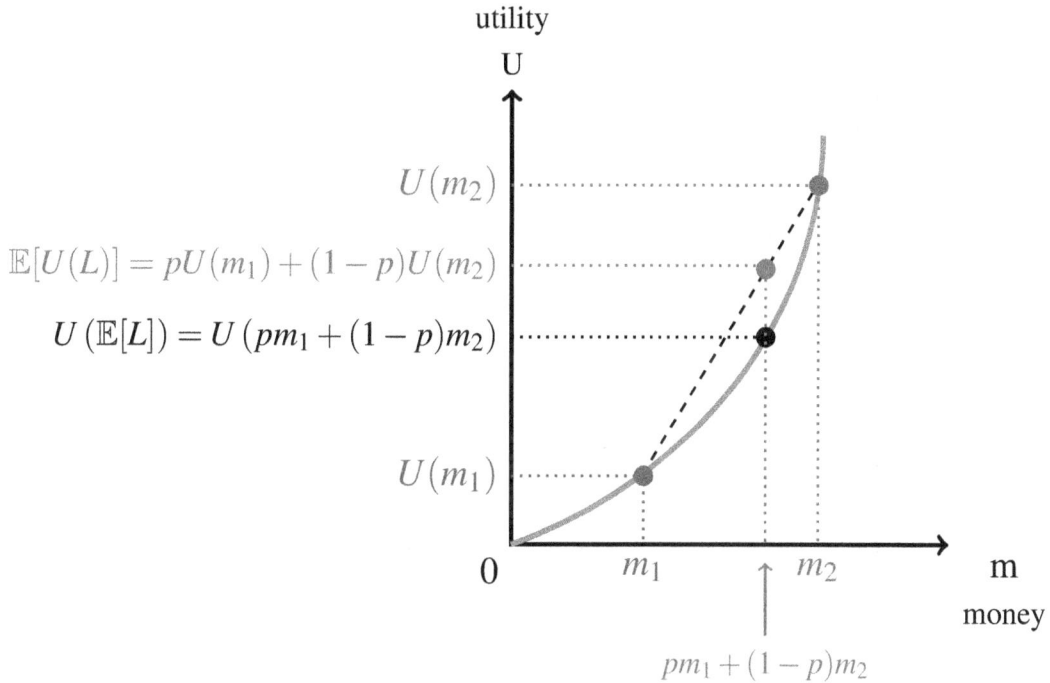

Figure 4.4: The utility function of a risk-averse individual is strictly concave.

Definition 4.1.2 A function $f : \mathbb{R}^+ \to \mathbb{R}$ is *strictly convex* if, for every $x, y \in \mathbb{R}$ and for every $p \in (0,1)$,
$$f(px + (1-p)y) < pf(x) + (1-p)f(y).$$

Ⓡ The vNM utility-of-money function of a risk-loving individual (that is, of an individual who is risk loving relative to every non-degenerate money lottery) is strictly convex.

4.1.4   Mixtures of risk attitudes

While we will tend to concentrate on risk neutrality and risk aversion – and we will typically assume that an individual is risk-neutral or risk-averse relative to *every* non-degenerate money lottery – it is possible for people to display different attitudes to risk for different money lotteries. Consider, for example, an individual whose vNM utility-of-money function is as shown in Figure 4.5. This individual displays risk love for money lotteries that involve small sums of money, risk neutrality for lotteries involving intermediate sums of money and risk aversion for lotteries involving "big stakes": the function is strictly convex for values of m between 0 and m_1, a straight line for values of m between m_1 and m_2 and strictly concave for values of m larger than m_2. Such an individual might be willing to buy a Powerball lottery ticket for \$1 (thus displaying risk love) while at the same time purchasing fire insurance for her house worth \$400,000 (thus displaying risk aversion).

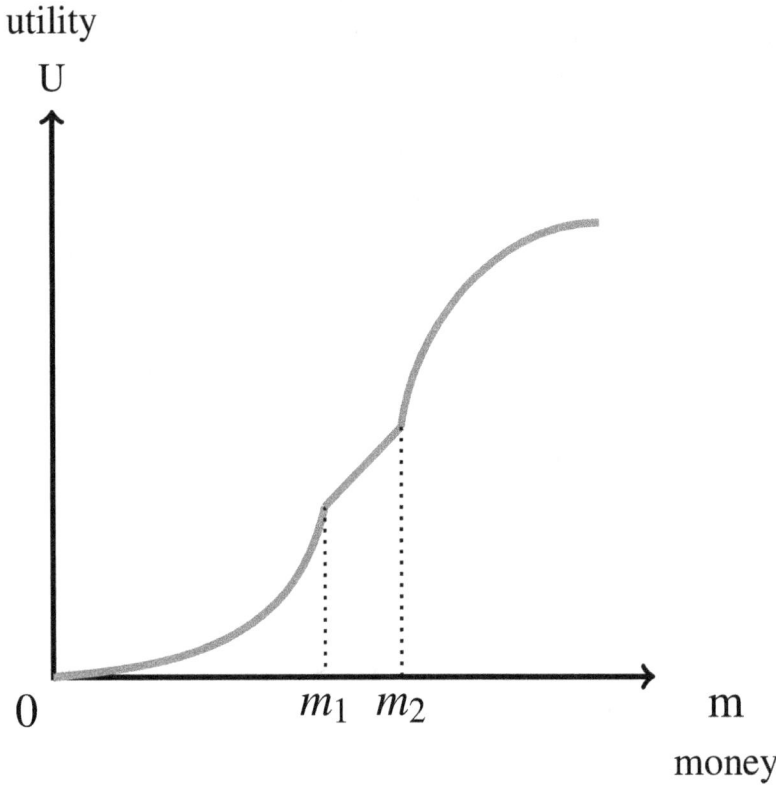

Figure 4.5: The utility function of an individual with different attitudes to risk for different lotteries.

4.1.5 Attitude to risk and the second derivative of the utility function

If the vNM utility-of-money function of an individual is a smooth function (or, at least, twice differentiable) then we can relate the attitude to risk (that is, the shape of the graph of the function) to the second-derivative of the utility function, using the following result from calculus.

Let $f : \mathbb{R}^+ \to \mathbb{R}$ be a twice differentiable function, then

- f is strictly concave if and only if $\frac{d^2 f}{dx^2}(x) < 0$, for every $x \in \mathbb{R}^+$,

- f is strictly convex if and only if $\frac{d^2 f}{dx^2}(x) > 0$, for every $x \in \mathbb{R}^+$,

- the graph of f is a straight line if and only if $\frac{d^2 f}{dx^2}(x) = 0$, for every $x \in \mathbb{R}^+$.

For example, an individual whose vNM utility-of-money function is $U(m) = \sqrt{m}$ is risk averse, since $\frac{dU}{dm} = \frac{1}{2\sqrt{m}}$ and thus $\frac{d^2 U}{dm^2} = -\frac{1}{4\sqrt{m^3}}$ which is negative for every $m > 0$. Figure 4.6 shows the graph of this function.

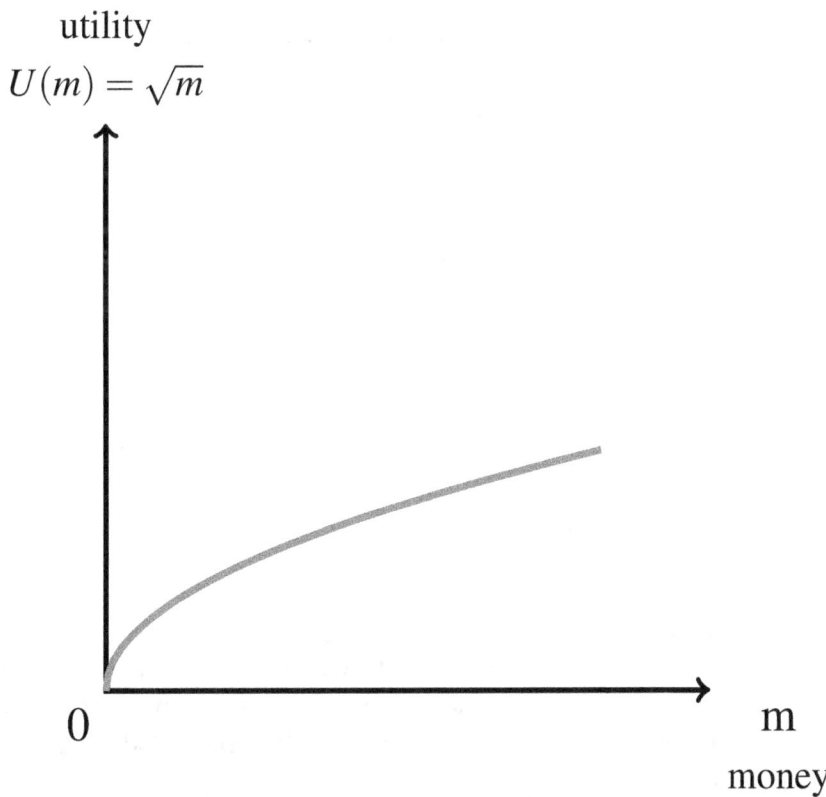

Figure 4.6: The graph of the utility function $U(m) = \sqrt{m}$.

On the other hand, an individual whose vNM utility-of-money function is $U(m) = \frac{m^2}{8}$ is risk averse, since $\frac{dU}{dm} = \frac{m}{4}$ and thus $\frac{d^2U}{dm^2} = \frac{1}{4} > 0$. Figure 4.7 shows the graph of this function.

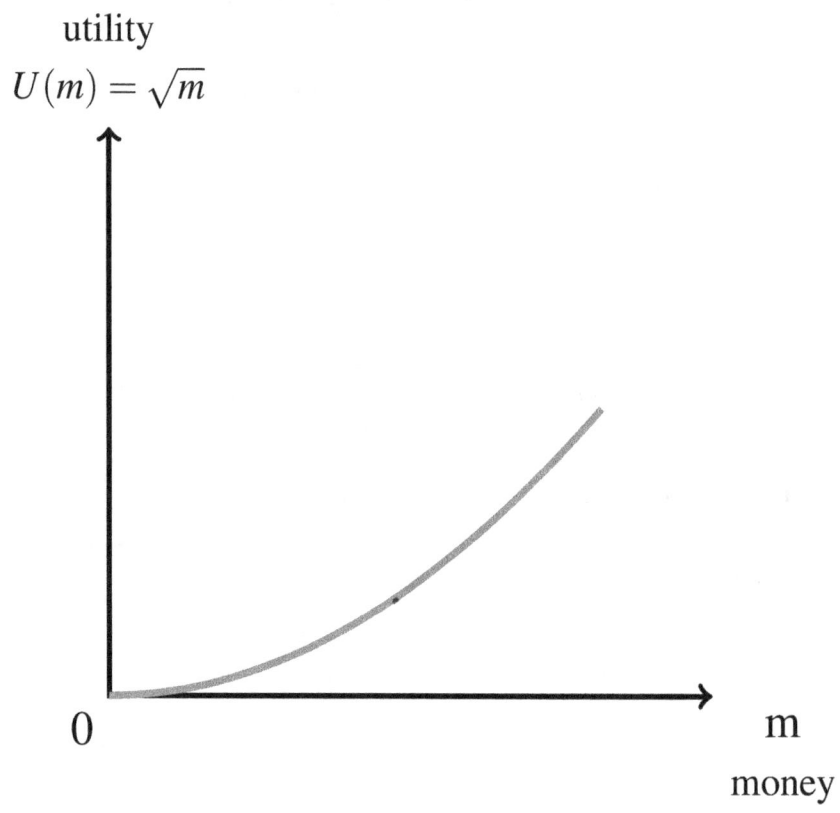

Figure 4.7: The graph of the utility function $U(m) = \frac{m^2}{8}$.

Test your understanding of the concepts introduced in this section, by going through the exercises in Section 4.5.1 at the end of this chapter.

4.2 Measures of risk aversion

Let us now focus on the case of risk aversion. Is it possible to measure the degree of risk aversion of an individual?

One possible measure of risk aversion is provided by the notion of *risk premium* defined in Chapter 2 (Section2.3), which we can now re-write using the notion of expected utility.

Consider an individual, whose initial wealth is $\$W \geq 0$, and a non-degenerate money lottery $M = \begin{pmatrix} \$x_1 & \$x_2 & \dots & \$x_n \\ p_1 & p_2 & \dots & p_n \end{pmatrix}$ (if $x_i < 0$ then we assume that $|x_i| \leq W$, that is, if x_i represents a loss then we assume that the loss is not larger than the initial wealth). As usual, let $\mathbb{E}[M] = p_1 x_1 + \dots + p_n x_n$ be the expected value of M. In terms of wealth levels, lottery M corresponds to the non-degenerate lottery $L = \begin{pmatrix} \$(W + x_1) & \$(W + x_2) & \dots & \$(W + x_n) \\ p_1 & p_2 & \dots & p_n \end{pmatrix}$

(given our assumption about the size of potential losses, $W + x_i \geq 0$, for every $i = 1, \ldots, n$), whose expected value is

$$\mathbb{E}[L] = W + \mathbb{E}[M].$$

If the individual has vNM preferences represented by the utility-of-money function $U(m)$, the expected utility of L is

$$\mathbb{E}[U(L)] = p_1 U(W + x_1) + \cdots + p_n U(W + x_n).$$

The risk premium associated with lottery L and utility function U is that amount of money R_{LU} such that the agent is indifferent between lottery L and the sum of money $\$(\mathbb{E}[L] - R_{LU})$ for sure:

$$U(\mathbb{E}[L] - R_{LU}) = \mathbb{E}[U(L)].$$

Thus R_{LU} is the maximum amount that an individual with vNM utility function U is willing to forego to exchange the risky prospect L for a non-risky (i.e. certain) one with the same expected value.

For example, consider the money lottery

$$M = \begin{pmatrix} \$11 & \$20 \\ \frac{3}{5} & \frac{2}{5} \end{pmatrix}$$

whose expected value is $\mathbb{E}[M] = \frac{3}{5} 11 + \frac{2}{5} 20 = \$14.6$, and an individual whose initial wealth is $W = \$5$ and whose vNM preferences can be represented by the utility-of-money function $U(m) = \sqrt{m}$. Then, in terms of wealth levels, the individual is facing the lottery

$$L = \begin{pmatrix} \$16 & \$25 \\ \frac{3}{5} & \frac{2}{5} \end{pmatrix}$$

whose expected value is $\mathbb{E}[L] = \$(14.6 + 5) = \$19.6$; the expected utility of lottery L is $\mathbb{E}[U(L)] = \frac{3}{5} \sqrt{16} + \frac{2}{5} \sqrt{25} = 4.4$. Thus, for this lottery and this individual, the risk premium is the solution to the equation $\sqrt{19.6 - R_{LU}} = 4.4$, which is $R_{LU} = \$0.24$.

On the other hand, if the individual's initial wealth is $\$110$ then lottery M corresponds to the wealth lottery

$$L' = \begin{pmatrix} \$121 & \$130 \\ \frac{3}{5} & \frac{2}{5} \end{pmatrix}$$

whose expected value is $\mathbb{E}[L'] = \$(14.6 + 110) = \$124.6$; the expected utility of lottery L' is $\mathbb{E}[U(L')] = \frac{3}{5} \sqrt{121} + \frac{2}{5} \sqrt{130} = 11.1607$. Hence, for this lottery and this individual, the risk premium is the solution to the equation $\sqrt{124.6 - R_{L'U}} = 11.1607$, which is $R_{L'U} = \$0.0388$.

Thus – as measured by the risk premium– the degree of risk aversion (incorporated in a given vNM utility function U) towards a given money lottery M, varies with the individual's initial wealth. In the above example, when the individual's initial wealth is only $\$5$, she is prepared to avoid the risky prospect M by reducing the expected value of the corresponding wealth lottery by an amount of up to 24 cents, but if her initial wealth is $\$110$ then she is only prepared to reduce the expected value of the corresponding wealth lottery by up to 4 cents.

(R) From now on we will use the expression *wealth lottery* to refer to a lottery whose outcomes are levels of wealth for the individual (such as lotteries L and L' above, constructed from the money lottery M by adding the individual's initial wealth to every outcome in M).

The reader should try to prove the following: suppose that, given a wealth lottery L and a vNM utility function U, the risk premium is r; then the risk premium remains r if the utility-of-money function U is replaced by a positive affine transformation V of U, that is, for every m, $V(m) = aU(m) + b$, with $a > 0$. In other words, if, for every m, $V(m) = aU(m) + b$, with $a > 0$, then $R_{LV} = R_{LU}$.

Instead of comparing, *for a fixed utility function*, the risk premium of a given money lottery across different levels of initial wealth, we can also compare the risk premium, *for a fixed wealth lottery*, for different utility functions (representing different preferences, hence different individuals). Figure 4.8 shows the risk premium for the wealth lottery $L = \begin{pmatrix} \$m_1 & \$m_2 \\ p & 1-p \end{pmatrix}$ and two different utility functions, U and V. Let R_{LU} be the risk premium associated with U and R_{LV} be the risk premium associated with V; then $R_{LV} = [pm_1 + (1-p)m_2] - \hat{m}_V > R_{LU} = [pm_1 + (1-p)m_2] - \hat{m}_U$, where $\hat{m}_V$ is the certainty equivalent of lottery L for V and $\hat{m}_U$ is the certainty equivalent of lottery L for U (see Chapter 2, Section 2.3 for the notion of certainty equivalent).

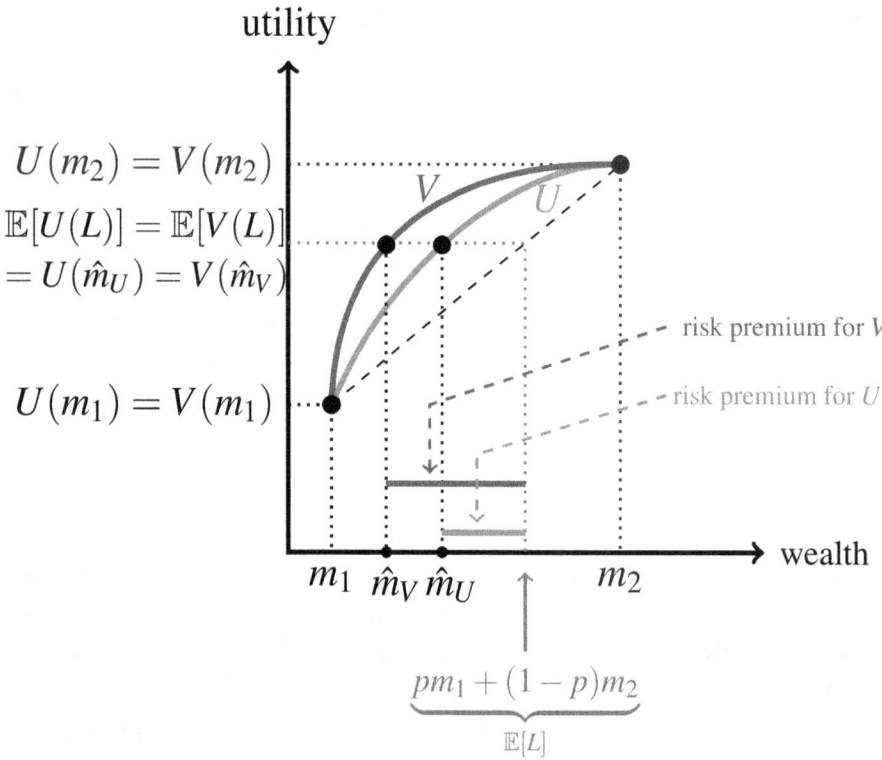

Figure 4.8: The graphs of two utility functions U and V and the risk premia corresponding to the wealth lottery that gives $\$m_1$ with probability p and $\$m_2$ with probability $(1-p)$.

Let us now focus on the issue of comparing different utility functions in terms of the the extent to which they express risk aversion. Using the notion of risk premium, one possibility is given in the following definition.

> **Definition 4.2.1** Let U and V be two concave vNM utility-of-money functions. We say that V incorporates *more* risk aversion than U if, for every non-degenerate wealth lottery L, $R_{LV} \geq R_{LU}$ (with strict inequality for at least one lottery).

Since we identified risk aversion with concavity of the vNM utility function, it seems that the more concave the utility function, the more risk averse the individual is. This intuition is confirmed in Figure 4.8 (on page 80): V is more concave than U and indeed it incorporates more risk aversion, as measured by the size of the risk premium.

Since we identified concavity with negativity of the second derivative of the utility function, one might be tempted to conclude that an individual with vNM utility-of-money function V is more risk-averse than an individual with vNM utility-of-money function U if, in absolute value, the second derivative of V is larger than the second derivative of U: $\left| \frac{d^2 V}{dm^2} \right| > \left| \frac{d^2 U}{dm^2} \right|$.

Unfortunately, this is not correct, because it violates the requirement that, if V is a positive affine transformation of U, then V and U represent the same preferences and thus the same degree of risk aversion (as was pointed out in the remark on page 80). For example, let $V(m) = 2U(m)$, for every $m \geq 0$. Then, for every m, $\left| \frac{d^2 V}{dm^2}(m) \right| = \left| 2\frac{d^2 U}{dm^2}(m) \right| > \left| \frac{d^2 U}{dm^2}(m) \right|$

and yet V and U represent the same preferences.

An expression involving the second derivative of the utility function is the following, which is known as the *Arrow-Pratt measure of absolute risk aversion*, denoted by $A_U(m)$:[2]

$$A_U(m) = -\frac{U''(m)}{U'(m)}.$$

The minus sign makes this expression positive (since $U'(m) > 0$, because the individual is assumed to prefer more money to less, and $U''(m) < 0$, since the individual is assumed to be risk averse).

Note that the Arrow-Pratt measure of absolute risk aversion is a *local* measure, since it varies with the amount of money considered; that is, typically, if $m_1 \neq m_2$ then $A_U(m_1) \neq A_U(m_2)$.

Let us verify that the Arrow-Pratt measure of risk aversion *is* invariant to affine transformations. Let a and b be real numbers, with $a > 0$, and let $V(m) = aU(m) + b$, for every $m \geq 0$. Then $V'(m) = aU'(m)$ and $V''(m) = aU''(m)$, so that $\frac{V''(m)}{V'(m)} = \frac{aU''(m)}{aU'(m)} = \frac{U''(m)}{U'(m)}$ and thus $A_V(m) = A_U(m)$.

Using the Arrow-Pratt measure of risk aversion we can introduce a second definition of "more risk averse".

---

[2] We denote the first derivative of U interchangeably by either $U'(m)$ or $\frac{dU}{dm}(m)$ and the second derivative interchangeably by either $U''(m)$ or $\frac{d^2 U}{dm^2}(m)$

Definition 4.2.2 Let U and V be two concave vNM utility-of-money functions. We say that V incorporates *more* risk aversion than U if, for every level of wealth $m > 0$, $A_V(m) \geq A_U(m)$ (with strict inequality for at least one m).

For example, according to Definition 4.2.2, which of $\sqrt{m}$ and $\ln(m)$ incorporates greater risk aversion? Let us compute the Arrow-Pratt measure of risk aversion for these two functions.

Since $\quad \frac{d}{dm}\sqrt{m} = -\frac{1}{2\sqrt{m}} \quad$ and $\quad \frac{d^2}{dm^2}\sqrt{m} = -\frac{1}{4\sqrt{m^3}}, \quad A_{\sqrt{}}(m) = \frac{1}{2m}.$

On the other hand, since $\quad \frac{d}{dm}\ln(m) = \frac{1}{m} \quad$ and $\quad \frac{d^2}{dm^2}\ln(m) = -\frac{1}{m^2}, \quad A_{\ln}(m) = \frac{1}{m}.$

Thus, since, for every $m > 0$, $\frac{1}{m} > \frac{1}{2m}$ we have that, for every $m > 0$, $A_{\ln}(m) > A_{\sqrt{}}(m)$ and thus, according to Definition 4.2.2, the utility function $\ln(m)$ incorporates more risk aversion than the utility function $\sqrt{m}$.

Note that, in general, there may be utility functions U and V that cannot be ranked according to Definition 4.2.2. For example, it may be that case $A_U(m) > A_V(m)$ for values of m in some interval and $A_U(m) < A_V(m)$ for values of m in some other interval: see Exercise 4.11.

Yet a third definition of "more risk averse" relies on the intuition that "more concave" means "more risk averse":

Definition 4.2.3 Let U and V be two concave vNM utility-of-money functions. We say that V incorporates *more* risk aversion than U if there exists a strictly increasing and concave function $f : \mathbb{R} \to \mathbb{R}$ such that, for every $m \geq 0$, $V(m) = f(U(m))$. In this case we say that V is a *concave transformation* of U.

For example, since $\ln(x)$ is a strictly increasing, concave function, $V(m) = \ln(\sqrt{m})$ is a concave transformation of $U(m) = \sqrt{m}$ and thus, according to Definition 4.2.3, V incorporates more risk aversion than U.

Of course, having three different definitions of greater risk aversion is rather confusing: which of the three is the "correct" definition? Furthermore, while the condition in Definition 4.2.2 is somewhat easier to verify, the condition in Definition 4.2.1 is not very practical, since it would require considering all possible wealth lotteries, and the condition in Definition 4.2.3 is also hard to verify: how can one tell if one function is a concave transformation of another? Luckily, it turns out that the three definitions are in fact equivalent. The following theorem was proved by John Pratt in 1964.[3]

---

[3] John W. Pratt, Risk aversion in the small and in the large, *Econometrica*, Vol. 32, No. 1/2, 1964, pp. 122-136.

> **Theorem 4.2.1** Let $U(m)$ and $V(m)$ be two functions. Then the following conditions are equivalent:
>
> 1. $R_{LV} \geq R_{LU}$, for every non-degenerate wealth lottery L.
>
> 2. $A_V(m) \geq A_U(m)$, for every m.
>
> 3. There exists a strictly increasing and concave function $f : \mathbb{R} \to \mathbb{R}$ such that $V(m) = f(U(m))$, for every $m \geq 0$.

The Arrow-Pratt measure of absolute risk aversion is not invariant to a change in the units of measurement. For example, if the agent's vNM utility-of-money function is $U(m) = \sqrt{m}$, where m is wealth measured in dollars, then her Arrow-Pratt measure of absolute risk aversion is, as we saw above, $A_{\sqrt{}}(m) = \frac{1}{2m}$; for example, when the agent's wealth is \$10, her Arrow-Pratt measure of absolute risk aversion is $A_{\sqrt{}}(10) = \frac{1}{2(10)} = \frac{1}{20} = 0.05$. Suppose now that we want to change our units of measurement from dollars to cents. The utility function then would be written as $V(y) = \sqrt{y}$ where y is wealth measured in cents (thus $y = 100m$) and her Arrow-Pratt measure of absolute risk aversion is $A_{\sqrt{}}(y) = \frac{1}{2y}$; so that when $y = 1,000\,cents$, that is, \$10, her Arrow-Pratt measure of absolute risk aversion is $A_{\sqrt{}}(1,000) = \frac{1}{2(1,000)} = \frac{1}{2,000} = 0.0005$: a different number, despite the fact that we are looking at the same preferences and the same wealth.

A related measure of risk aversion, which is immune from this problem (that is, is invariant to changes in units of measurement) is the *Arrow-Pratt measure of relative risk aversion*, denoted by $r_U(m)$:

$$r_U(m) = -m \frac{U''(m)}{U'(m)}.$$

Thus $r_U(m) = m A_U(m)$.

While the Arrow-Pratt measure of *absolute* risk aversion measures the rate at which marginal utility (that is, the first derivative of the utility function) decreases when wealth is increased by one monetary unit (e.g. \$1), the Arrow-Pratt measure of *relative* risk aversion measures the rate at which marginal utility decreases when wealth is increased by 1%.[4]

> Test your understanding of the concepts introduced in this section, by going through the exercises in Section 4.5.2 at the end of this chapter.

---

[4] In other words, $r_U(m)$ is the absolute value of the wealth elasticity of marginal utility, $U'(m)$, with respect to m.

4.3 Some noteworthy utility functions

In the previous section we considered some specific utility-of-money functions.

For the square root function $\sqrt{m}$ we found that the Arrow-Pratt measure of absolute risk aversion is $A_{\sqrt{}}(m) = \frac{1}{2m}$, which is decreasing in m. Thus an individual with this vNM utility function displays less and less risk aversion as her wealth increases.[5]

The natural logarithm function $\ln(m)$ is similar: the Arrow-Pratt measure of absolute risk aversion is also decreasing in m: $A_{\ln}(m) = \frac{1}{m}$.[6]

Consider now the following utility-of-money function, whose graph is shown in Figure 4.9:

$$U(m) = 1 - e^{-m} = 1 - \frac{1}{e^m}.$$

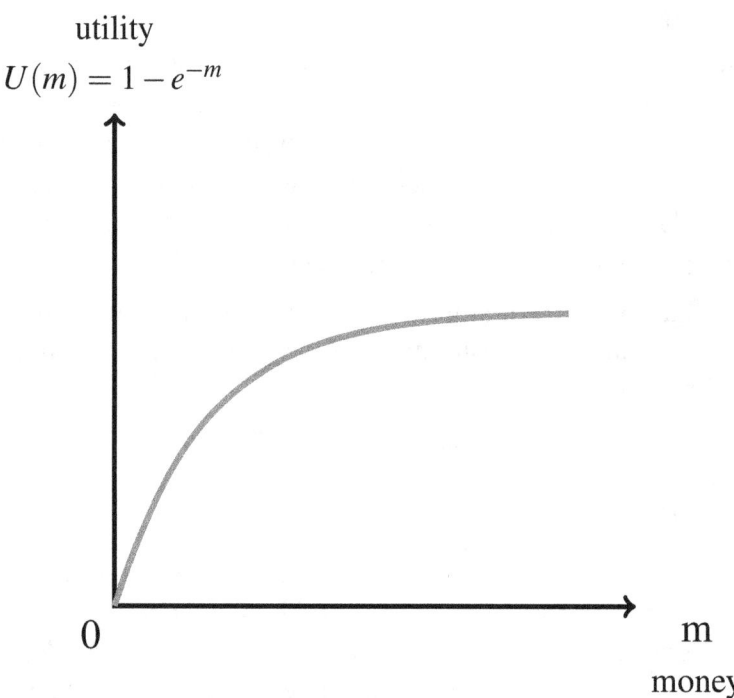

Figure 4.9: The graphs of the utility function $U(m) = 1 - e^{-m}$.

Since $\frac{d}{dm}\left(1 - e^{-m}\right) = e^{-m}$ and $\frac{d^2}{dm^2}\left(1 - e^{-m}\right) = -e^{-m}$ it follows that the Arrow-Pratt measure of absolute risk aversion for this function is a constant:

$$A(m) = -\frac{-e^{-m}}{e^{-m}} = 1.$$

---

[5] On the other hand, the Arrow-Pratt measure of *relative* risk aversion is constant: $r_{\sqrt{}}(m) = m A_{\sqrt{}}(m) = m\frac{1}{2m} = \frac{1}{2}$.

[6] And the Arrow-Pratt measure of *relative* risk aversion is constant: $r_{\ln}(m) = m A_{\ln}(m) = m\frac{1}{m} = 1$.

Indeed, this is a special case of the class of CARA (Constant Absolute Risk Aversion) utility functions, which is the class of functions of the form

$$U(m) = 1 - e^{-\lambda m} = 1 - \frac{1}{e^{\lambda m}}$$

where λ is a positive constant. In fact, $\frac{d}{dm}\left(1 - e^{-\lambda m}\right) = \lambda e^{-\lambda m}$ and $\frac{d^2}{dm^2}\left(1 - e^{-\lambda m}\right) = -\lambda^2 e^{-\lambda m}$ so that the Arrow-Pratt measure of absolute risk aversion is equal to λ.

We saw above that the utility function $\ln(m)$ is characterized by constant relative risk aversion. That is not the only function with this property. The class of CRRA (Constant Relative Risk Aversion) utility functions contains, besides the natural logarithm function,[7] the functions of the form

$$U(m) = \frac{m^{(1-\lambda)}}{1-\lambda} \quad \text{with } \lambda > 0, \lambda \neq 1.$$

For these functions the Arrow-Pratt measure of absolute risk aversion is $A_U(m) = \frac{\lambda}{m}$ so that the Arrow-Pratt measure of relative risk aversion is $r_U(m) = mA_U(m) = \lambda$.

> Test your understanding of the concepts introduced in this section, by going through the exercises in Section 4.5.3 at the end of this chapter.

4.4 Higher risk

In the previous section we answered the following questions:

- For a given money lottery M involving changes in wealth, how does a risk-averse individual view the corresponding wealth lottery at different levels of initial wealth? Typically (but not necessarily), individuals display less risk aversion as their initial wealth increases.

- How can we determine if one individual, whose utility-of-money function is $U(m)$, is more or less risk averse than another individual, whose utility-of-money function is $V(m)$? We considered three alternative definitions of "more risk averse" and saw that they are equivalent.

In this section we ask a different question, namely: when can we say that a money lottery, L, is "more risky" than another money lottery, M?

In order to address this issue we fix a set of non-negative monetary prizes, $\$m_1, \$m_2, \dots, \$m_n$ with the convention that they are ordered from smallest to largest, that is,

$$0 \leq m_1 < m_2 < \cdots < m_n.$$

A lottery over $\{m_1, m_2, \dots, m_n\}$ coincides with a probability distribution over this set.

---

[7] And, more generally, the logarithmic functions $\log_a(m)$ with $a > 1$.

Let L be one such lottery, whose probabilities are $\{p_1, p_2, \ldots, p_n\}$ (p_i is the probability of prize $\$m_i$, for every $i = 1, 2, \ldots, n)$[8] and let M be another lottery, whose probabilities are $\{q_1, q_2, \ldots, q_n\}$:

$$L = \begin{pmatrix} \$m_1 & \$m_2 & \cdots & \$m_n \\ p_1 & p_2 & \cdots & p_n \end{pmatrix} \quad \text{and} \quad M = \begin{pmatrix} \$m_1 & \$m_2 & \cdots & \$m_n \\ q_1 & q_2 & \cdots & q_n \end{pmatrix}.$$

(R) Note that we allow for the possibility that some of the p_i's and q_i's are zero.

We shall denote by $P : \{m_1, m_2, \ldots, m_n\} \to [0, 1]$ the *cumulative* distribution corresponding to the distribution $\{p_1, p_2, \ldots, p_n\}$ and by $Q : \{m_1, m_2, \ldots, m_n\} \to [0, 1]$ the *cumulative* distribution corresponding to the distribution $\{q_1, q_2, \ldots, q_n\}$, that is, for every $i = 1, 2, \ldots, n$ (denoting $P(m_i)$ by P_i and $Q(m_i)$ by Q_i)

$$P_i = p_1 + \cdots + p_i \quad \text{and} \quad Q_i = q_1 + \cdots + q_i$$

(clearly, $P_1 = p_1$, $Q_1 = q_1$ and $P_n = Q_n = 1$). For example, if

$$L = \begin{pmatrix} \$12 & \$26 & \$40 & \$58 & \$80 & \$96 \\ \frac{1}{20} & \frac{7}{20} & 0 & \frac{4}{20} & 0 & \frac{8}{20} \end{pmatrix}$$

then the corresponding cumulative distribution is as follows:

$$\begin{array}{ccccccc} & \$12 & \$26 & \$40 & \$58 & \$80 & \$96 \\ \text{cumulative } P : & \frac{1}{20} & \frac{8}{20} & \frac{8}{20} & \frac{12}{20} & \frac{12}{20} & \frac{20}{20} \end{array}$$

4.4.1 First-order stochastic dominance

The following definition captures one (rather obvious) way in which a lottery M can be viewed as unambiguously better than another lottery L.

Definition 4.4.1 Given two lotteries

$$L = \begin{pmatrix} \$m_1 & \$m_2 & \cdots & \$m_n \\ p_1 & p_2 & \cdots & p_n \end{pmatrix} \quad \text{and} \quad M = \begin{pmatrix} \$m_1 & \$m_2 & \cdots & \$m_n \\ q_1 & q_2 & \cdots & q_n \end{pmatrix}$$

we say that L *first-order stochastically dominates* M (and write $L >_{FSD} M$) if

$$P_i \leq Q_i \quad \text{for ever } i = 1, 2, \ldots, n, \quad \text{with at least one strict inequality.}$$

---

[8]Thus p is a function $p : \{m_1, \ldots, m_n\} \to [0, 1]$ and, for every $i = 1, \ldots, m$, we denote $p(m_i)$ by p_i.

For example,

$$L = \begin{pmatrix} \$26 & \$40 & \$58 & \$80 & \$96 \\ \frac{7}{20} & 0 & \frac{3}{20} & \frac{1}{20} & \frac{9}{20} \end{pmatrix} >_{FSD} M = \begin{pmatrix} \$26 & \$40 & \$58 & \$80 & \$96 \\ \frac{7}{20} & 0 & \frac{4}{20} & 0 & \frac{9}{20} \end{pmatrix}$$

as can be seen from the cumulative distributions:

		$26	$40	$58	$80	$96
cumulative for L,	P :	$\frac{7}{20}$	$\frac{7}{20}$	$\frac{10}{20}$	$\frac{11}{20}$	1
cumulative for M,	Q :	$\frac{7}{20}$	$\frac{7}{20}$	$\frac{11}{20}$	$\frac{11}{20}$	1

It should be clear that if lottery L first-order stochastically dominates lottery M, then L assigns higher probabilities to higher prizes relative to M. It follows that the expected value of L is greater than the expected value of M: $\mathbb{E}[L] > \mathbb{E}[M]$; thus a risk-neutral person prefers L to M. However, the same is true for any attitude to risk.[9]

> **Theorem 4.4.1** Let L and M be two money lotteries (over the same set of prizes). Then
>
> $$L >_{FSD} M$$
>
> if and only if
>
> $$\mathbb{E}[U(L)] > \mathbb{E}[U(M)], \text{ for every strictly increasing utility function } U.$$

4.4.2 Mean preserving spread and second-order stochastic dominance

The notion of first-order stochastic dominance does not really capture the fact that a money lottery is less risky than another one; it captures a different notion, namely that of a money lottery being unambiguously better than another one. On the other hand, the notion of *second-order* stochastic dominance does capture the property of being unambiguously less risky. Second-order stochastic dominance is based on the notion of a "mean preserving spread".

Intuitively, a mean preserving spread of a probability distribution is an operation that takes probability from a point and moves it to each side of that point in such a way that the expected value remains the same.

---

[9]The theorem can be proved using Abel's Lemma, which says that if $a_1, \ldots, a_n$ and $b_1, \ldots, b_n$ are real numbers, then, letting $A_i = a_1 + \cdots + a_i$ and $B_i = b_1 + \cdots + b_i$, $\sum\limits_{i=1}^{n} a_i b_i = \sum\limits_{i=1}^{n-1} A_i(b_i - b_{i+1}) + A_n b_n$ (see `https://planetmath.org/abelslemma`). To prove Theorem 4.4.1 using Abel's Lemma, let $a_i = q_i - p_i$ and $b_i = U(m_i)$.

Let L be the following money lottery, whose expected value is $\mathbb{E}[L] = 5$:

$$L = \begin{pmatrix} \$2 & \$3 & \$4 & \$5 & \$9 \\ \frac{1}{3} & 0 & \frac{1}{3} & 0 & \frac{1}{3} \end{pmatrix}.$$

Now let us construct a new lottery M by taking the probability assigned to the prize \$4, namely $\frac{1}{3}$, and spreading it equally between the prizes \$3 and \$5, as shown inn Figure 4.10. It is easy to check that the expected value of M is the same as the expected value of L, namely 5.

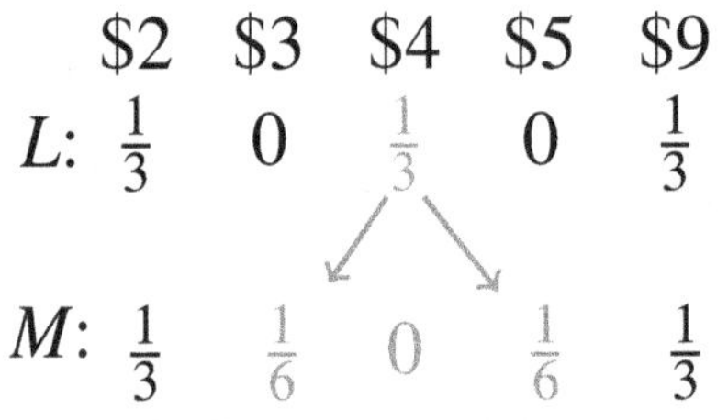

$$
\begin{array}{cccccc}
 & \$2 & \$3 & \$4 & \$5 & \$9 \\
L: & \frac{1}{3} & 0 & \frac{1}{3} & 0 & \frac{1}{3} \\
 & & & \swarrow \searrow & & \\
M: & \frac{1}{3} & \frac{1}{6} & 0 & \frac{1}{6} & \frac{1}{3}
\end{array}
$$

Figure 4.10: A mean-preserving spread.

Intuitively, a risk-averse person should dislike the change from L to M because it involves more risk: the prize of \$4 has been replaced with a non-degenerate "sub-lottery" with expected value of \$4. By definition of risk aversion, the sub-lottery is worse than its expected value.

To perform a 'worsening" of lottery L it is not even necessary to spread out the entire probability of prize \$4; for example, we could merely take away half that probability, namely $\frac{1}{6}$, and spread it equally between the prizes \$3 and \$5 thus obtaining the alternative lottery

$$M' = \begin{pmatrix} \$2 & \$3 & \$4 & \$5 & \$9 \\ \frac{1}{3} & \frac{1}{12} & \frac{1}{6} & \frac{1}{12} & \frac{1}{3} \end{pmatrix}.$$

It is easy to check that also the expected value of M' is 5. In Exercise 4.18 the reader is asked to verify that an individual with utility-of-money function $U(m) = \sqrt{m}$ strictly prefers L to M' and M' to M.

In fact, according to the next definition, M is a mean-preserving spread of M', which, in turn, is a mean-preserving spread of L.

Before giving the formal definition of a mean-preserving spread, let us gain some intuition, as follows. Start with a lottery

$$L = \begin{pmatrix} \$m_1 & \$m_2 & \dots & \$m_n \\ p_1 & p_2 & \dots & p_n \end{pmatrix}$$

and fix three monetary prizes m_i, m_j and m_k with $m_i < m_j < m_k$ and assume that m_j has positive probability in L, that is, $p_j > 0$. Since m_j is strictly between m_i and m_k, there is a $\delta \in (0,1)$ such that $m_j = (1 - \delta)m_i + \delta m_k$, in fact

$$\delta = \frac{m_j - m_i}{m_k - m_i}. \tag{$\blacklozenge$}$$

Now focus on the part of lottery L that involves the three prizes m_i, m_j and m_k:

$$\begin{pmatrix} \ldots & \$m_i & \ldots & \$m_j & \ldots & \$m_k & \ldots \\ \ldots & \$p_i & \ldots & \$p_j & \ldots & \$p_k & \ldots \end{pmatrix}$$

Let $\alpha \in (0,1)$ and let us reduce the probability of m_j from p_j to $p_j - \alpha p_j$ and spread the probability αp_j between m_i and m_k in the proportions $(1-\delta)$ and δ, respectively, where δ is given by ($\blacklozenge$). This is shown in Figure 4.11.

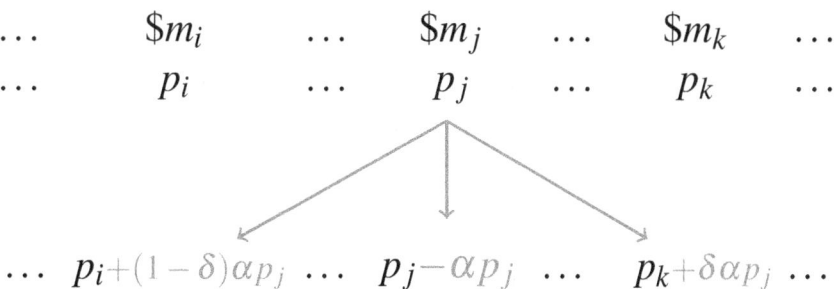

Figure 4.11: A mean-preserving spread.

Let M be the new lottery so constructed. Thus L and M differ **only** in the probabilities assigned to prizes m_i, m_j and m_k. The contribution of these prizes to the calculation of the expected value of the initial lottery L is

$$p_i m_i + p_j m_j + p_k m_k$$

while the contribution of these prizes to the calculation of the expected value of the new lottery M is

$$\left[p_i + (1-\delta)\alpha p_j \right] m_i + \left[p_j - \alpha p_j \right] m_j + \left[p_k + \delta \alpha p_j \right] m_k$$

$$= p_i m_i + p_j m_j + p_k m_k + \alpha p_j \underbrace{\left[(1-\delta)m_i + \delta m_k - m_j \right]}_{=0 \text{ because } (1-\delta)m_i + \delta m_k = m_j}$$

$$= p_i m_i + p_j m_j + p_k m_k.$$

Hence $\mathbb{E}[L] = \mathbb{E}[M]$.

We are now ready to give the definition of a mean-preserving spread.[10]

---

[10]The notion of a mean preserving spread of a probability distribution was introduced by Michael Rothschild and Joseph Stiglitz in "Increasing risk I: A definition", *Journal of Economic Theory*, 1970, Vol. 2, pp. 225-243. Their definition involved re-assigning probabilities across *four* different points, but that definition is equivalent to one that is based on reassigning probabilities across *three* different points, as shown by Eric Rasmusen and Emmanuel Petrakis, "Defining the mean-preserving spread: 3-pt versus 4-pt", in: *Decision making under risk and uncertainty: new models and empirical findings*, edited by John Geweke, Amsterdam: Kluwer, 1992. Rasmusen and Petrakis' definition is different from ours, but equivalent to it. Their definition is as follows. Take three points a_1, a_2, a_3 with $a_1 < a_2 < a_3$; a mean-preserving spread is a triple of probabilities $\gamma_1, \gamma_2, \gamma_3$ such that (1) $\gamma_1 + \gamma_3 = \gamma_2 \le p_2$ (where p_2 is the initial probability of a_2) and (2) $\gamma_1 a_1 - \gamma_2 a_2 + \gamma_3 a_3 = 0$. The initial probability of a_i is p_i and the modified probabilities are $p_1 + \gamma_1, p_2 - \gamma_2, p_3 + \gamma_3$. To convert it into our definition let $\alpha = \frac{\gamma_1 + \gamma_3}{p_2}$ and $\delta = \frac{a_2 - a_1}{a_3 - a_1}$. Invert the operations to go from our definition to theirs.

Definition 4.4.2 Let

$$L = \begin{pmatrix} \$m_1 & \$m_2 & \ldots & \$m_n \\ p_1 & p_2 & \ldots & p_n \end{pmatrix} \quad \text{and} \quad M = \begin{pmatrix} \$m_1 & \$m_2 & \ldots & \$m_n \\ q_1 & q_2 & \ldots & q_n \end{pmatrix}.$$

be two money lotteries. We say that *M is obtained from L by a mean-preserving spread*, and write

$$L \to_{MPS} M$$

if there are three prizes m_i, m_j, m_k with $m_i < m_j < m_k$ such that:

(1) for very $t \in \{1, \ldots, n\} \setminus \{i, j, k\}$, $q_t = p_t$ and

(2) for some $\alpha \in (0, 1]$

$$q_i = p_i + (1 - \delta)\alpha p_j, \quad q_j = p_j - \alpha p_j, \quad q_k = p_k + \delta\alpha p_j \quad \text{with } \delta = \frac{m_j - m_i}{m_k - m_i}.$$

Definition 4.4.3 Let

$$L = \begin{pmatrix} \$m_1 & \$m_2 & \ldots & \$m_n \\ p_1 & p_2 & \ldots & p_n \end{pmatrix} \quad \text{and} \quad M = \begin{pmatrix} \$m_1 & \$m_2 & \ldots & \$m_n \\ q_1 & q_2 & \ldots & q_n \end{pmatrix}.$$

be two money lotteries. We say that *L second-order stochastically dominates M*, stochastic dominance!second-order and write

$$L >_{SSD} M$$

if *M* can be obtained from *L* by a finite sequence of mean-preserving spreads, that is, if there is a sequence of money lotteries $\langle L_1, L_2, \ldots, L_m \rangle$ (with $m \geq 2$) such that:

(1) $L_1 = L$,

(2) $L_m = M$ and

(3) for every $i = 1, \ldots, m - 1$, $L_i \to_{MPS} L_{i+1}$.

As remarked above, a risk-averse person ought to be made worse off by a mean preserving spread. This intuition is confirmed by the following theorem.[11]

Theorem 4.4.2 Let L and M be two money lotteries (over the same set of prizes). Then

$$L >_{SSD} M$$

if and only if

$\mathbb{E}[U(L)] > \mathbb{E}[U(M)]$, for every strictly increasing and concave utility function U.

Test your understanding of the concepts introduced in this section, by going through the exercises in Section 4.5.4 at the end of this chapter.

4.5 Exercises

The solutions to the following exercises are given in Section 4.6 at the end of this chapter.

4.5.1 Exercises for Section 4.1: vNM preferences over money lotteries

Exercise 4.1 Jennifer's von Neumann-Morgenstern utility-of-money function is $U(m) = 20\sqrt{m} - 4$. Consider the following lottery, where the outcomes are possible levels of wealth for Jennifer:

$$L = \begin{pmatrix} \$8 & \$18 & \$24 & \$28 & \$30 \\ \frac{2}{5} & \frac{1}{5} & \frac{1}{10} & \frac{1}{10} & \frac{1}{5} \end{pmatrix}$$

(a) What is the expected value of L?

(b) What is the expected utility of L?

(c) Calculate $\frac{d}{dm}U(m)$.

(d) Calculate $\frac{d^2}{dm^2}U(m)$.

(e) Is Jennifer risk-averse, risk-neutral or risk-loving?

---

[11]This result is best known to economists from the 1970 paper by Rothschild and Stiglitz mentioned in Footnote 10. However, in a later article (Michael Rothschild and Joseph Stiglitz, Addendum to 'Increasing risk I: A definition', *Journal of Economic Theory*, 1972, Vol. 5, p. 306) the authors themselves acknowledged that their main result could have been derived from earlier contributions by mathematicians.

Exercise 4.2 Consider again the wealth lottery of Exercise 4.1, but a different agent: Jim, whose vNM utility-of-money function is $U(m) = \sqrt{m}$. Answer the same questions as in Exercise 4.1 but referring to Jim.

Exercise 4.3 What attitude to risk is incorporated in the following vNM utility-of-money functions? Base your answer on the sign of the second derivative of the utility function.

(a) $\ln(m+1)$

(b) $8 + m^{1.65}$

(c) $2 + 7m$.

Exercise 4.4 Let m denote the amount of money (measured in millions of dollars) and suppose that it varies in the interval $[0, 1]$. John's utility-of-money function is given by:

$$U(m) = -m^2 + 2m - 4.$$

(a) What is John's attitude to risk?

Jenny, on the other hand, has the following utility function:

$$V(m) = -3\left(m^2 - 2m\right).$$

(b) What is Jenny's attitude to risk?

(c) Do John and Jenny have the same preferences?

(d) Give an example of two utility functions that incorporate the same attitude to risk but do not represent the same preferences for lotteries.

4.5.2   Exercises for Section 4.2: Measures of risk aversion

Exercise 4.5 As in Exercise 4.1, consider Jennifer, whose vNM utility-of-money function is $U(m) = 20\sqrt{m} - 4$, and the lottery

$$L = \left(\begin{array}{ccccc} \$8 & \$18 & \$24 & \$28 & \$30 \\ \frac{2}{5} & \frac{1}{5} & \frac{1}{10} & \frac{1}{10} & \frac{1}{5} \end{array} \right)$$

(a) Calculate the risk premium for lottery L for Jennifer.

(b) Calculate Jennifer's Arrow-Pratt measure of absolute risk aversion for $m = 900$ and for $m = 1,600$.

Exercise 4.6 As in Exercise 4.2, consider Jim, whose vNM utility-of-money function is $V(m) = \sqrt{m}$, and the lottery

$$L = \left(\begin{array}{ccccc} \$8 & \$18 & \$24 & \$28 & \$30 \\ \frac{2}{5} & \frac{1}{5} & \frac{1}{10} & \frac{1}{10} & \frac{1}{5} \end{array} \right)$$

(a) Calculate the risk premium for lottery L for Jim.

(b) Calculate Jim's Arrow-Pratt measure of absolute risk aversion for $m = 900$ and for $m = 1,600$.

Exercise 4.7 As in Exercise 4.4, let m denote the amount of money, measured in millions of dollars, and suppose that it varies in the interval $[0,1]$. John's utility-of-money function is given by: $U(m) = -m^2 + 2m - 4$ while Jenny's utility function is: $V(m) = -3\left(m^2 - 2m\right)$. Calculate the Arrow-Pratt measures of absolute and relative risk aversion for John and Jenny and compare them.

Exercise 4.8 Amy faces the wealth lottery $\left(\begin{array}{ccc} \$24 & \$12 & \$48 \\ \frac{2}{6} & \frac{3}{6} & \frac{1}{6} \end{array} \right)$ and tells you that she considers it equivalent to getting $18 for sure.

(a) Calculate the risk premium for lottery L for Amy.

(b) What is Amy's attitude to risk?

(c) Could Amy's vNM utility-of-money function be $U(m) = \sqrt{m}$?

Exercise 4.9 Bill is risk neutral.

(a) How does he rank the following lotteries?

$$L_1 = \left(\begin{array}{cccc} \$24 & \$12 & \$48 & \$6 \\ \frac{1}{6} & \frac{2}{6} & \frac{1}{6} & \frac{2}{6} \end{array} \right) \qquad L_2 = \left(\begin{array}{ccc} \$180 & \$0 & \$90 \\ \frac{1}{20} & \frac{17}{20} & \frac{2}{20} \end{array} \right)$$

(b) What is the risk premium associated with lottery L_1 for Bill?

(c) What is the risk premium associated with lottery L_2 for Bill?

Exercise 4.10 Consider the following money lottery, where the outcomes are *changes* in wealth:

$$M = \begin{pmatrix} -\$50 & \$120 \\ \frac{1}{4} & \frac{3}{4} \end{pmatrix}.$$

Berta's vNM utility-of-money function is $U(m) = \ln(m)$.

(a) Suppose that Berta's inital wealth is $80. Write the wealth lottery corresponding to lottery M above and calculate the risk premium for this lottery for Berta.

(b) Suppose that Berta's inital wealth is $200. Write the wealth lottery corresponding to lottery M above and calculate the risk premium for this lottery for Berta.

Exercise 4.11 Consider the wealth lottery $L = \begin{pmatrix} \$120 & \$180 & \$260 \\ \frac{2}{5} & \frac{2}{5} & \frac{1}{5} \end{pmatrix}$ and the following vNM utility-of-money functions defined for $m \in [0, 300]$:

$$U(m) = \sqrt{m} \quad \text{and} \quad V(m) = -\left(\frac{m}{10} - 36\right)^2 + \frac{m}{20} + 1,400.$$

(a) Write an equation whose solution gives R_{LU} (the risk premium for lottery L and utility function U) and verify that the solution is $R_{LU} = 3.6949$.

(b) Write an equation whose solution gives R_{LV} (the risk premium for lottery L and utility function V) and verify that the solution is $R_{LV} = 6.848$.

(c) Using the Arrow-Pratt measure of absolute risk aversion, which of U and V incorporates greater risk aversion?

4.5.3 **Exercises for Section 4.3: Some noteworthy utility functions**

Exercise 4.12 Plot the following utility functions in the same diagram:

$$U(m) = 1 - e^{-m} \quad \text{and} \quad V(m) = 1 - e^{-3m}.$$

Exercise 4.13 Consider the utility-of-money function $U(m) = m^a$, where a is a constant such that $0 < a < 1$. For this function is the Arrow-Pratt measure of absolute risk aversion decreasing, constant or increasing?

Exercise 4.14 Consider the quadratic utility-of-money function $U(m) = cm - \frac{m^2}{2}$, where c is a positive constant and $m \in [0, c)$. For this function is the Arrow-Pratt measure of absolute risk aversion decreasing, constant or increasing?

4.5.4 Exercises for Section 4.4: Higher risk

Exercise 4.15 Consider the following lotteries:

$$L = \begin{pmatrix} \$26 & \$40 & \$58 & \$80 & \$96 \\ \frac{6}{20} & \frac{4}{20} & \frac{2}{20} & \frac{1}{20} & \frac{7}{20} \end{pmatrix} \quad \text{and} \quad M = \begin{pmatrix} \$26 & \$40 & \$58 & \$80 & \$96 \\ \frac{5}{20} & \frac{4}{20} & \frac{2}{20} & \frac{2}{20} & \frac{7}{20} \end{pmatrix}$$

Does one dominate the other in terms of first-order stochastic dominance?

Exercise 4.16 Consider the following lotteries:

$$L = \begin{pmatrix} \$26 & \$40 & \$58 & \$80 & \$96 \\ \frac{6}{20} & \frac{4}{20} & \frac{2}{20} & 0 & \frac{8}{20} \end{pmatrix} \quad \text{and} \quad M = \begin{pmatrix} \$26 & \$40 & \$58 & \$80 & \$96 \\ \frac{5}{20} & \frac{4}{20} & \frac{2}{20} & \frac{2}{20} & \frac{7}{20} \end{pmatrix}$$

Does one dominate the other in terms of first-order stochastic dominance?

Exercise 4.17 Consider the lotteries of Exercise 4.16. Since it is not the case that M dominates L in terms of first-order stochastic dominance, by Theorem 4.4.1 there must be an increasing utility-of-money function U such that $\mathbb{E}[U(L)] > \mathbb{E}[U(M)]$. Construct such a function. Note that you don't need to define a function over the entire set of non-negative real numbers: it is enough to define a function over the set $\{26, 40, 58, 80, 96\}$.

Exercise 4.18 Consider the following lotteries, which were discussed at the beginning of Section 4.4.2:

$$L = \begin{pmatrix} \$2 & \$3 & \$4 & \$5 & \$9 \\ \frac{1}{3} & 0 & \frac{1}{3} & 0 & \frac{1}{3} \end{pmatrix}$$

$$M' = \begin{pmatrix} \$2 & \$3 & \$4 & \$5 & \$9 \\ \frac{1}{3} & \frac{1}{12} & \frac{1}{6} & \frac{1}{12} & \frac{1}{3} \end{pmatrix} \quad \text{and} \quad M = \begin{pmatrix} \$2 & \$3 & \$4 & \$5 & \$9 \\ \frac{1}{3} & \frac{1}{6} & 0 & \frac{1}{6} & \frac{1}{3} \end{pmatrix}.$$

Show that an individual with utility-of-money function $U(m) = \sqrt{m}$ strictly prefers M to L' and L' to L.

Exercise 4.19 Consider the following lotteries:

$$L = \begin{pmatrix} \$4 & \$16 & \$25 & \$36 & \$49 \\ \frac{3}{40} & \frac{9}{40} & \frac{18}{40} & \frac{8}{40} & \frac{2}{40} \end{pmatrix} \quad \text{and} \quad M = \begin{pmatrix} \$4 & \$16 & \$25 & \$36 & \$49 \\ \frac{23}{200} & \frac{9}{40} & \frac{3}{8} & \frac{8}{40} & \frac{17}{200} \end{pmatrix}.$$

(a) Calculate $\mathbb{E}[L]$.

(b) Calculate $\mathbb{E}[M]$.

(c) Calculate the expected utility of L for an individual whose utility-of-money function is $U(m) = \sqrt{m}$.

(d) Calculate the expected utility of M for an individual whose utility-of-money function is $U(m) = \sqrt{m}$.

(e) Show that M is a mean-preserving spread of L according to Definition 4.4.2.

Exercise 4.20 Show that $L >_{SSD} M$, where

$$L = \begin{pmatrix} \$6 & \$23 & \$44 & \$51 & \$70 \\ \frac{1}{3} & \frac{1}{12} & \frac{1}{6} & \frac{1}{12} & \frac{1}{3} \end{pmatrix} \quad \text{and} \quad M = \begin{pmatrix} \$6 & \$23 & \$44 & \$51 & \$70 \\ \frac{77}{192} & \frac{11}{94} & 0 & 0 & \frac{4349}{9024} \end{pmatrix}$$

by constructing a two-step mean-preserving spread from L to M.

4.6   Solutions to Exercises

Solution to Exercise 4.1

(a) The expected value of L is $\frac{2}{10} \times 30 + \frac{1}{10} \times 28 + \frac{1}{10} \times 24 + \frac{2}{10} \times 18 + \frac{4}{10} \times 8 = 18$.

(b) The expected utility of L is

$$\tfrac{2}{10}(20\sqrt{30}-4) + \tfrac{1}{10}(20\sqrt{28}-4) + \tfrac{1}{10}(20\sqrt{24}-4) + \tfrac{2}{10}(20\sqrt{18}-4) + \tfrac{4}{10}(20\sqrt{8}-4)$$

$$= 77.88.$$

(c) $\frac{d}{dm}(20\sqrt{m}-4) = 20\frac{1}{2\sqrt{m}} = \frac{10}{\sqrt{m}}$.

(d) $\frac{d^2}{dm^2}(20\sqrt{m}-4) = 10\left(-\frac{1}{2}\right)m^{-\frac{3}{2}} = -\frac{5}{\sqrt{m^3}} < 0$, for every $m > 0$.

(e) Jennifer is risk-averse since the second derivative of her utility function is negative for every $m > 0$.   □

Solution to Exercise 4.2

   (a) The expected value is, of course, the same, namely 18.

   (b) The expected utility of L is

$$\tfrac{2}{10}\sqrt{30}+\tfrac{1}{10}\sqrt{28}+\tfrac{1}{10}\sqrt{24}+\tfrac{2}{10}\sqrt{18}+\tfrac{4}{10}\sqrt{8}=4.094.$$

Note that this is equal to $\frac{77.88}{20}+\frac{1}{5}$ (recall that 77.88 was the expected utility for Jennifer). Indeed, Jim's utility function, call it V, can be obtained from Jennifer's utility function, call it $U(m)$, by applying the following affine transformation $V(m)=\frac{1}{20}U(m)+\frac{1}{5}$; hence Jennifer and Jim have the same preferences.

   (c) $\frac{d\sqrt{m}}{dm}=\frac{1}{2\sqrt{m}}$.

   (d) $\frac{d^2\sqrt{m}}{dm^2}=-\frac{1}{4\sqrt{m^3}}$.

   (e) Jim is risk-averse (he has the same preferences as Jennifer).   □

Solution to Exercise 4.3

   (a) $\frac{d^2}{dm^2}\ln(m+1)=-\frac{1}{(m+1)^2}<0$, for every $m\geq 0$. Thus risk aversion.

   (b) $\frac{d^2}{dm^2}(8+m^{1.65})=\frac{1.0725}{m^{0.35}}>0$, for every $m>0$. Thus risk love.

   (c) $\frac{d^2}{dm^2}(2+7m)=0$. Thus risk neutrality.   □

Solution to Exercise 4.4

   (a) $U''(m)=-2<0$. Thus John is risk averse.

   (b) $V''(m)=-6<0$. Thus Jenny is risk averse.

   (c) Since $V(m)=3U(m)+12$, that is, V is an affine transformation of U, John and Jenny have the same preferences.

   (d) There are, of course, many examples. One example is $U(m)=\sqrt{m}$ and $V(m)=\ln(m+1)$.   □

Solution to Exercise 4.5

   (a) Recall from Exercise 4.1 that the expected value of L is 18. The risk premium is the value of R that solves the equation $20\sqrt{18-R}-4=77.88$. The solution is $R=\$1.24$.

   (b) The Arrow-Pratt measure of absolute risk aversion is

$$A(m)=-\frac{U''(m)}{U'(m)}=-\frac{-\frac{5}{\sqrt{m^3}}}{\frac{10}{\sqrt{m}}}=\frac{1}{2m}$$

Thus $A(900)=\frac{1}{1,800}$ and $A(1,600)=\frac{1}{3,200}$.   □

Solution to Exercise 4.6

(a) Again, the expected value of L is 18. The risk premium is the value of R that solves the equation $\sqrt{18 - R} = 4.094$. The solution is $R = \$1.24$: the same as for Jennifer (as it should be, since they have the same preferences).

(b) The Arrow-Pratt measure of absolute risk aversion is

$$A(m) = -\frac{V''(m)}{V'(m)} = -\frac{-\frac{1}{4\sqrt{m^3}}}{\frac{1}{2\sqrt{m}}} = \frac{1}{2m}$$

the same as for Jennifer (as it should be, since they have the same preferences). Thus $A(900) = \frac{1}{1,800}$ and $A(1,600) = \frac{1}{3,200}$. □

Solution to Exercise 4.7
We already know from Exercise 4.4 that John and Jennifer have the same preferences. This is confirmed by the fact that the Arrow-Pratt measures are the same for both individuals:

$$A_U(m) = A_V(m) = \frac{1}{1-m} \quad \text{and} \quad r_U(m) = r_V(m) = \frac{m}{1-m}.$$

□

Solution to Exercise 4.8

(a) The expected value of lottery $\begin{pmatrix} \$24 & \$12 & \$48 \\ \frac{2}{6} & \frac{3}{6} & \frac{1}{6} \end{pmatrix}$ is $\frac{2}{6}24 + \frac{3}{6}12 + \frac{1}{6}48 = 22$. Thus the risk premium is $\$(22 - 18) = \$4$.

(b) Amy is risk-averse since she considers the lottery to be equivalent to a sum of money which is *less* than the expected value of the lottery (hence she prefers the expected value of the lottery for sure to the lottery).

(c) If $U(m)$ is Amy's vNM utility-of-money function, then it must be that $U(18) = \mathbb{E}[U(L)]$, where $\mathbb{E}[U(L)] = \frac{2}{6}U(24) + \frac{3}{6}U(12) + \frac{1}{6}U(48)$. Since $\sqrt{18} = 4.2426$, while $\frac{2}{6}\sqrt{24} + \frac{3}{6}\sqrt{12} + \frac{1}{6}\sqrt{48} = 4.5197$, it cannot be that $U(m) = \sqrt{m}$. □

Solution to Exercise 4.9

(a) The expected value of both lotteries is 18, hence Bill is indifferent between the two.

(b) Zero.

(c) Zero. □

Solution to Exercise 4.10

(a) When Berta's initial wealth is $80, the corresponding wealth lottery is $L = \begin{pmatrix} \$30 & \$200 \\ \frac{1}{4} & \frac{3}{4} \end{pmatrix}$, whose expected value is $157.5. The risk premium is given by the solution to

$$\ln(157.5 - R) = \tfrac{1}{4}\ln(30) + \tfrac{3}{4}\ln(200)$$

which is $33.0304.

(b) When Berta's initial wealth is $200, the corresponding wealth lottery is $L = \begin{pmatrix} \$150 & \$320 \\ \frac{1}{4} & \frac{3}{4} \end{pmatrix}$, whose expected value is $277.5. The risk premium is given by the solution to

$$\ln(277.5 - R) = \tfrac{1}{4}\ln(150) + \tfrac{3}{4}\ln(320)$$

which is $12.7199. $\square$

Solution to Exercise 4.11 We are considering the wealth lottery $L = \begin{pmatrix} \$120 & \$180 & \$260 \\ \frac{2}{5} & \frac{2}{5} & \frac{1}{5} \end{pmatrix}$. The expected value of L is 172.

(a) R_{LU} is the solution to $\sqrt{172 - R} = \tfrac{2}{5}\sqrt{120} + \tfrac{2}{5}\sqrt{180} + \tfrac{1}{5}\sqrt{260}$. The solution is $R_{LU} = 3.6949$.

(b) R_{LV} is the solution to

$$-\left(\tfrac{172-R}{10} - 36\right)^2 + \tfrac{172-R}{20} + 1,400 =$$
$$\tfrac{2}{5}\left[-\left(\tfrac{120}{10} - 36\right)^2 + \tfrac{120}{20} + 1,400\right]$$
$$+ \tfrac{2}{5}\left[-\left(\tfrac{180}{10} - 36\right)^2 + \tfrac{180}{20} + 1,400\right]$$
$$+ \tfrac{1}{5}\left[-\left(\tfrac{260}{10} - 36\right)^2 + \tfrac{260}{20} + 1,400\right].$$

The solution is $R_{LV} = 6.848$.

(c) $A_U(m) = \tfrac{1}{2m}$ and $A_V(m) = \tfrac{1}{362.5-m}$. The two are equal when $m = 120.833$, $A_U(m) > A_V(m)$ for $m \in (0, 120.833)$ and $A_U(m) < A_V(m)$ for $m \in (120.833, 300]$. Thus U incorporates greater risk aversion than V for values of m in the interval $(0, 120.833)$ and less risk aversion than V in the interval $(120.833, 300]$. $\square$

Solution to Exercise 4.12   See Figure 4.12.   □

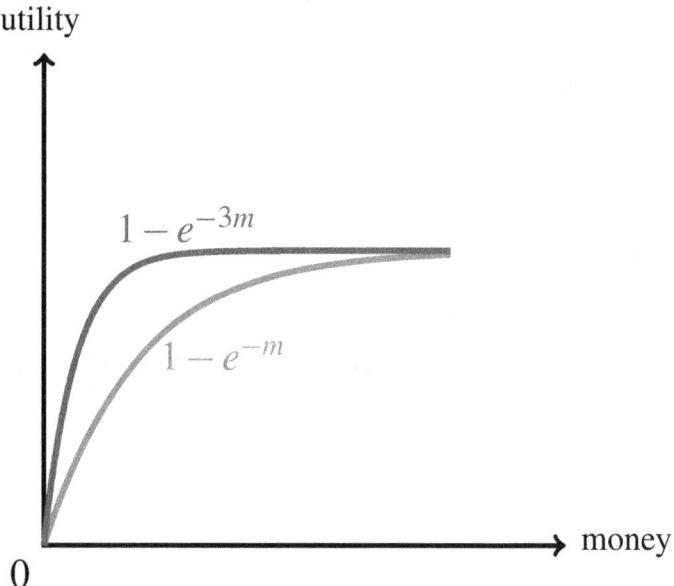

Figure 4.12: The graphs of $1 - e^{-m}$ and $1 - e^{-3m}$.

Solution to Exercise 4.13

$\frac{d}{dm}m^a = \frac{a}{m^{1-a}}$ and $\frac{d^2}{dm^2}m^a = \frac{-a(1-a)}{m^{2-a}}$. Thus $A(m) = \frac{1-a}{m}$ which is decreasing in m.   □

Solution to Exercise 4.14

$\frac{d}{dm}\left(cm - \frac{m^2}{2}\right) = c - m$ and $\frac{d^2}{dm^2}\left(cm - \frac{m^2}{2}\right) = -1$. Thus $A(m) = \frac{1}{c-m}$ which is *increasing* in m. In fact, $\frac{d}{dm}\left(\frac{1}{c-m}\right) = \frac{1}{(c-m)^2} > 0$.   □

Solution to Exercise 4.15

The lotteries are:

$$M = \left(\begin{array}{ccccc} \$26 & \$40 & \$58 & \$80 & \$96 \\ \frac{5}{20} & \frac{4}{20} & \frac{2}{20} & \frac{2}{20} & \frac{7}{20} \end{array} \right) \quad \text{and} \quad L = \left(\begin{array}{ccccc} \$26 & \$40 & \$58 & \$80 & \$96 \\ \frac{6}{20} & \frac{4}{20} & \frac{2}{20} & \frac{1}{20} & \frac{7}{20} \end{array} \right)$$

By constructing the corresponding cumulative distribution functions one can see that $M >_{FSD} L$ ($Q_i \leq P_i$ for every $i = 1, \ldots, 5$ and $Q_3 < P_3$):

	$m_1 = \$26$	$m_2 = \$40$	$m_3 = \$58$	$m_4 = \$80$	$m_5 = \$96$
cumulative for L, P:	$\frac{6}{20}$	$\frac{10}{20}$	$\frac{12}{20}$	$\frac{13}{20}$	1
cumulative for M, Q:	$\frac{5}{20}$	$\frac{9}{20}$	$\frac{11}{20}$	$\frac{13}{20}$	1

□

Solution to Exercise 4.16

The lotteries are:

$$L = \begin{pmatrix} \$26 & \$40 & \$58 & \$80 & \$96 \\ \frac{6}{20} & \frac{4}{20} & \frac{2}{20} & 0 & \frac{8}{20} \end{pmatrix} \quad \text{and} \quad M = \begin{pmatrix} \$26 & \$40 & \$58 & \$80 & \$96 \\ \frac{5}{20} & \frac{4}{20} & \frac{2}{20} & \frac{2}{20} & \frac{7}{20} \end{pmatrix}$$

By constructing the corresponding cumulative distribution functions one can see that, according to the criterion of first-order dominance, it is neither the case that L dominates M (since, for example, $P_1 = \frac{6}{20} > Q_1 = \frac{5}{20}$) nor the case that M dominates L (since $Q_4 = \frac{13}{20} > P_4 = \frac{12}{20}$):

		$26	$40	$58	$80	$96
cumulative for L,	P:	$\frac{6}{20}$	$\frac{10}{20}$	$\frac{12}{20}$	$\frac{12}{20}$	1
cumulative for M,	Q:	$\frac{5}{20}$	$\frac{9}{20}$	$\frac{11}{20}$	$\frac{13}{20}$	1

□

Solution to Exercise 4.17

The lotteries are:

$$L = \begin{pmatrix} \$26 & \$40 & \$58 & \$80 & \$96 \\ \frac{6}{20} & \frac{4}{20} & \frac{2}{20} & 0 & \frac{8}{20} \end{pmatrix} \quad \text{and} \quad M = \begin{pmatrix} \$26 & \$40 & \$58 & \$80 & \$96 \\ \frac{5}{20} & \frac{4}{20} & \frac{2}{20} & \frac{2}{20} & \frac{7}{20} \end{pmatrix}$$

Since L assigns an additional probability of $\frac{1}{20}$ to $96 (relative to M), it is sufficient to have a "big jump" in utility going from $80 to $96. For example, consider the folllowing utility function:

	$26	$40	$58	$80	$96
Utility U:	1	2	3	4	10

Then $\mathbb{E}[U(L)] = \frac{6}{20}1 + \frac{4}{20}2 + \frac{2}{20}3 + \frac{8}{20}10 = 5$ and $\mathbb{E}[U(M)] = \frac{5}{20}1 + \frac{4}{20}2 + \frac{2}{20}3 + +\frac{2}{20}4 + \frac{7}{20}10 = 4.85$. Thus an individual with this (strictly increasing) utility function prefers lottery L to lottery M. One can also easily construct a strictly increasing utility function according to which lottery M is preferred to lottery L (big jump at $80, small jump at $96). □

Solution to Exercise 4.18

The lotteries are:

$$M = \begin{pmatrix} \$2 & \$3 & \$4 & \$5 & \$9 \\ \frac{1}{3} & 0 & \frac{1}{3} & 0 & \frac{1}{3} \end{pmatrix}$$

$$L' = \begin{pmatrix} \$2 & \$3 & \$4 & \$5 & \$9 \\ \frac{1}{3} & \frac{1}{12} & \frac{1}{6} & \frac{1}{12} & \frac{1}{3} \end{pmatrix} \quad \text{and} \quad L = \begin{pmatrix} \$2 & \$3 & \$4 & \$5 & \$9 \\ \frac{1}{3} & \frac{1}{6} & 0 & \frac{1}{6} & \frac{1}{3} \end{pmatrix}.$$

$$\mathbb{E}[U(M)] = \tfrac{1}{3}\sqrt{2} + \tfrac{1}{3}\sqrt{4} + \tfrac{1}{3}\sqrt{9} = 2.1381$$
$$> E[U(L')] = \tfrac{1}{3}\sqrt{2} + \tfrac{1}{12}\sqrt{3} + \tfrac{1}{6}\sqrt{4} + \tfrac{1}{12}\sqrt{5} + \tfrac{1}{3}\sqrt{9} = 2.1354$$
$$> E[U(L)] = \tfrac{1}{3}\sqrt{2} + \tfrac{1}{6}\sqrt{3} + \tfrac{1}{16}\sqrt{5} + \tfrac{1}{3}\sqrt{9} = 2.1328.$$

□

Solution to Exercise 4.19

The lotteries are:

$$L = \begin{pmatrix} \$4 & \$16 & \$25 & \$36 & \$49 \\ \frac{3}{40} & \frac{9}{40} & \frac{18}{40} & \frac{8}{40} & \frac{2}{40} \end{pmatrix} \quad \text{and} \quad M = \begin{pmatrix} \$4 & \$16 & \$25 & \$36 & \$49 \\ \frac{23}{200} & \frac{9}{40} & \frac{3}{8} & \frac{8}{40} & \frac{17}{200} \end{pmatrix}.$$

(a) $\mathbb{E}[L] = \frac{3}{40}4 + \frac{9}{40}16 + \frac{18}{40}25 + \frac{8}{40}36 + \frac{2}{40}49 = 24.8$.

(b) $\mathbb{E}[M] = \frac{23}{200}4 + \frac{9}{40}16 + \frac{3}{8}25 + \frac{8}{40}36 + \frac{17}{200}49 = 24.8$.

(c) $\mathbb{E}[U(L)] = \frac{3}{40}\sqrt{4} + \frac{9}{40}\sqrt{16} + \frac{18}{40}\sqrt{25} + \frac{8}{40}\sqrt{36} + \frac{2}{40}\sqrt{49} = 4.85$

(d) $\mathbb{E}[M] = \frac{23}{200}\sqrt{4} + \frac{9}{40}\sqrt{16} + \frac{3}{8}\sqrt{25} + \frac{8}{40}\sqrt{36} + \frac{17}{200}\sqrt{49} = 4.8$.

(e) We have that $m_1 = 4, m_2 = 16, m_3 = 25, m_4 = 36, m_5 = 49$, $p_2 = q_2$ and $p_4 = q_4$. Thus the change involves prizes m_1, m_3 and m_5, that is, $i = 1, j = 3$, $k = 5$. To find α solve $\frac{18}{40} - \alpha\frac{18}{40} = \frac{3}{8}$ which gives $\alpha = \frac{1}{6}$. Then verify that $p_1 + \left(1 - \frac{m_3 - m_1}{m_5 - m_1}\right)\alpha p_3 = q_1$ and $p_5 + \left(\frac{m_3 - m_1}{m_5 - m_1}\right)\alpha p_3 = q_5$; indeed $\frac{3}{40} + \left(1 - \frac{25-4}{49-4}\right)\frac{1}{6}\left(\frac{18}{40}\right) = \frac{23}{200}$ and $\frac{2}{40} + \left(\frac{25-4}{49-4}\right)\frac{1}{6}\left(\frac{18}{40}\right) = \frac{17}{200}$ □

Solution to Exercise 4.20

The lotteries are:

$$L = \begin{pmatrix} \$6 & \$23 & \$44 & \$51 & \$70 \\ \frac{1}{3} & \frac{1}{12} & \frac{1}{6} & \frac{1}{12} & \frac{1}{3} \end{pmatrix} \quad \text{and} \quad M = \begin{pmatrix} \$6 & \$23 & \$44 & \$51 & \$70 \\ \frac{77}{192} & \frac{11}{94} & 0 & 0 & \frac{4349}{9024} \end{pmatrix}.$$

Let us perform a first mean-preserving spread (MPS) on L by reducing the probability of $m_3 = 44$ to 0 (hence $\alpha = 1$) and spreading it out to $m_1 = 6$ and $m_5 = 70$ (thus $\delta = \frac{44-6}{70-6} = \frac{38}{64}$); then the probability of m_1 becomes $\frac{1}{3} + \left(1 - \frac{38}{64}\right)\frac{1}{6} = \frac{77}{192}$ and the probability of m_5 becomes $\frac{1}{3} + \left(\frac{38}{64}\right)\frac{1}{6} = \frac{83}{192}$. Call the resulting lottery M'. Then

$$M' = \begin{pmatrix} \$6 & \$23 & \$44 & \$51 & \$70 \\ \frac{77}{192} & \frac{1}{12} & 0 & \frac{1}{12} & \frac{83}{192} \end{pmatrix}.$$

Now perform a second MPS on M' by reducing the probability of $m_4 = 51$ to 0 (hence $\alpha = 1$) and spreading it out to $m_2 = 23$ and $m_5 = 70$ (thus $\delta = \frac{51-23}{70-23} = \frac{28}{47}$); then the probability of m_2 becomes $\frac{1}{12} + \left(1 - \frac{28}{47}\right)\frac{1}{12} = \frac{11}{94}$ and the probability of m_5 becomes

$\frac{83}{192} + \left(\frac{28}{47}\right)\frac{1}{12} = \frac{4349}{9024}$ thus yielding

$$M = \begin{pmatrix} \$6 & \$23 & \$44 & \$51 & \$70 \\ \frac{77}{192} & \frac{11}{94} & 0 & 0 & \frac{4349}{9024} \end{pmatrix}.$$

It can be verified that $\mathbb{E}[L] = \mathbb{E}[M'] = \mathbb{E}[M] = 38.8333$. $\qquad\square$

5. Insurance: Part 2

5.1 Binary lotteries and indifference curves

In this chapter we complete the analysis of insurance that we started in Chapter 2 by considering the point view of the potential customer. Before we do so, we need to develop the analysis of binary money lottery, which are lotteries that involve only two prizes.

Fix a value of p (with $0 < p < 1$) and consider all the lotteries of the form

$$\begin{pmatrix} \$x & \$y \\ p & 1-p \end{pmatrix} \quad \text{with } x \geq 0 \text{ and } y \geq 0.$$

Thus we think of x and y as variables, while **p is a constant**.

We can identify a binary lottery with a point (x,y) in the positive quadrant of the cartesian plane. If $x = y$ then the lottery (x,x) lies on the 45°-line out of the origin and represents the situation where the individual gets x with probability p and x with probability $(1-p)$, that is, she gets x for sure; if $x > y$ the point lies below the 45°-line and if $x < y$ the point lies above the 45°-line.

Consider an individual whose utility-of-money function is $U(m)$. We assume that $U'(m) > 0$ (for every $m \geq 0$), that is, that the individual prefers more money to less. Given a lottery (x,y), the individual's expected utility is given by: $pU(x) + (1-p)U(y)$. Given two lotteries $A = (x_1, y_1)$ and $B = (x_2, y_2)$, the individual will prefer A to B if and only if

$$\mathbb{E}[U(A)] = pU(x_1) + (1-p)U(y_1) > \mathbb{E}[U(B)] = pU(x_2) + (1-p)U(y_2),$$

she will prefer B to A if the above inequality is reversed and will be indifferent between A and B if $\mathbb{E}[U(A)] = \mathbb{E}[U(B)]$. For example, if $p = \frac{1}{4}$ and the individual is risk neutral (so that we can take the identity function $U(m) = m$ as her vNM utility function) then the individual will be indifferent among the following lotteries, since their expected value is the same (namely 85): (130, 70), (100, 80), (85, 85) and (16, 108).

> **Definition 5.1.1** An *indifference curve* is a set of points (lotteries) in the (x, y) plane among which the individual is indifferent. For every point (x, y) there is an indifference curve that goes through that point. Since $U'(m) > 0$, for every m, each indifference curve will be downward-sloping.[a]
>
> ───────────
>
> [a]In order for expected utility to remain constant, if one coordinate is increased then the other coordinate must be decreased.

We want to relate the shape of the indifference curves of an individual to her attitude towards risk.

5.1.1 Case 1: risk neutrality

As remarked above, for a risk-neutral person we can take the identity function $U(m) = m$ as her vNM utility-of-money function, so that expected utility and expected value coincide. Fix an arbitrary lottery $A = (x_A, y_A)$ and let us try to find another lottery $B = (x_B, y_B)$ that lies on the same indifference curve. Then it must be that $px_A + (1 - p)y_A = px_B + (1 - p)y_B$ which can be written as

$$\overbrace{\underbrace{\frac{y_A - y_B}{x_A - x_B}}_{run}}^{rise} = -\frac{p}{1 - p}.$$

Thus indifference curves are straight lines with slope $-\frac{p}{1-p}$, as shown in Figure 5.1.

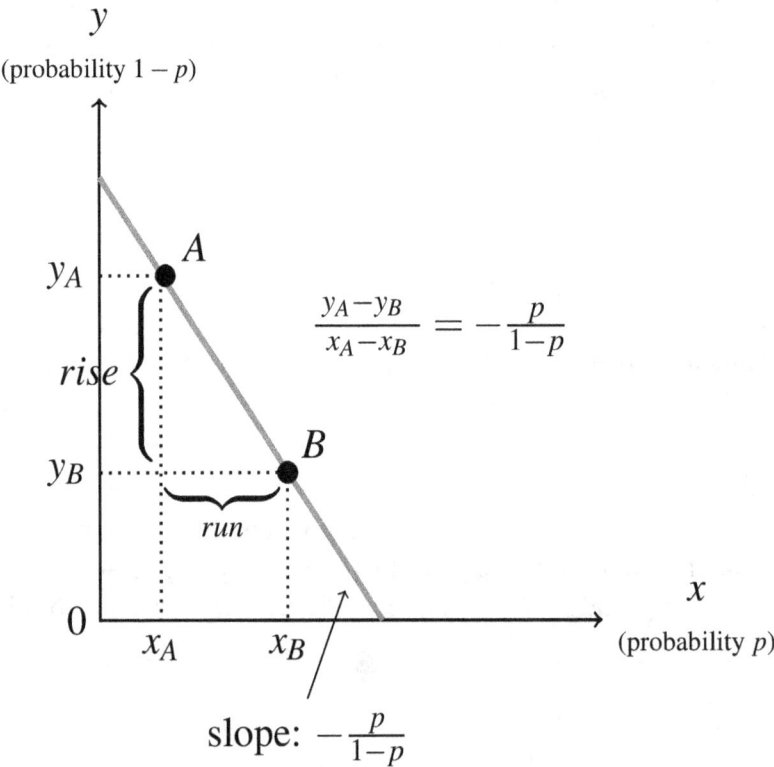

Figure 5.1: An indifference curve for a risk-neutral individual.

5.1.2 Case 2: risk aversion

Now consider the case of a risk-averse individual. Recall from Chapter 4 that the utility-of-money function $U(m)$ of a risk-averse individual is strictly concave, that is, for every $x > 0$ and $y > 0$ and for every $t \in (0,1)$,

$$U(tx + (1-t)y) > tU(x) + (1-t)U(y). \tag{5.1}$$

We now show that, if we take two lotteries A and B that yield the same expected utility (so that they lie on the same indifference curve) then all the lotteries on the line segment joining A and B (apart from A and B themselves) correspond to higher levels of expected utility than A and B. Hence, since the utility function is assumed to be strictly increasing, it follows that the indifference curve to which A and B belong, must lie *below* the line segment that joins A and B, that is, the indifference curve must be convex towards the origin.

As before, fix an arbitrary $p \in (0,1)$ and consider all the lotteries of the form

$$\left(\begin{array}{cc} \$x & \$y \\ p & 1-p \end{array} \right)$$

which can be identified with points in the positive quadrant of the cartesian plane (x,y).

Let $A = (x_A, y_A)$ and $B = (x_B, y_B)$ lie on the same indifference curve, that is,

$$\underbrace{pU(x_A) + (1-p)U(y_A)}_{=\mathbb{E}[U(A)]} = \underbrace{pU(x_B) + (1-p)U(y_B)}_{=\mathbb{E}[U(B)]} = \hat{u}.$$

Fix an arbitrary $t \in (0,1)$ and consider the point $C = tA + (1-t)B$ on the line segment joining A and B, which represents the lottery

$$C = \left(\begin{array}{cc} tx_A + (1-t)x_B & ty_A + (1-t)y_B \\ p & 1-p \end{array} \right).$$

Then

$$\mathbb{E}[U(C)] = p\,U(tx_A + (1-t)x_B) + (1-p)\,U(ty_A + (1-t)y_B). \tag{5.2}$$

By (5.1),

$$U(tx_A + (1-t)x_B) > tU(x_A) + (1-t)U(x_B) \tag{5.3}$$
$$U(ty_A + (1-t)y_B) > tU(y_A) + (1-t)U(y_B). \tag{5.4}$$

Thus, from (5.2)-(5.4) we get that

$$\mathbb{E}[U(C)] > p\left[tU(x_A) + (1-t)U(x_B)\right] + (1-p)\left[tU(y_A) + (1-t)U(y_B)\right]$$

$$= t\left[pU(x_A) + (1-p)U(y_A)\right] + (1-t)\left[pU(x_B) + (1-p)U(y_B)\right]$$

$$= t\mathbb{E}[U(A)] + (1-t)\mathbb{E}[U(B)]$$

$$= t\hat{u} + (1-t)\hat{u} = \hat{u}.$$

All of this is illustrated in Figure 5.2.

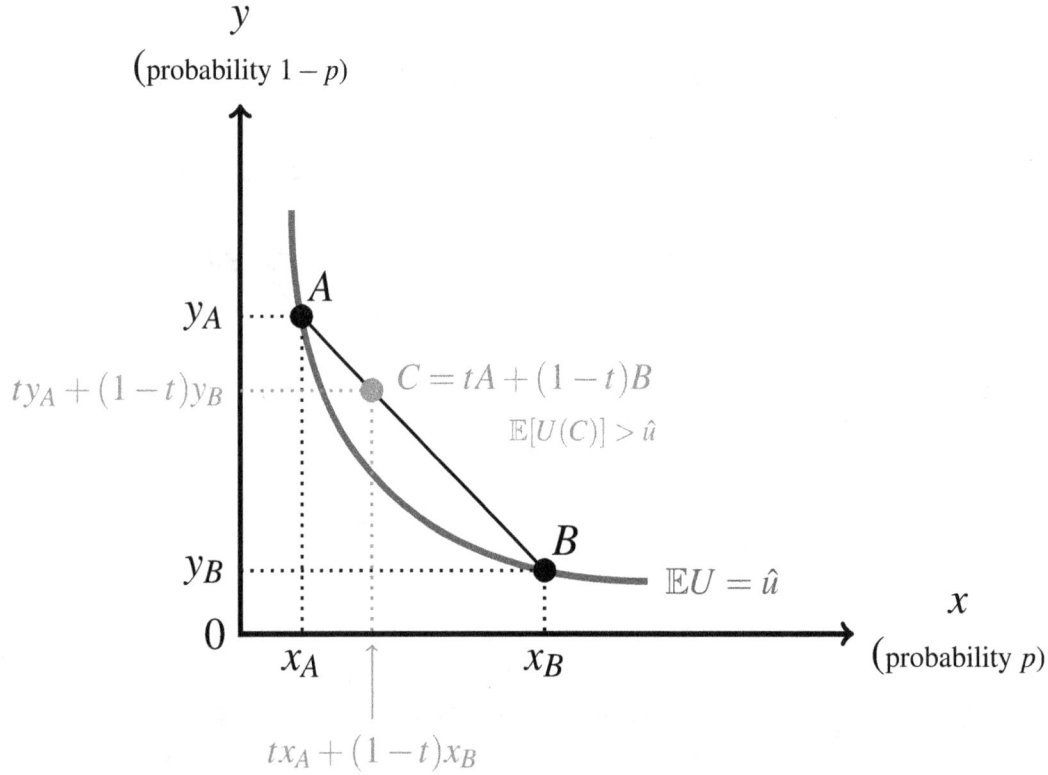

Figure 5.2: Indifference curves for a risk-averse individual are convex.

5.1.3 Case 3: risk love

Now consider the case of a risk-loving individual. Recall from Chapter 4 that the utility-of-money function $U(m)$ of a risk-loving individual is strictly convex, that is, for every $x > 0$ and $y > 0$ and for every $t \in (0,1)$,

$$U(tx + (1-t)y) < tU(x) + (1-t)U(y). \tag{5.5}$$

With an argument similar to the one used in the previous section, one can show that, if we take two lotteries A and B that yield the same expected utility – so that they lie on the same indifference curve – all the lotteries on the line segment joining A and B (apart from A and B themselves) correspond to *lower* levels of expected utility than A and B . Hence, since the utility function is assumed to be strictly increasing, it follows that the indifference curve to which A and B belong, must lie *above* the line segment that joins A and B, that is, the indifference curve must be concave towards the origin, as shown in Figure 5.3.

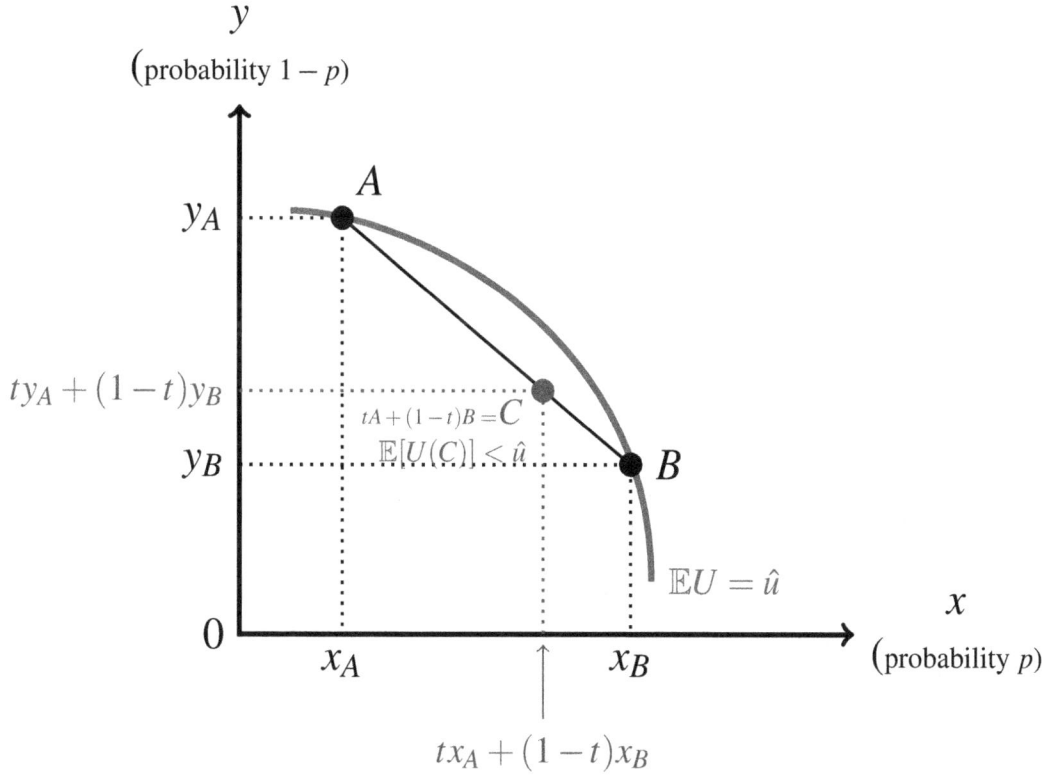

Figure 5.3: Indifference curves for a risk-loving individual are concave.

5.1.4 **The slope of an indifference curve**

We saw above that the indifference curves of a risk-neutral individual are straight lines and thus have a constant slope, which is equal to $-\frac{p}{1-p}$. On the other hand, the indifference curves of a risk-averse individual are convex towards the origin and thus do *not* have a constant slope: indeed the slope decreases as we move along the curve in the direction of an increase in the horizontal coordinate (and a decrease in the vertical coordinate). For a risk-loving individual the opposite is true: the slope of an indifference curve increases as we move along the curve in the direction of an increase in the horizontal coordinate.

How can we compute the slope of an indifference curve at a point? Let $A = (x_A, y_A)$ and consider a point B on the same indifference curve as A, so that $\mathbb{E}[U(A)] = \mathbb{E}[U(B)]$. Let us choose this point B to be "very close" to A, so that $B = (x_A + \delta, y_A + \varepsilon)$ with δ and ε close to 0 (one must be positive and the other negative). By hypothesis,

$$\underbrace{pU(x_A) + (1-p)U(y_A)}_{\mathbb{E}[U(A)]} = \underbrace{pU(x_A + \delta) + (1-p)U(y_A + \varepsilon)}_{\mathbb{E}[U(B)]} \tag{5.6}$$

Since B is close to A (that is, δ and ε are small), we can approximate the values of $U(x_A + \delta)$ and $U(y_A + \varepsilon)$ using the derivative of U (that is, using a first-order Taylor expansion):

$$\begin{aligned} U(x_A + \delta) &= U(x_A) + U'(x_A)\,\delta \\ U(y_A + \varepsilon) &= U(y_A) + U'(y_A)\,\varepsilon. \end{aligned} \tag{5.7}$$

Replacing (5.7) into (5.6) we get

$$\begin{aligned} pU(x_A) + (1-p)U(y_A) &= p\left[U(x_A) + U'(x_A)\delta\right] + (1-p)\left[U(y_A) + U'(y_A)\varepsilon\right] \\ &= pU(x_A) + (1-p)U(y_A) + pU'(x_A)\delta + (1-p)U'(y_A)\varepsilon \end{aligned} \tag{5.8}$$

from which we get that

$$pU'(x_A)\delta + (1-p)U'(y_A)\varepsilon = 0,$$

that is,

$$\frac{\overbrace{\varepsilon}^{rise}}{\underbrace{\delta}_{run}} = -\frac{p}{1-p}\frac{U'(x_A)}{U'(y_A)}.$$

Thus the slope of an indifference curve at a point $A = (x_A, y_A)$ is given by[1]

$$\boxed{-\frac{p}{1-p}\frac{U'(x_A)}{U'(y_A)}} \tag{5.9}$$

---

[1]Alternatively, one can derive the slope of an indifference curve at a point by using the implicit function theorem, which says the following. Let $F : \mathbb{R}^2 \to \mathbb{R}$ be a continuously differentiable function and $(x_0, y_0) \in \mathbb{R}^2$ a point such that $F(x_0, y_0) = c$; if $\frac{\partial F}{\partial y}(x_0, y_0) \neq 0$ then there is an interval $(x_0 - \varepsilon, x_0 + \varepsilon)$ and a differentiable function $f : (x_0 - \varepsilon, x_0 + \varepsilon) \to \mathbb{R}$ such that (1) $F(x_0, f(x_0)) = y_0$, (2) $F(x, f(x)) = c$ for every $x \in (x_0 - \varepsilon, x_0 + \varepsilon)$ and (3) $f'(x_0) = -\frac{\frac{\partial F}{\partial x}(x_0, y_0)}{\frac{\partial F}{\partial y}(x_0, y_0)}$. To apply the implicit function theorem in this context, let $F(x, y) = pU(x) + (1-p)U(y)$ and let $A = (x_A, y_A)$ be a point where $pU(x_A) + (1-p)U(y_A) = \hat{u}$.

In the case of risk neutrality U' is constant and thus $U'(x_A) = U'(y_A)$ so that $\frac{U'(x_A)}{U'(y_A)} = 1$; hence the slope becomes $-\frac{p}{1-p}$ at every point, consistently with what we saw above.

Now let us see what (5.9) implies for a concave utility-of-money function, that is, for the case of **risk aversion**. When the utility function is *concave*, the second derivative is negative ($U''(m) < 0$), which means that *the first derivative is decreasing*, that is,

$$\text{if} \quad m_1 < m_2 \quad \text{then} \quad U'(m_1) > U'(m_2) \quad \left(\text{or} \quad \frac{U'(m_1)}{U'(m_2)} > 1\right),$$

as shown in Figure 5.4.

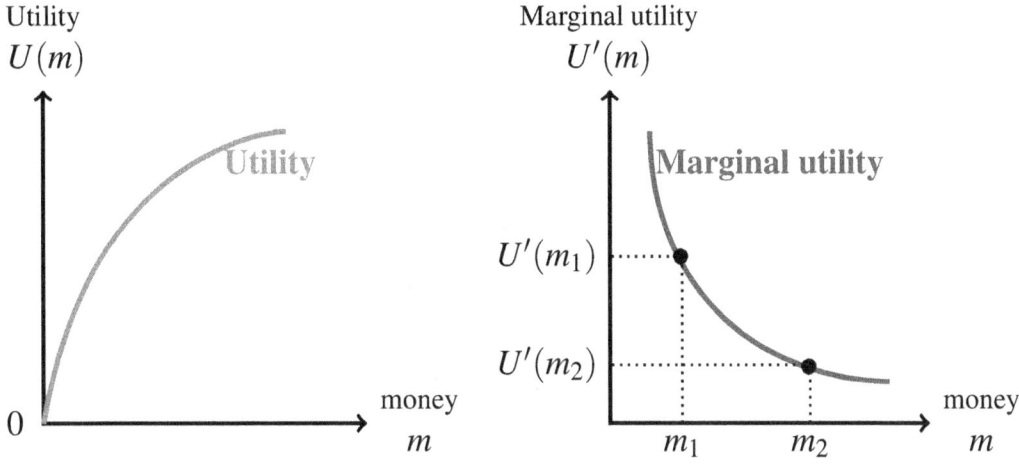

Figure 5.4: When the utility function is concave, marginal utility is decreasing.

At a point $A = (x, y)$ **above** the 45° line (where $x < y$) we have that $\frac{U'(x)}{U'(y)} > 1$ so that

$$-\frac{p}{1-p}\frac{U'(x)}{U'(y)} < -\frac{p}{1-p} \quad \text{or} \quad \frac{p}{1-p}\frac{U'(x)}{U'(y)} > \frac{p}{1-p}.$$

Hence the indifference curve is **steeper** than the straight line with slope $-\frac{p}{1-p}$.

Conversely, at a point $A = (x, y)$ **below** the 45° line (where $x > y$) we have that $\frac{U'(x)}{U'(y)} < 1$ so that

$$-\frac{p}{1-p}\frac{U'(x)}{U'(y)} > -\frac{p}{1-p} \quad \text{or} \quad \frac{p}{1-p}\frac{U'(x)}{U'(y)} < \frac{p}{1-p}.$$

Hence the indifference curve is **less steep** than the straight line with slope $-\frac{p}{1-p}$.

Finally at a point **on** the 45° line (where $x = y$) we have that $\frac{U'(x)}{U'(y)} = 1$ so that

$$-\frac{p}{1-p}\frac{U'(x)}{U'(y)} = -\frac{p}{1-p};$$

hence the straight line with slope $-\frac{p}{1-p}$ is **tangent to** the indifference curve.

■ **Example 5.1** This example is illustrated in Figure 5.5. Let $p = \frac{2}{5}$ and $U(m) = \sqrt{m}$ and consider all the lotteries of the form $\begin{pmatrix} \$x & \$y \\ \frac{2}{5} & \frac{3}{5} \end{pmatrix}$. Since, $U'(m) = \frac{1}{2\sqrt{m}}$, $\frac{U'(x)}{U'(y)} = \frac{\sqrt{y}}{\sqrt{x}}$ (for $x > 0$ and $y > 0$).

Consider three points: (25,100), (64,64) and (121,36). The expected utility of these three lotteries is the same, namely 8; hence these three points belong to the same indifference curve.[2]

- Point (64,64) is on the 45° line and the slope of the indifference curve at that point is

$$-\frac{p}{1-p}\left(\frac{\sqrt{64}}{\sqrt{64}}\right) = -\frac{p}{1-p} = -\frac{2}{3}.$$

- Point (25,100) is above the 45° line and the slope of the indifference curve at that point is

$$-\frac{p}{1-p}\left(\frac{\sqrt{100}}{\sqrt{25}}\right) = -\frac{2}{3}\left(\frac{10}{5}\right) = -\frac{4}{3}.$$

- Point (121,36) is below the 45° line and the slope of the indifference curve at that point is

$$-\frac{p}{1-p}\left(\frac{\sqrt{36}}{\sqrt{121}}\right) = -\frac{2}{3}\left(\frac{6}{11}\right) = -\frac{4}{11}.$$

■

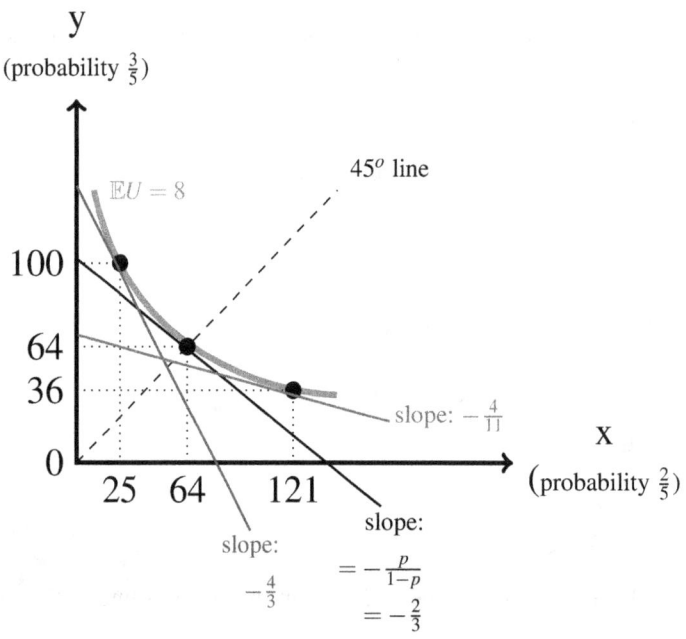

Figure 5.5: The graph for Example 5.1.

---

[2]The equation of the indifference curve is obtained by solving for y the equation $\frac{2}{5}\sqrt{x} + \frac{3}{5}\sqrt{y} = 8$. The solution is $y = \frac{4}{9}(20 - \sqrt{x})^2$.

We will omit the case of risk love (convex utility function, concave indifference curves). The reader should convince himself/herself that in this case an indifference curve is less steep than the line of slope $-\frac{p}{1-p}$ at a point above the 45° line and steeper at a point below the 45° line.

> Test your understanding of the concepts introduced in this section, by going through the exercises in Section 5.5.1 at the end of this chapter.

5.2 Back to insurance

We can now return to the topic of insurance, which we partially analyzed in Chapter 2. We begin by recalling the general set-up.

Consider an individual whose current wealth is $\$W_0$. She faces the possibility of a loss in the amount of $\$\ell$ ($0 < \ell \leq W_0$) with probability p ($0 < p < 1$). An insurance contract can be expressed as a pair of wealth levels (W_1, W_2), where W_1 is wealth in the bad state (if the loss occurs) and W_2 is wealth in the good state (if the loss does not occur); the amount $(W_0 - W_2)$ is the contract's premium and the amount $W_2 - W_1$ is the deductible. If $W_1 = W_2$ the contract offers full insurance, while if $W_1 < W_2$ the contract offers partial insurance.

We saw in Chapter 2 that, through any point in the (W_1, W_2) plane, we can draw an isoprofit line which contains all the contracts that yield the same profit to the insurer. Recall that

$$\text{isoprofit lines are straight lines with slope } -\frac{p}{1-p}.$$

The isoprofit line that goes through the no-insurance point $NI = (W_0 - \ell, W_0)$ is the zero-profit line. Points below the zero-profit line represent profitable contracts, while points above the zero-profit line correspond to contracts that would involve a loss for the insurer. Thus no insurer would be willing to offer a contract that lies above the zero-profit line.

We can now ask the question: what contracts would be acceptable to the individual under consideration?

If the individual purchases insurance contract (W_1, W_2) then she faces the following money lottery:

$$\begin{pmatrix} \$W_1 & \$W_2 \\ p & 1-p \end{pmatrix}.$$

We focus on a risk-averse individual who has von Neumann-Morgenstern preferences, so that her preferences over possible insurance contracts can be represented by means of a vNM utility-of-money function $U(m)$ (which is increasing and strictly concave). A contract (W_1, W_2) will be acceptable to the individual if it yields at least as high an expected utility as the no-insurance option, that is, if

$$pU(W_1) + (1-p)U(W_2) \geq pU(W_0 - \ell) + (1-p)U(W_0).$$

Using the tools developed in this chapter, we can draw the individual's indifference curve that goes through the no-insurance point *NI*: it will be a decreasing and convex curve; we shall call it the *reservation indifference curve*. Points below the reservation indifference curve represent contracts that would yield lower expected utility than the no-insurance option; thus the individual would reject any such contracts, if offered to her. Only contracts represented by points on or above the reservation indifference curve will be acceptable to the individual.

Thus the set of *mutually beneficial insurance contracts* is given by the area bounded below by the reservation indifference curve, bounded above by the zero-profit line and bounded on the right by the 45^0 line; it is shown as a shaded area in Figure 5.6.

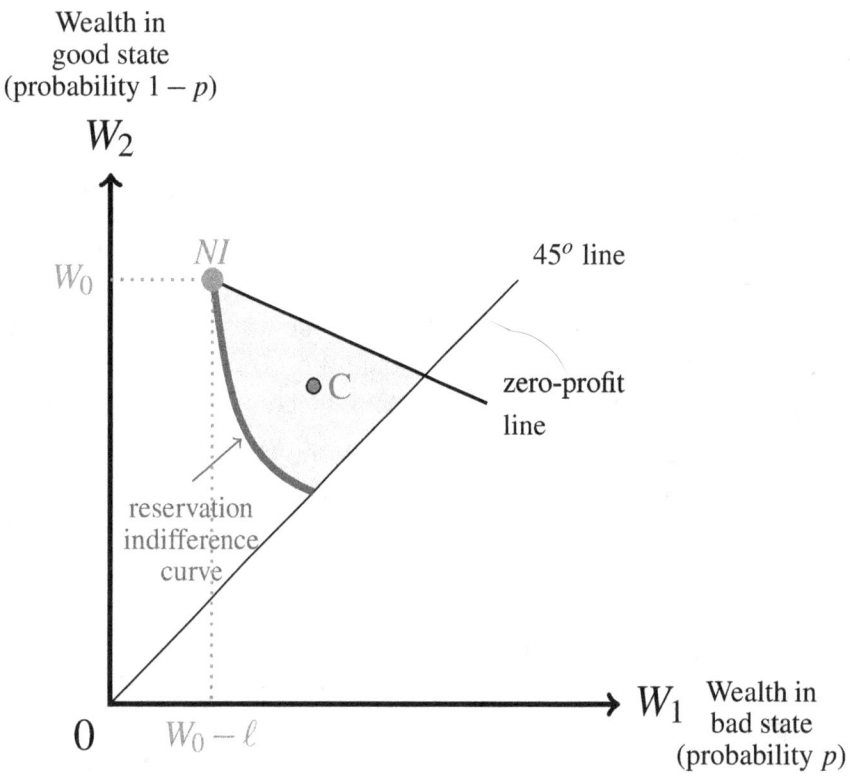

Figure 5.6: The shaded area is the set of mutually beneficial insurance contracts.

Contract *C* in Figure 5.6 is above the reservation indifference curve and thus yields higher expected utility than the no-insurance option (that is, *C* is strictly preferred to *NI* by the potential customer) and is below the zero-profit line and thus yields positive profit to the insurer.

In Figure 5.6 the reservation indifference curve that goes through the no-insurance (*NI*) point is steeper at that point than the zero-profit line. This follows from the analysis in Section 5.1.4. Indeed this is true of any point that lies above the 45° line. Let $A = (W_1^A, W_2^A)$ be a contract that lies above the 45° line. Then, by (5.9) the slope, at point *A*, of the indifference curve that goes through *A* is equal to

$$\boxed{-\frac{p}{1-p}\left(\frac{U'(W_1^A)}{U'(W_2^A)}\right)}$$

(5.10)

Recall that the slope of the isoprofit line that goes through any point in the wealth diagram is $-\frac{p}{1-p}$. By the remark on page 111,

- At any point **above** the 45° line the indifference curve is steeper than the isoprofit line that goes through that point.

- At any point **on** the 45° line the indifference curve is tangent to (has the same slope as) the isoprofit line that goes through that point.

This is shown in Figure 5.7. Any contract that lies in the area above the indifference curve that goes through contract A and below the isoprofit line through A, such as point B in Figure 5.7, represents a contract that is better than A for the potential customer (B yields higher expected utility than A) and is better than A for the insurance company (B yields higher profits than A).

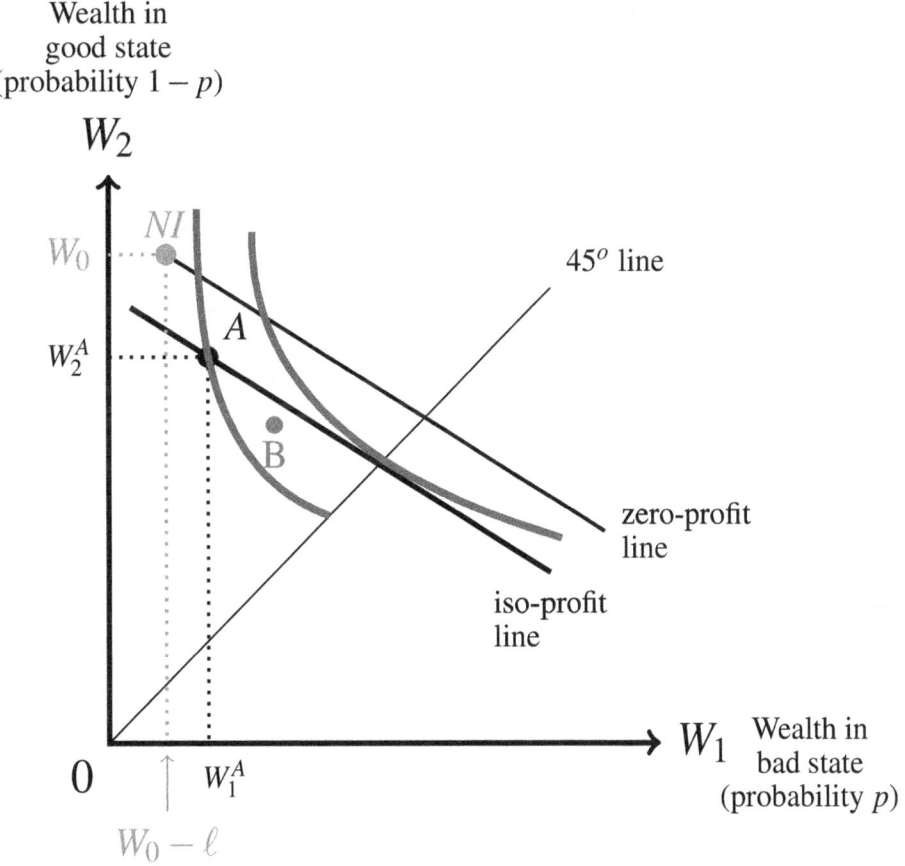

Figure 5.7: The relative slope of an indifference curve and an isoprofit line.

The profit-maximizing contract for a monopolist

Without making use of expected utility theory, we showed in Chapter 2 (Section 2.6.3) that a profit-maximizing monopolist would offer a full-insurance contract to a potential customer, at a premium that makes her indifferent between insuring and not insuring. We can now confirm this result with the tools developed in this chapter. Consider an arbitrary partial-insurance contract that is acceptable to the potential customer (that is, that lies on or above the reservation indifference curve), such as point A in Figure 5.7. Such a contract is not profit maximizing, because the monopolist could replace it with a contract above the indifference curve through A and below the iso-profit line through A (such as contract B in Figure 5.7) and (1) the potential customer would be even happier with the new contract and (2) the monopolist would increase its profits. Since this argument applies to *any* partial-insurance contract (that is, to any point above the 45° line), we deduce that a profit-maximizing monopolist would offer a full-insurance contract.[3] Of all the full-insurance contracts that are acceptable to the potential customer (that is, that are not below the reservation indifference curve) the one that yields the highest profit to the insurer is at the intersection of the reservation indifference curve and the 45° line: contract C in Figure 5.8. The corresponding premium, denoted by h^{max}, is such that:

$$U(W_0 - h_{max}) = pU(W_0 - \ell) + (1-p)U(W_0). \qquad (5.11)$$

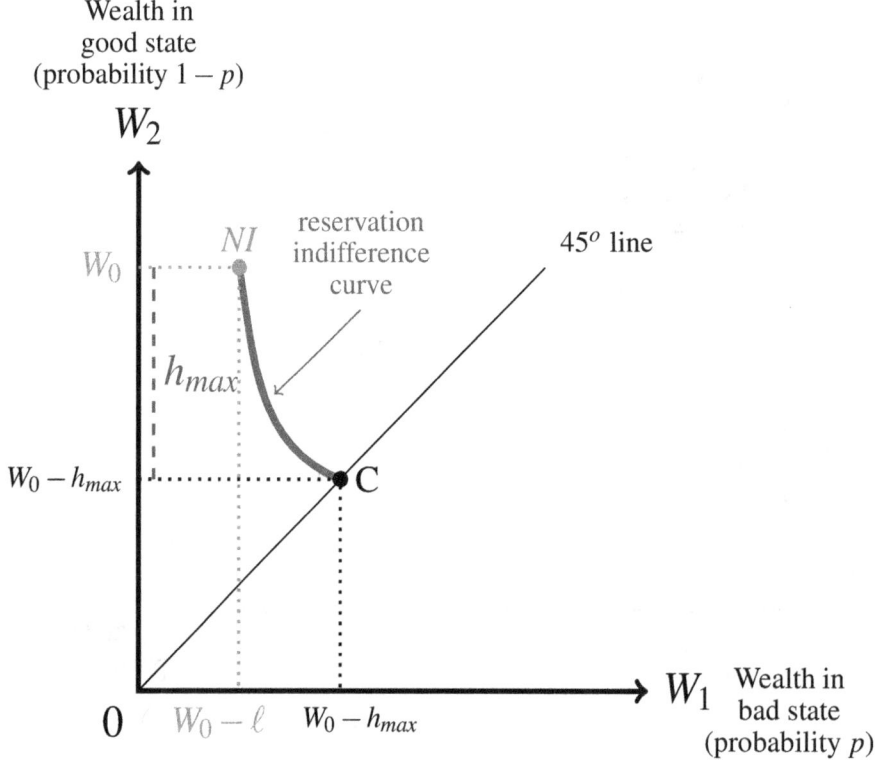

Figure 5.8: Contract C is the full-insurance contract that would be offered by a monopolist.

---

[3]Recall that, at any point on the 45° line, the indifference curve is tangent to the isoprofit line.

Recall the definition of risk premium, R_L, of a money lottery L: it is the amount by which the expected value of lottery L can be reduced to leave the individual indifferent between the amount $\$(\mathbb{E}[L] - R_L)$ for sure and the lottery itself. Using this definition and (5.11) it is clear that, since $\mathbb{E}[NI] = W_0 - p\ell$,

$$h_{max} = p\ell + R_{NI}$$

where $NI = \begin{pmatrix} W_0 - \ell & W_0 \\ p & 1-p \end{pmatrix}$ is the no-insurance lottery. That is, h_{max} *is equal to the expected loss plus the risk premium of the no-insurance lottery.*

For example, if $W_0 = 1,600$, $\ell = 700$, $p = \frac{1}{10}$ and $U(m) = \sqrt{m}$ then h_{max} is given by the solution to the equation

$$\sqrt{1,600-h} = \frac{1}{10}\sqrt{1,600-700} + \frac{9}{10}\sqrt{1,600}$$

which is $h^{max} = 79$. Hence the risk premium of the NI lottery is

$$R_{NI} = h_{max} - p\ell = 79 - \frac{1}{10}700 = \$9.$$

5.2.2 Perfectly competitive industry with free entry

Without making use of expected utility theory, we showed in Chapter 2 (Section 2.6.4) that, at an equilibrium in a perfectly competitive industry with free entry, all the insurance firms offer the same contract, namely the full insurance contract with "fair" premium equal to the expected loss $p\ell$. We can now confirm this result with the tools developed in this chapter.

Recall that a free-entry competitive equilibrium is a situation where

1. each firm in the industry makes zero profits, and

2. there is no unexploited profit opportunity in the industry, that is, there is no currently-not-offered contract that would attract some custmers and yield positive profit to a firm that offered that contract.

By the zero-profit condition (Point 1), any equilibrium contract must be on the zero-profit line. By the no-profitable-opportunity condition (Point 2), it cannot be a partial-insurance contract, such as contract A in Figure 5.9, because a new entrant (or an existing firm) could offer a contract in the region above the indifference curve through point A and below the iso-profit line through point A, such as contract B in Figure 5.9; such a contract would induce all those customers who were purchasing contract A to switch to B and would yield positive profits to the insurance firm offering it. The only contract that is immune to this is the contract at the intersection of the zero-profit line and the 45° line (contract D in Figure 5.9).

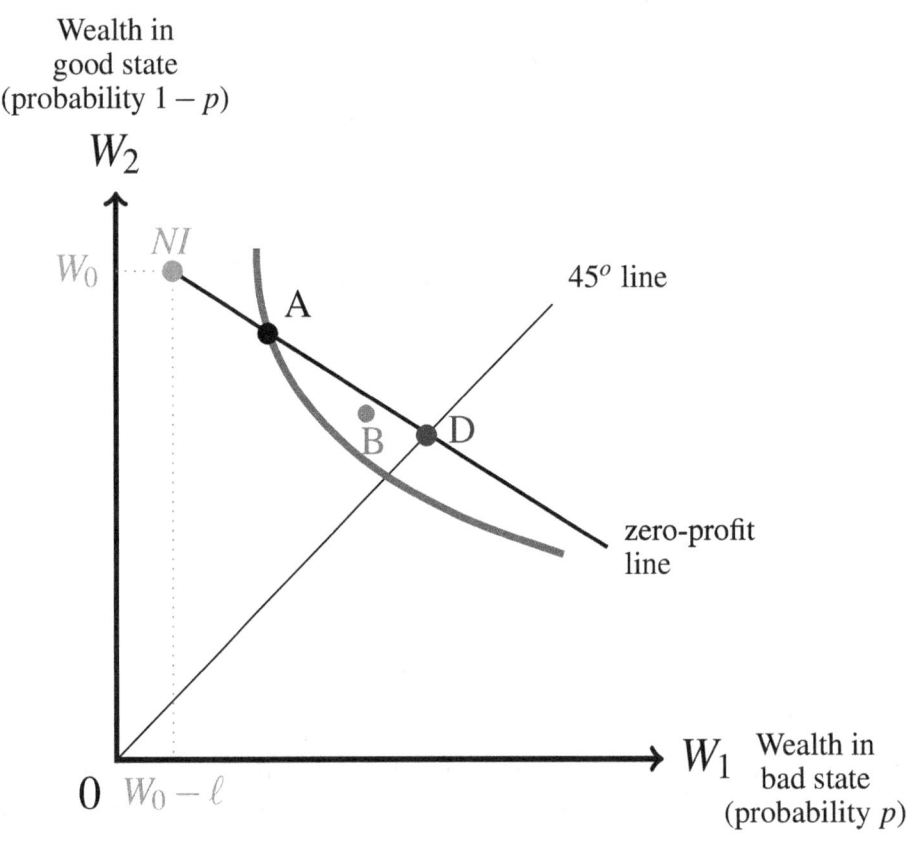

Figure 5.9: Contract D is the full-insurance contract that would be offered at a free-entry competitive equilibrium.

> Test your understanding of the concepts introduced in this section, by going through the exercises in Section 5.5.2 at the end of this chapter.

5.3 Choosing from a menu of contracts

It is often the case that insurance companies offer, not just a single contract, but a menu of contracts and potential customers are allowed to choose which contract to purchase from this menu. Typically, customers are given a choice between a higher premium with higher coverage (= lower deductible) or a lower premium with lower coverage (= higher deductible). The offered menu consists of either a list of contracts or a formula that relates premium to deductible. In this section we discuss how the potential customer chooses a contract from a given menu.

5.3.1 Choosing from a finite menu

In the case where the menu consists of a finite list of contracts, the potential customer will first determine which of the offered contracts is best for her (that is, yields the highest expected utility) then choose the best contract, provided that it is better than the no-insurance alternative.

For example, consider an individual whose initial wealth is $1,000. He faces a potential loss of $400, with probability 20% and has the following vNM utility-of-money function $U(m) = \sqrt{m}$. Suppose that the insurance company offers the following options:

	premium	deductible
Contract 1:	$82	0
Contract 2:	$62	$100
Contract 3:	$40	$200

The expected utility of each contract is as follows:

Contract 1: $\sqrt{1,000-82} = 30.2985$

Contract 2: $0.2\sqrt{1,000-162}+0.8\sqrt{1,000-62} = 30.2911$

Contract 3: $0.2\sqrt{1,000-240}+0.8\sqrt{1,000-40} = 30.3007$

This *if* he decides to insure, he will choose Contract 3. To see if he does decide to insure we need to compare the expected utility of the best contract, namely Contract 3, with the expected utility of no insurance, which is $0.2\sqrt{1,000-400}+0.8\sqrt{1,000} = 30.1972$. Since Contract 3 (the best of the three offered contracts) is better than no insurance, he will purchase Contract 3.

5.3.2   Choosing from a continuum of options

Suppose now that the insurance company offers a continuum of options in the form of a formula relating premium and deductible. For example, consider an individual who is facing a potential loss of \$4,100 and is told by the insurance company that she can choose any deductible $d \in [0, 4100]$; the corresponding premium h is then calculated according to the following formula:

$$h = 820 - \frac{1}{5}d. \tag{5.12}$$

Thus the following are some of the many possible contracts that the individual can choose from:

deductible	premium
0	\$820
\$100	\$800
\$140	\$792
\$260	\$768
...	...

The set of possible choices is infinite, since any $d \in [0, 4100]$ can be chosen by the individual. Thus we can think of (5.12) as a line, similar to the budget line faced by a consumer. We shall call it the *insurance budget line*.

It is useful to translate the line of equation (5.12) – which is expressed in terms of premium and deductible – into a line in the wealth diagram (W_1, W_2). This is easily done by recalling that $h = W_0 - W_2$ and $d = W_2 - W_1$:

$$W_0 - W_2 = 820 - \frac{1}{5}(W_2 - W_1), \quad \text{that is,} \quad W_2 = \left(\frac{5W_0}{4} - 1025\right) - \frac{W_1}{4}. \tag{5.13}$$

For example, if $W_0 = 6,000$ then (5.13) becomes $W_0 - W_2 = 820 - \frac{1}{5}(W_2 - W_1)$, that is,

$$W_2 = 6,475 - \frac{W_1}{4}. \tag{5.14}$$

Note that the line (in the wealth space) corresponding to equation (5.14) goes through the no-insurance point $NI = (1900, 6000)$; in fact, replacing W_1 with the value 1900 in (5.14) we get $W_2 = 6000$.

The insurance budget line of equation (5.14) is shown in Figure 5.10.

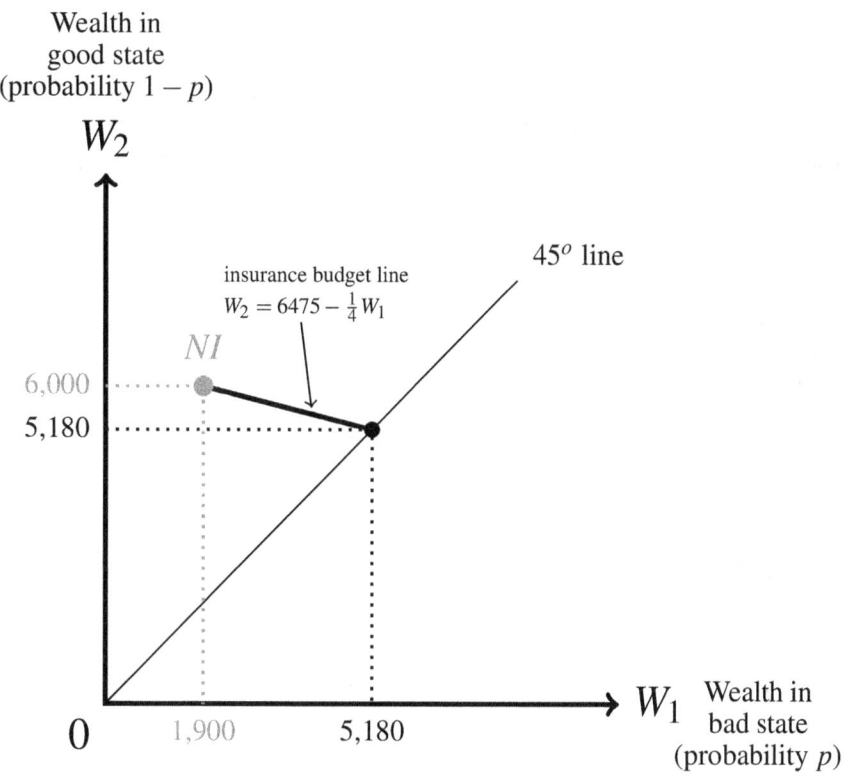

Figure 5.10: The insurance budget line $W_2 = 6,475 - \frac{W_1}{4}$.

We will consider insurance budget lines defined by equations of the form

$$h = a - bd \qquad \text{with } a > 0, \ b > 0, \ d \in [0, \ell] \text{ and } a - b\ell \geq 0, \tag{5.15}$$

which – translated into the wealth space (by replacing h with $(W_0 - W_2)$ and d with $(W_2 - W_1)$) – becomes

$$W_2 = \frac{W_0 - a}{1 - b} - \frac{b}{1 - b} W_1. \tag{5.16}$$

If (5.15) is such that $a - b\ell = 0$ then the insurance budget line in the wealth space (defined by (5.16)) goes through the no-insurance point $NI = (W_0 - \ell, W_0)$,[4] while if $a - b\ell > 0$ then the insurance budget line in the wealth space (defined by (5.16)) goes through a point vertically below NI.[5]

---

[4] For example, the zero-profit line falls into this category.

[5] For example, an isoprofit line corresponding to a positive level of profit will fall into this category.

What contract, if any, would the individual choose from the insurance budget line?

We start with the case where the insurance budget line goes through the *NI* point. There are three cases to consider.

Case 1: the reservation indifference curve is, at *NI*, as steep as, or less steep than, the insurance budget line, as shown in Figure 5.11. It follows that the entire insurance budget line lies below the reservation indifference curve and thus **the individual will choose not to insure**.

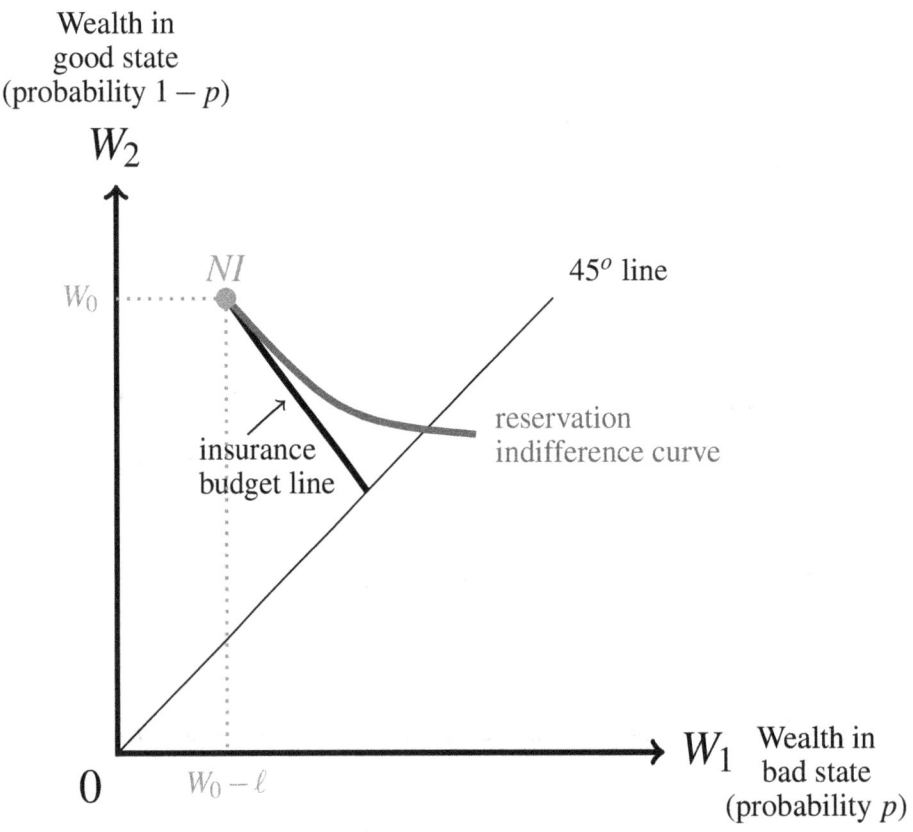

Figure 5.11: Case 1: the insurance budget line lies below the reservation indifference curve.

In the example above, where $W_0 = 6,000$, $\ell = 4,100$ and the insurance budget line is given by the equation $W_2 = 6,475 - \frac{W_1}{4}$, we will be in Case 1 if and only if

$$\frac{p}{1-p}\left(\frac{U'(1,900)}{U'(6,000)}\right) \leq \frac{1}{4}.$$

For instance, if $U(m) = \ln(m)$, then Case 1 occurs if and only if $p \leq \frac{19}{259} = 0.0734$.

For Cases 2 and 3 below we assume that reservation indifference curve is steeper at *NI* than the insurance budget line.

Case 2: the indifference curve that goes through the point at the intersection of the 45° line and the insurance budget line is steeper than, or as steep as, the insurance budget line at that point, as shown in Figure 5.12.[6]

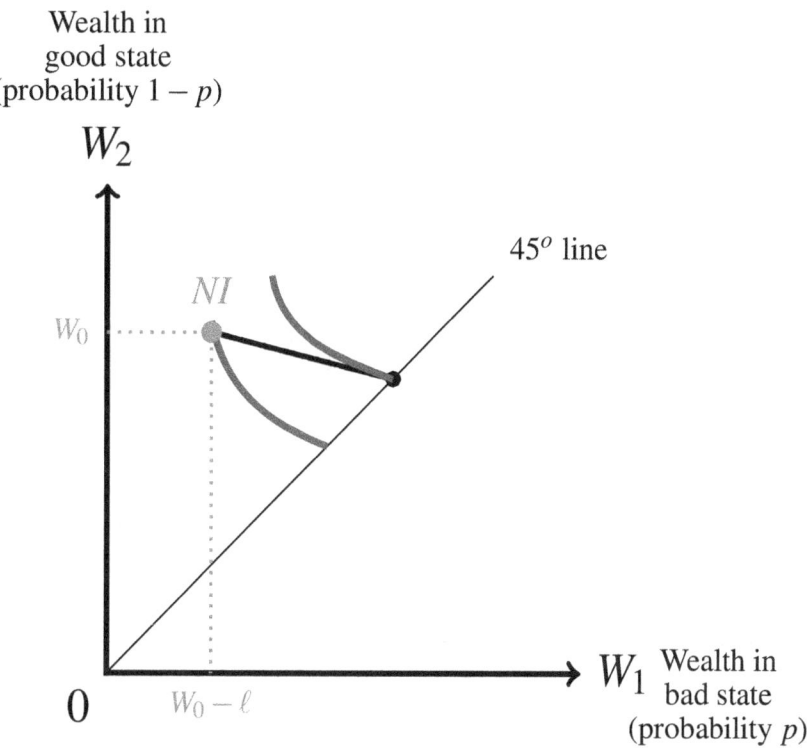

Figure 5.12: Case 2: the individual chooses full insurance.

In this case, insurance is better than no insurance and the best contract (that is, the contract that yields the highest expected utility) is the **full insurance** contract (the point at the intersection of the 45° line and the insurance budget).

In the example above, where the insurance budget line is given by the equation $W_2 = 6{,}475 - \frac{W_1}{4}$, we will be in Case 2 if and only if (recall that the slope of any indifference curve at any point on the 45° line is $-\frac{p}{1-p}$)

$$\frac{p}{1-p} \geq \frac{1}{4} \quad \text{i.e.} \quad p \geq \frac{1}{5}.$$

---

[6] The indifference curve will be, at that point, as steep as the insurance budget line if and only if the insurance budget line is the zero-profit line, since that slope will be $-\frac{p}{1-p}$. It is steeper if and only if the insurance budget line is less steep than the zero-profit line, which implies that all the contracts on the insurance budget line – with the exception of the *NI* point – yield negative profits; thus it is unlikely that an insurance company would offer such menu (unless it is subsidized by the government).

Case 3: the indifference curve that goes through the point at the intersection of the 45° line and the insurance budget line is less steep than the insurance budget line at that point, as shown in Figure 5.13.

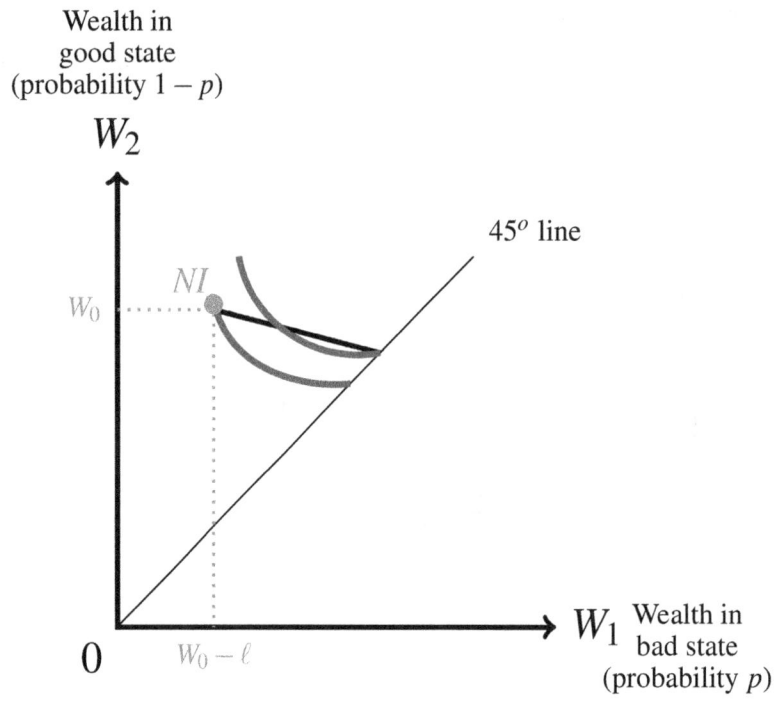

Figure 5.13: Case 3: the individual chooses partial insurance.

In this case, there are partial-insurance contracts on the insurance budget line that are better than full insurance (and than no insurance). Thus the individual will choose a partial insurance contract.

Which of the many partial-insurance contracts will she choose? It cannot be a contract where the indifference curve through it is either steeper, or less steep, than the insurance budget line: in the former case there would be contracts on the budget line to the right of that contract that would be better and in the latter case there would be contracts on the budget line to the left of that contract that would be better. Hence the best contract is the one at which the slope of the indifference curve at that point is equal to the slope of the insurance budget line, that is, it is a contract at which the indifference curve through it is *tangent to* the insurance budget line: it is that contract $C = \left(W_1^C, W_2^C\right)$ such that, letting $W_2 = \alpha - \beta W_1$ be the equation of the budget line (with $\alpha > 0$ and $\beta > 0$),

$$W_2^C = \alpha - \beta W_1^C \quad \text{and} \quad \frac{p}{1-p}\left(\frac{U'(W_1^C)}{U'(W_2^C)}\right) = \beta. \tag{5.17}$$

The optimal contract (which satisfies (5.17)) is shown in Figure 5.14.

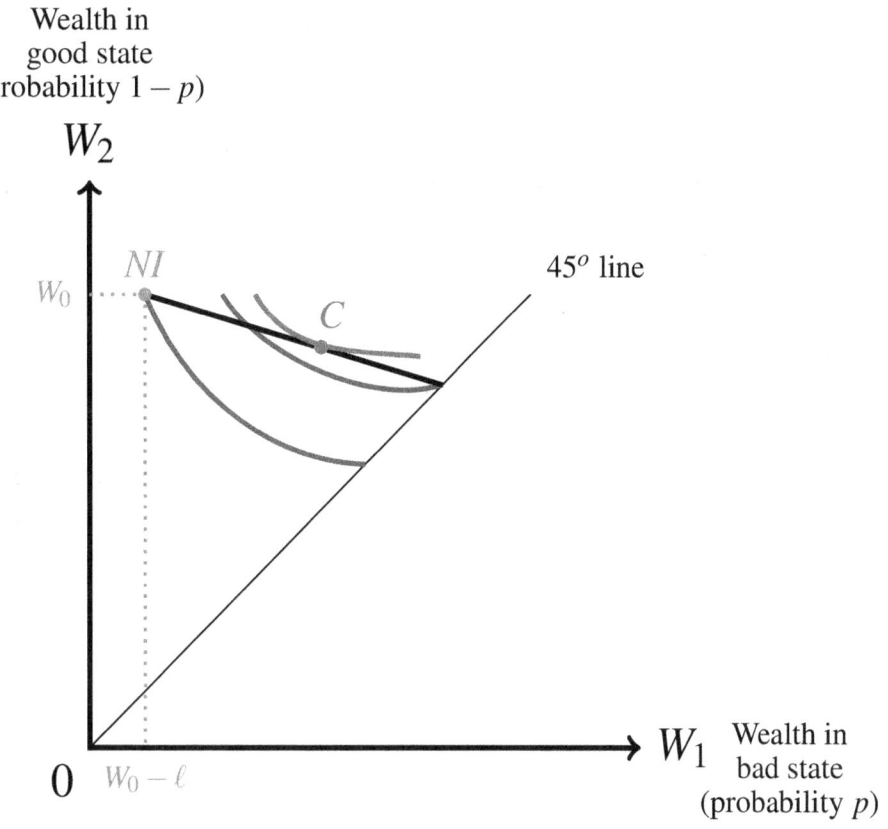

Figure 5.14: The best contract in Case 3.

In the example above, where $W_0 = 6,000$, $\ell = 4,100$ and the insurance budget line is given by the equation $W_2 = 6,475 - \frac{W_1}{4}$, we will be in Case 3 if and only if[7]

$$\frac{p}{1-p}\left(\frac{U'(1,900)}{U'(6,000)}\right) > \frac{1}{4} \quad \text{and} \quad \frac{p}{1-p} < \frac{1}{4}.$$

For instance, if $U(m) = \ln(m)$, then Case 3 occurs if and only if $p > \frac{19}{259}$ and $p < \frac{1}{5}$, that is, if and only if $p \in \left[\frac{19}{259}, \frac{1}{5}\right]$. Fix a value of p in this range and continue to assume that $U(m) = \ln(m)$. Then the optimal contract $C = (W_1^C, W_2^C)$ is given by the solution to

$$W_2 = 6,475 - \frac{W_1}{4} \quad \text{and} \quad \frac{p}{1-p}\left(\frac{W_2}{W_1}\right) = \frac{1}{4}.$$

For example, if $p = \frac{1}{7}$ then the optimal contract is $C = (3700, 5550)$, that is, the individual will choose a deductible of $5,550 - 3,700 = \$1,850$ with a corresponding premium of $6,000 - 5,550 = \$450$.

---

[7] The first inequality says that the reservation indifference curve is steeper at NI than the insurance budget line. The second inequality says that the indifference curve that goes through the point on the 45° line that lies on the insurance budget line is less steep at that point than the budget line.

So far we have assumed that the insurance budget line goes through the no-insurance point *NI*. If it does not then, given the assumptions stated in (5.15) on page 121, it will go through a point vertically below the no-insurance point. There are several possibilities.

A **first possibility** is that the insurance budget line lies entirely below the reservation indifference curve (this situation is similar to Case 1 considered above). In such a case the individual will choose not to insure, since any of the offered contracts yields a lower expected utility than no insurance.

A **second possibility** is that there are points on the insurance budget line that are above the reservation indifference curve, as well as points that are below the reservation indifference curve. This case can be further subdivided into two sub-cases.

The **first sub-case** is that there is only one point of intersection between the insurance budget line and the reservation indifference curve, as shown in Figure 5.15. In this case the entire segment of the budget line to the right of the intersection point lies above the reservation indifference curve.

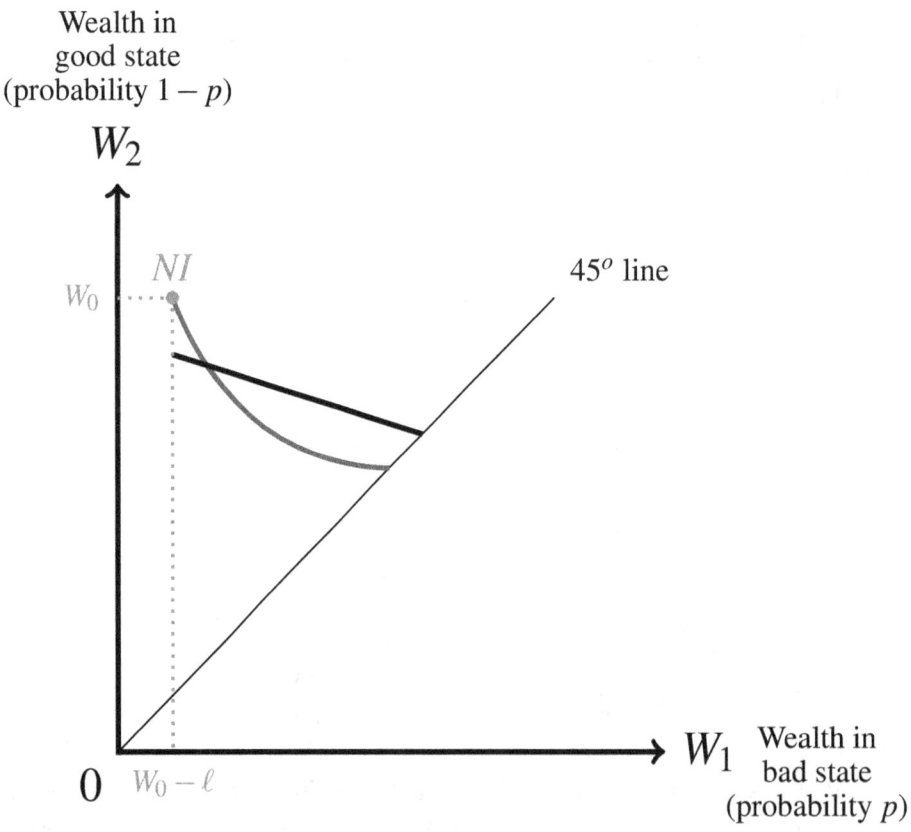

Figure 5.15: The case where the insurance budget line does not go through *NI*.

In this case,

- if the indifference curve that goes through the point at the intersection of the 45° line and the insurance budget line is - at that point - *steeper than, or as steep as,* the insurance budget line (as shown in the left panel of Figure 5.16), then the best contract for the individual is the full-insurance contract;

- if the indifference curve that goes through the point at the intersection of the 45° line and the insurance budget line is - at that point - *less steep than* the insurance budget line (as shown in the right panel of Figure 5.16), then the best contract for the individual is a partial-insurance contract, namely a point at which there is a tangency between the budget line and the indifference curve that goes through that point (point C in the right panel of Figure 5.16).

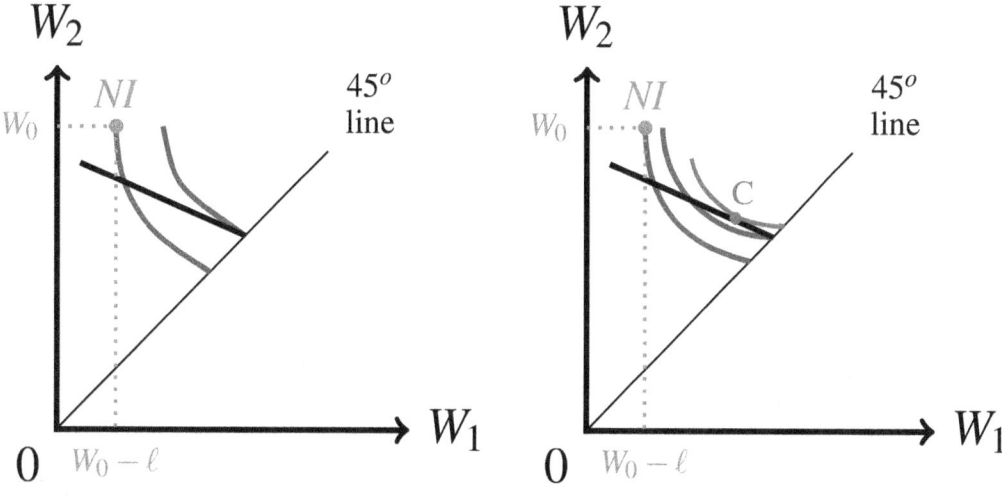

Figure 5.16: In this case the individual chooses full insurance.

For example, let $W_0 = 3,600$, $\ell = 1,100$ and $p = \frac{1}{5}$. Suppose that the insurance company is willing to offer any contact that yields a profit of \$10. Then premium and deductible are related by the equation $h - p(\ell - d) = 10$, that is, $h = 230 - \frac{d}{5}$. Let us translate it into a line in the wealth space: $3,600 - W_2 = 230 - \frac{1}{5}(W_2 - W_1)$, that is,

$$W_2 = 4,212.5 - \frac{W_1}{4}.$$

This is the equation of the isoprofit line corresponding to a profit-level of 10. Call B the point of intersection of the budget line and the 45° line. Then the slope of the isoprofit line is equal to the slope, at point B, of the indifference curve that goes through point B. Hence we are in the subcase shown in the left panel of Figure 5.16 and the individual will choose the full-insurance contract, with a premium of \$230 (assuming, of course, that the utility-of-money function is such that the reservation indifference curve crosses the insurance budget line).

On the other hand, if the insurance budget line is steeper than an isoprofit line, then we are in the case shown in the right panel of Figure 5.16 and the individual will choose a partial-insurance contract.

The **second sub-case** is that there are two points of intersection between the insurance budget line and the reservation indifference curve, as shown in Figure 5.17.

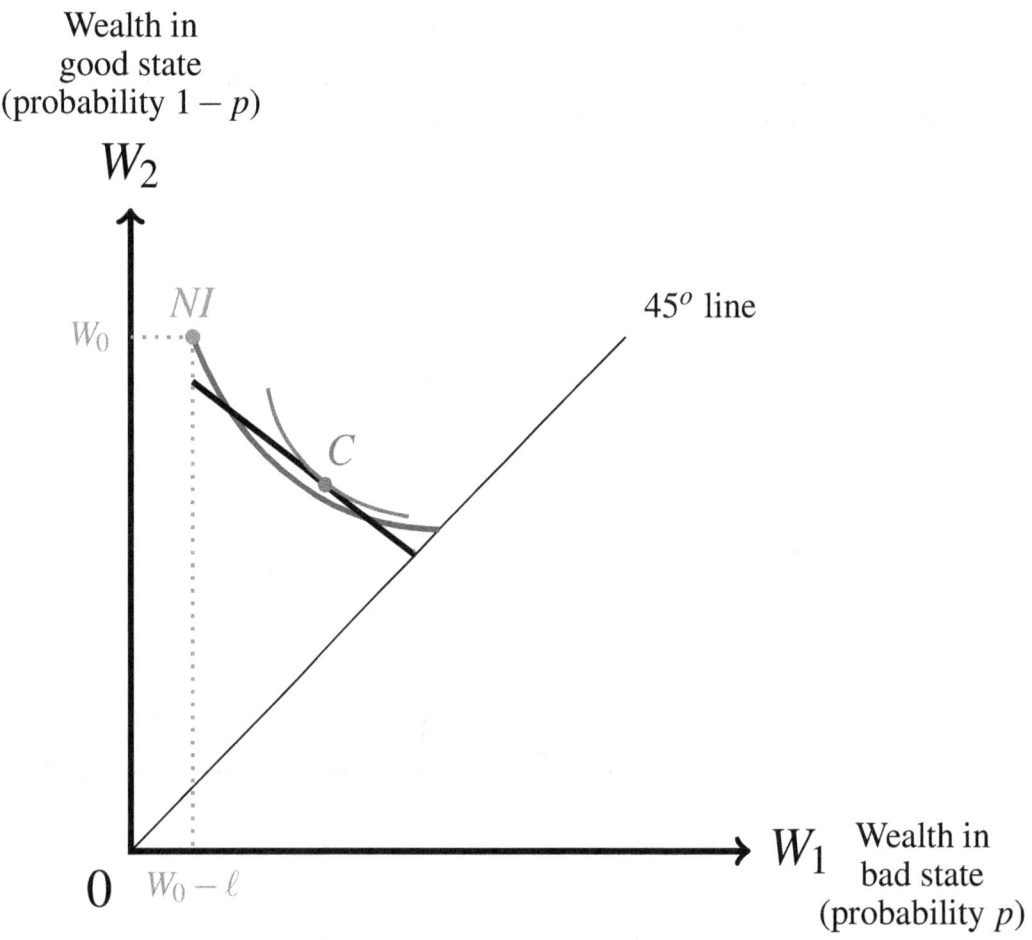

Figure 5.17: In this case the individual chooses partial insurance.

In this case the individual will choose a partial-insurance contract, namely the contract on the insurance budget line at which there is a tangency between the budget line and the indifference curve that goes through that point (shown as point C in Figure 5.17).

We will not consider cases where the insurance budget line does not cover the entire range $[0, \ell]$ of possible deductibles and is thus a smaller segment than considered so far; it should be clear, however, that the method would be the same, namely based on comparing the relative slopes of indifference curves and the budget line. An example of this is given in Exercise 5.16.

We can summarize the discussion of this section as follows. Let

$$W_2 = \alpha - \beta W_1$$

be the equation of the insurance budget line (with $\alpha > 0$ and $\beta > 0$). To determine whether the individual will buy insurance and, if so, what contract she will choose, we can proceed as follows.[8]

Let B be the full-insurance contract on the insurance budget line (thus $W_1^B = W_2^B = \frac{\alpha}{1+\beta}$) and recall that the slope, at point B, of the indifference curve that goes through B is $\frac{p}{1-p}$ (where, as usual, p denotes the probability of loss).

1. If $\mathbb{E}[U(B)] \geq \mathbb{E}[U(NI)]$, then the individual will buy insurance[9] and

   (a) if $\frac{p}{1-p} \geq \beta$ she will choose the full-insurance contract B;

   (b) if $\frac{p}{1-p} < \beta$ she will choose partial insurance, namely that contract $C = \left(W_1^C, W_2^C\right)$ such that

   $$W_2^C = \alpha - \beta W_1^C \qquad \text{and} \qquad \frac{p}{1-p}\left(\frac{U'(W_1^C)}{U'(W_2^C)}\right) = \beta.$$

2. If $\mathbb{E}[U(B)] < \mathbb{E}[U(NI)]$ then

   (a) if the insurance budget line does not intersect the reservation indifference curve, that is, if the there is no solution to the equation

   $$pU(W_0 - \ell) + (1-p)U(W_0) = pU(W_1) + (1-p)U(\alpha - \beta W_1)$$

   in the range $(W_0 - \ell, W_0)$, then the individual will not buy insurance;

   (b) if the insurance budget line intersects the reservation indifference curve at two points, that is, if the there are two solutions to the equation

   $$pU(W_0 - \ell) + (1-p)U(W_0) = pU(W_1) + (1-p)U(\alpha - \beta W_1)$$

   in the range $(W_0 - \ell, W_0)$, then the individual will choose partial insurance, namely the contract $C = \left(W_1^C, W_2^C\right)$ such that

   $$W_2^C = \alpha - \beta W_1^C \qquad \text{and} \qquad \frac{p}{1-p}\left(\frac{U'(W_1^C)}{U'(W_2^C)}\right) = \beta.$$

> Test your understanding of the concepts introduced in this section, by going through the exercises in Section 5.5.3 at the end of this chapter.

---

[8] The reader should convince herself/himself that, indeed, the following steps cover all the cases considered in this section.

[9] Here and elsewhere we are implicitly assuming that if the individual is indifferent between insuring and not insuring then she will choose to insure.

5.4   Mutual insurance

After an exceptional spate of wildfires in the western United States in 2017 and 2018, several insurance companies notified residents in brush-heavy areas that their homeowner-insurance policies would not be renewed because the location of their homes posed an unacceptable fire risk. For example, on August 6, 2018, CBS News reported that[10]

> facing mounting losses, some property insurers are pulling back from selling policies in California and other western states where wildfire risk is elevated. In California alone, damages had mounted to at least $12 billion by early 2018.

Clearly, the unavailability of insurance makes a risk-averse individual worse off. Is there anything that he/she can do mitigate the welfare loss due to the inability to but insurance?

Imagine that Ann and Bob are friends who live in high-risk areas that insurers have decided to no longer cover. To make things simple, imagine that Ann and Bob have the same initial wealth $\$W_0$ and their homes are of equal value, so that they both face the same potential loss of $\$\ell$ if a fire occurs; furthermore, assume that they face the same probability p of a fire occurring. Without insurance they both face the same money lottery, namely

$$NI = \left(\begin{array}{cc} W_0 & W_0 - \ell \\ 1-p & p \end{array} \right)$$

One possible course of action for Ann and Bob is to resort to *mutual-insurance*, that is, to insure each other by signing the following contract:

I agree to the following:

1. in the event that we both suffer a loss (due to a fire) or in the event that none of us suffers a loss, then no transfer of money will take place between us,

2. in the event that only one of us suffers a loss of $\$\ell$ (due to a fire), the other one (who did not suffer a loss) will give $\$\frac{\ell}{2}$ to the person who suffered the loss, that is, will cover 50% of his/her loss.

Would such a contract make them better off relative to no insurance? Let us assume they leave in locations that are far apart, so that the event of a fire in Ann's area can plausibly be treated as independent of the event of a fire in Bob's area. When two events are independent, the probability of them jointly occurring is equal to the product of the individual probabilities. Thus the probabilities can be computed as follows:

event:	no fire	fire only at Ann's	fire only at Bob's	fire at both locations
probability:	$(1-p)^2$	$p(1-p)$	$p(1-p)$	p^2

Thus, each individual will suffers a loss of $\$\frac{\ell}{2}$ (either in the form of a payment to a less lucky friend or in the form of a loss of ℓ followed by a reimbursement, in the amount of $\frac{\ell}{2}$,

---

from the luckier friend) with probability $2p(1-p)$, so that the contract will give rise to the following money lottery for each of them ('MI' stands for 'Mutual Insurance'):

$$MI = \begin{pmatrix} W_0 & W_0 - \frac{\ell}{2} & W_0 - \ell \\ (1-p)^2 & 2p(1-p) & p^2 \end{pmatrix}$$

Assuming that Ann has vNM preferences over money lotteries and prefers more money to less (a similar argument applies to Bob), we can represent her preferences by means of a normalized vNM utility function as follows, with $0 < a < 1$:

money:	W_0	$W_0 - \frac{\ell}{2}$	$W_0 - \ell$
utility:	1	a	0

Then the expected utilities of the two lotteries are:

$$\mathbb{E}[U(NI)] = 1 - p, \quad \text{and}$$

$$\mathbb{E}[U(MI)] = (1-p)^2 + 2p(1-p)a = (1-p)[1 + p(2a-1)].$$

Consider first the case where Ann is risk neutral. Then it must be that $a = \frac{1}{2}$. In fact, the lottery $\begin{pmatrix} W_0 - \frac{\ell}{2} \\ 1 \end{pmatrix}$ and the lottery $\begin{pmatrix} W_0 & W_0 - \ell \\ \frac{1}{2} & \frac{1}{2} \end{pmatrix}$ have the same expected value, namely $W_0 - \frac{\ell}{2}$ and thus Ann must be indifferent between them. The expected utility of the former is a and the expected utility of the latter is $\frac{1}{2}$; thus $a = \frac{1}{2}$. When $a = \frac{1}{2}$, $(2a-1) = 0$ and thus $\mathbb{E}[U(NI)] = \mathbb{E}[U(MI)]$ so that Ann does not gain from signing the contract: with the contract she is as well off as without the contract.

Next consider first the case where Ann is risk averse. Then it must be that $a > \frac{1}{2}$. In fact, the lottery $\begin{pmatrix} W_0 - \frac{\ell}{2} \\ 1 \end{pmatrix}$, whose expected utility is a, gives for sure the expected value of the lottery $\begin{pmatrix} W_0 & W_0 - \ell \\ \frac{1}{2} & \frac{1}{2} \end{pmatrix}$, whose expected utility is $\frac{1}{2}$. By definition of risk aversion, Ann prefers the former lottery to the latter. Hence $a > \frac{1}{2}$. When $a > \frac{1}{2}$, $(2a-1) > 0$ and thus $(1-p)[1 + p(2a-1)] > 1 - p$ so that $\mathbb{E}[U(MI)] > E[U(NI)]$, that is, Ann is better off with the contract than without the contract.

Thus we have shown that two *risk-averse individuals can make themselves better off by signing a mutual-insurance agreement*, according to which they share the losses equally, whoever incurs the losses.

The astute reader will have realized that there was no need for a detailed proof of the fact that a risk-averse individual will prefer lottery *MI* to lottery *NI*, since it follows from the analysis of Chapter 4 (Section 4.4.2): lottery *NI* can be obtained from lottery *MI* by means of a mean-preserving spread. First of all, the reader should verify that $\mathbb{E}[NI] = \mathbb{E}[MI] = W_0 - p\ell$. Secondly, by taking the probability of outcome $\left(W_0 - \frac{\ell}{2}\right)$, namely $2p(1-p)$, and spreading it equally to each of the other outcomes we obtain lottery *NI*; in fact, $(1-p)^2 + \frac{1}{2}2p(1-p) = 1 - p$ and $p^2 + \frac{1}{2}2p(1-p) = p$.

> Test your understanding of the concepts introduced in this section, by going through the exercises in Section 5.5.4 at the end of this chapter.

5.5 Exercises

The solutions to the following exercises are given in Section 5.6 at the end of this chapter.

5.5.1 Exercises for Section 5.1: Binary lotteries and indifference curves

Exercise 5.1 Consider all the lotteries of the form $\begin{pmatrix} \$x & \$y \\ \frac{1}{3} & \frac{2}{3} \end{pmatrix}$ with $x \geq 0$ and $y \geq 0$.

Assume that the individual in question is risk neutral.

(a) Write the equation of the indifference curve that goes through point $(x = 6, y = 10)$.

(b) Write the equation of the indifference curve that goes through point (10,8).

(c) Write the equation of the indifference curve that goes through point (4,9).

Exercise 5.2 Consider all the lotteries of the form $\begin{pmatrix} \$x & \$y \\ \frac{1}{3} & \frac{2}{3} \end{pmatrix}$ with $x \geq 0$ and $y \geq 0$.

Consider an individual with von Neumann-Morgenstern utility-of-money function $U(m) = \ln(m)$.

(a) Calculate the expected utility of lottery $A = \begin{pmatrix} \$10 & \$40 \\ \frac{1}{3} & \frac{2}{3} \end{pmatrix}$.

(b) Calculate the expected utility of lottery $B = \begin{pmatrix} \$10 & \$10 \\ \frac{1}{3} & \frac{2}{3} \end{pmatrix}$.

(c) Calculate the slope of the indifference curve at point $A = (10, 40)$.

(d) Calculate the slope of the indifference curve at point $B = (10, 10)$.

(e) In the (x, y)-plane draw the indifference curve that goes to point $A = (10, 40)$ and the indifference curve that goes to point $B = (10, 10)$.

Exercise 5.3 Repeat Parts (a)-(e) of the previous question for the case of an individual who is risk neutral.

Exercise 5.4 Consider all the lotteries of the form $\begin{pmatrix} \$x & \$y \\ \frac{2}{3} & \frac{1}{3} \end{pmatrix}$ with $x \geq 0$ and $y \geq 0$.

Consider an individual with von Neumann-Morgenstern utility-of-money function $U(m) = \ln(m)$.

(a) Write an equation whose solutions give the set of lotteries that the individual considers just as good as lottery $A = \begin{pmatrix} \$4 & \$4 \\ \frac{2}{3} & \frac{1}{3} \end{pmatrix}$.

(b) Solve the equation of Part (a) and obtain a function $y = f(x)$ whose graph is the indifference curve that goes through point $(4,4)$.

(c) Write an equation whose solutions give the set of lotteries that the individual considers just as good as lottery $B = \begin{pmatrix} \$9 & \$4 \\ \frac{2}{3} & \frac{1}{3} \end{pmatrix}$.

(d) Solve the equation of Part (c) and obtain a function $y = g(x)$ whose graph is the indifference curve that goes through point $(9,4)$.

(e) Calculate the slope of the indifference curve at point $A = (4,4)$.

(f) Calculate the slope of the indifference curve at point $B = (9,4)$.

Exercise 5.5 Consider all the lotteries of the form $\begin{pmatrix} \$x & \$y \\ \frac{1}{5} & \frac{4}{5} \end{pmatrix}$ with $x \geq 0$ and $y \geq 0$.

Let $A = (100, 25)$, $B = (4, 49)$ and $C = (40, 40)$.

(a) Draw the indifference curves that go through points A, B and C for an individual with von Neumann-Morgenstern utility-of-money function $U(m) = \sqrt{m}$.

(b) Draw the indifference curves that go through points A, B and C for a risk-neutral individual.

5.5.2 Exercises for Section 5.2: Back to insurance

Exercise 5.6 Adam's current wealth is $\$80,000$. With probability $\frac{1}{20}$ he faces a loss of $\$30,000$. His vNM utility-of-money function is $U(m) = \ln(m)$.

(a) Calculate the slope of Adam's reservation indifference curve at the no-insurance point NI.

(b) Calculate the slope of the iso-profit curve that goes through point NI.

(c) Calculate the maximum premium that Adam is willing to pay for full insurance.

(d) Calculate the increase in Adam's utility relative to no insurance if he obtains full insurance at the "fair" premium (that is, at a premium that yields zero profits to the insurer).

(e) Consider contract $A = (80,000 - h, \ 80,000 - h)$. Calculate the slope at point A of Adam's indifference curve that goes through point A.

Exercise 5.7 Frank has a wealth of $\$W_0$. With probability $p = \frac{1}{10}$ he faces a loss of $\$\ell$. The maximum he is willing to pay for full insurance is $800. The risk premium associated with the lottery corresponding to no insurance is $500.

(a) What is the value of ℓ?

(b) What is the maximum profit that a monopolist can make by selling insurance to Frank?

Exercise 5.8 Bob owns a house. The value of the land is $75,000 while the value of the building is $110,000. The rest of his wealth consists of the balance of his bank account, which is $10,000. Thus his current wealth is $195,000. Bob lives in an area where there is a 5% probability that a fire will completely destroy his house during any year (while the land will not be affected by a fire). Bob's utility function is given by:

$$U(m) = 800 - (20 - m)^2$$

where $m \in [0, 20]$ denotes money measured in $10,000 (thus, for example, $m = 11$ means $110,000).

(a) What is Bob's expected loss if he does not insure?

(b) What is Bob's expected *wealth* if he does not insure?

(c) What is Bob's expected *utility* if he does not insure?

(d) What is Bob's expected utility if he purchases an insurance contract with premium $1,200 and deductible $20,000?

(e) What is the slope of Bob's reservation indifference curve at the no-insurance point?

(f) Let A be the point in the wealth diagram that corresponds to the insurance contract with premium $1,200 and deductible $20,000. What is the slope, at point A, of Bob's indifference curve that goes through point A?

(g) Does the indifference curve that goes through point A of Part (f) lie above or below the reservation indifference curve?

(h) What is the maximum premium that Bob would be willing to pay for full insurance?

Exercise 5.9 Beth's vNM utility-of-money function is $U(m) = \alpha - \beta e^{-m}$, where α and β are positive constants. [Recall that $e \approx 2.71828$ and $\frac{d}{dx}e^x = e^x$.]

(a) What is Beth's attitude to risk?

(b) What is Beth's Arrow-Pratt measure of absolute risk aversion?

(c) Show that if Beth's initial wealth is W_0 and she is faced with a potential loss ℓ with probability p, the maximum premium that she is willing to pay for full insurance is the same whatever her initial wealth, that is, it is independent of W_0.

Exercises for Section 5.3: Choosing from a menu of contracts

Exercise 5.10 Barbara has a wealth of $80,000 and faces a potential loss of $20,000 with probability 10%. Her utility-of-money function is $U(m) = \sqrt{m}$. An insurance company offers her the following menu of contracts:

	premium	deductible
Contract 1:	$2,340	$500
Contract 2:	$2,280	$1,000
Contract 3:	$2,220	$1,500
Contract 4:	$2,160	$2,000

(a) What is Barbara's expected utility if she does not insure?

(b) For each contract calculate the corresponding expected utility and determine which contract, if any, Barbara will choose.

Exercise 5.11 You have the following vNM utility-of-money function: $U(m) = \ln(m)$. Your initial wealth is $10,000 and you face a potential loss of $4,000 with probability $\frac{1}{6}$. An insurance company offers you the following menu of choices: if you choose deductible d (with $0 \le d \le 4,000$) then your premium is $h = 800 - 0.2d$.

(a) Translate the equation $h = 800 - 0.2d$ into an equation in terms of wealth levels.

(b) Compare the slope of the reservation indifference curve at the no-insurance point NI to the slope of the insurance budget line. Are there contracts that are better for you than no insurance?

(c) Which contract will you choose from the menu?

(d) Compare expected utility if you do not insure with expected utility if you purchase the best contract from the menu.

(e) What is the insurance company's expected profit from the contract of Part (c)?

(f) Prove the result of Part (c) directly by expressing expected utility as a function of the deductible d and by maximizing that expression.

Exercise 5.12 You have the following vNM utility-of-money function: $U(m) = \sqrt{m}$. Your initial wealth is $576 and you face a potential loss of $176 with probability $\frac{1}{16}$. An insurance company offers you the following menu of choices: if you choose deductible d (with $0 \le d \le 176$) then your premium is $h = \frac{1}{9}(176 - d)$.

(a) Translate the equation $h = \frac{1}{9}(176 - d)$ into an equation in terms of wealth levels.

(b) Compare the slope of the reservation indifference curve at the no-insurance point NI to the slope of the insurance budget line. Are there contracts that are better for you than no insurance?

Exercise 5.13 [Note: in this exercise the data is the same as in Exercise 5.12, but we have changed the probability of loss from $\frac{1}{16}$ to $\frac{1}{7}$.]

Your vNM utility-of-money function is $U(m) = \sqrt{m}$; your initial wealth is $576 and you face a potential loss of $176 with probability $\frac{1}{7}$. An insurance company offers you the following menu of choices: if you choose deductible d (with $0 \le d \le 176$) then your premium is $h = \frac{1}{9}(176 - d)$.

(a) Translate the equation $h = \frac{1}{9}(176 - d)$ into an equation in terms of wealth levels.

(b) Compare the slope of the reservation indifference curve at the no-insurance point NI to the slope of the insurance budget line. Are there contracts that are better for you than no insurance?

(c) Which contract will you choose from the menu?

(d) Compare expected utility if you do not insure with expected utility if you purchase the best contract from the menu.

(e) What is the insurance company's expected profit from the contract of Part (c)?

(f) Confirm the result of Part (c) by expressing expected utility as a function of the deductible d and by finding the maximum of that function in the interval $[0, 400]$.

Exercise 5.14 David's vNM utility-of-money function is $U(m) = 1 - (m+1)^{-1}$, where m is money measured in thousands of dollars (thus, for example, $m = 6$ means $6,000$).

(a) What is David's attitude to risk?

(b) Calculate the Arrow-Pratt measure of absolute risk aversion for David.

David's initial wealth is $8,000 and he faces a potential loss of $3,000 with probability $\frac{1}{10}$. An insurance company offers him insurance at the following terms:

> choose the amount (of your potential loss) that you would like to be covered (thus a number in the range from 0 to 3,000); for every dollar of **coverage** you will pay $\$\gamma$ as premium (with $0 < \gamma < 1$).

(c) Write an equation that expresses the premium in terms of the deductible. [Recall that the deductible is that part of the loss that is **not** covered.].

(d) Translate the equation of Part (c) into an equation in terms od David's wealth levels.

(e) Does the insurance budget line of Part (d) go through the no-insurance point NI?

(f) For what values of γ will David choose not to insure?

(g) For what values of γ will Davis purchase full insurance?

(h) Assuming that the value of γ is in the range where David chooses partial insurance, write a system of two equations whose solution gives the contract that David will choose.

Exercise 5.15 Anna's vNM utility-of-money function is $U(m) = \ln(m)$. Her initial wealth is $3,600 and she faces a potential loss of $2,700 with 25% probability. An insurance company is offering Anna any contract such that premium h and deductible d satisfy the following equation: $h = 810 - \frac{3}{10}d$.

(a) Translate the equation $h = 810 - \frac{3}{10}d$ into an equation in terms of wealth levels.

(b) Does the equation found in Part (a) correspond to an isoprofit line?

(c) Does the insurance budget line of Part (a) go through the no-insurance point?

(d) Are there any contracts on the insurance budget line that Anna prefers to no insurance?

(e) What is the best contract on the insurance budget line for Anna?

(f) Calculate Anna's expected utility at the following points:

    (1) *NI* (no insurance),

    (2) the full-insurance contracts that belongs to the budget line, and

    (3) the contract found in Part (e).

(g) Prove the result of Part (e) directly by expressing expected utility as a function of the deductible d and by maximizing that expression.

Exercise 5.16 Kate has an initial wealth of $W_0 = \$1,600$ and faces a potential loss of $\ell = \$576$ with probability 20%. Her von Neumann-Morgenstern utility-of-money function is $U(m) = \sqrt{m}$. An insurance company is offering the following menu of contracts:

$$h = 152 - \frac{3}{10}d.$$

However, the deductible is restricted to the interval $[0, 360]$ (hence the largest deductible is 360 rather than 576).

Let $A = \left(W_1^A, W_2^A\right)$ be the point in wealth space corresponding to the contract $(h = 44, d = 360)$.

(a) Translate the insurance budget line $h = 152 - \frac{3}{10}d$ ($d \in [0, 360]$) into a budget line in wealth space (give the range of values).

(b) Does contract A lie on, below or above the reservation indifference curve?

(c) Calculate the slope, at point A, of the indifference curve that goes through A, compare it to the slope of the insurance budget line and deduce which contract from the offered menu will be chosen by Kate.

5.5.4   **Exercises for Section 5.4: Mutual insurance**

Exercise 5.17 Carla and Don have the same initial wealth, namely $32,400, and face the same potential loss, namely $18,000, with the same probability, namely $\frac{1}{5}$.
Carla's vNM utility-of-money function is

$$U_C(m) = \sqrt{m}$$

while Don's is

$$U_D(m) = 1 - \frac{1}{\frac{m}{10,000} + 1}.$$

They are unable to obtain insurance on the market, so they have decided to write a mutual insurance contract, according to which any losses are shared equally between them.

Assuming that the event that Carla suffers a loss is independent of the event that Don suffers a loss, show that signing the mutual insurance contract has made each of them better off relative to no insurance.

Exercise 5.18 Ann, Carla and Dana have the same initial wealth, namely $40,000, and face the same potential loss, namely $30,000, with the same probability, namely $\frac{1}{5}$. They have the same vNM preferences, represented by the vNM utility-of-money function $U(m) = \sqrt{m}$. They are unable to obtain insurance on the market and have decided to sign a mutual insurance contract, according to which any losses suffered by any of them will be shared equally by all three of them. Assume that the event that any of them suffers a loss is independent of the event(s) that the other(s) also suffer a loss.

(a) Calculate the probabilities of the following events:
   1. All three of them suffer a loss.
   2. Exactly two of them suffer a loss.
   3. Exactly one of them suffers a loss.
   4. None of them suffers a loss.

(b) Show that each of them is better off with the mutual insurance contract relative to no insurance.

Exercise 5.19 In this exercise we consider the benefit of mutual insurance when there is no independence, that is, when one person suffering a loss makes it more likely that the other person would also suffer a loss.

We consider two individuals, Albert an Ben, who have the same initial wealth, namely \$40,000, and face the same potential loss of \$30,000 due to wildfire, with the same probability, namely $\frac{1}{5}$. They have the same vNM preferences, represented by the vNM utility-of-money function $U(m) = \sqrt{m}$.

Since they live not far apart from each other if a fire occurs at one of the two properties then the probability that there will be a fire at the other property is greater than $\frac{1}{5}$. If the events were independent then the probabilities would be as follows:

fire at both	fire at one only	no fires
$\frac{1}{25}$	$\frac{8}{25}$	$\frac{16}{25}$

However, due to correlation, the probabilities are as follows:

fire at both	fire at one only	no fires
$\frac{3}{30}$	$\frac{7}{30}$	$\frac{20}{30}$

Suppose that Albert and Ben are unable to obtain insurance on the market. Are they better off with no insurance or with a mutual insurance agreement (according to which any losses suffered by either of them will be shared equally by both)?

5.6 Solutions to Exercises

Solution to Exercise 5.1

The slope of every indifference curve is $-\frac{\frac{1}{3}}{\frac{2}{3}} = -\frac{1}{2}$. Thus the equation of any indifference curve is of the form $y = a - \frac{1}{2}x$.

(a) To find the value of a for the indifference curve that goes through point $(6,10)$ solve the equation $10 = a - \frac{1}{2}6$ to get $a = 13$. Thus the equation of the indifference curve that goes through point $(6,10)$ is $y = 13 - \frac{1}{2}x$.

(b) To find the value of a for the indifference curve that goes through point $(10,8)$ solve the equation $8 = a - \frac{1}{2}10$ to get $a = 13$. Thus the equation of the indifference curve that goes through point $(10,8)$ is $y = 13 - \frac{1}{2}x$. Hence the two lotteries $(6,10)$ and $(10,8)$ lie on the same indifference curve; indeed, they have the same expected value, namely $\frac{26}{3}$.

(c) To find the value of a for the indifference curve that goes through point $(4,9)$ solve the equation $9 = a - \frac{1}{2}4$ to get $a = 11$. Thus the equation of the indifference curve that goes through point $(4,9)$ is $y = 11 - \frac{1}{2}x$. □

Solution to Exercise 5.2

(a) The expected utility of lottery $A = \begin{pmatrix} \$10 & \$40 \\ \frac{1}{3} & \frac{2}{3} \end{pmatrix}$ is $\frac{1}{3}\ln(10) + \frac{2}{3}\ln(40) = 3.227$.

(b) The expected utility of lottery $B = \begin{pmatrix} \$10 & \$10 \\ \frac{1}{3} & \frac{2}{3} \end{pmatrix}$ is $\frac{1}{3}\ln(10) + \frac{2}{3}\ln(10) = 3.303$.

(c) The indifference curve that goes through $A = (10, 40)$ is the set of lotteries that yield an expected utility of 3.227. It is a convex curve since the utility function U incorporates risk aversion. The slope of the indifference curve at point A is equal to

$$-\frac{p}{1-p}\left(\frac{U'(10)}{U'(40)}\right) = -\frac{\frac{1}{3}}{\frac{2}{3}}\left(\frac{\frac{1}{10}}{\frac{1}{40}}\right) = -2.$$

(d) Similarly, the indifference curve that goes through $B = (10, 10)$ is the set of lotteries that yield an expected utility of 2.303. It is a convex curve. The slope of the indifference curve at point B is equal to

$$-\frac{p}{1-p}\frac{U'(10)}{U'(10)} = -\frac{\frac{1}{3}}{\frac{2}{3}}\frac{\frac{1}{10}}{\frac{1}{10}} = -\frac{1}{2}.$$

(e) The two indifference curves are shown in Figure 5.18.   □

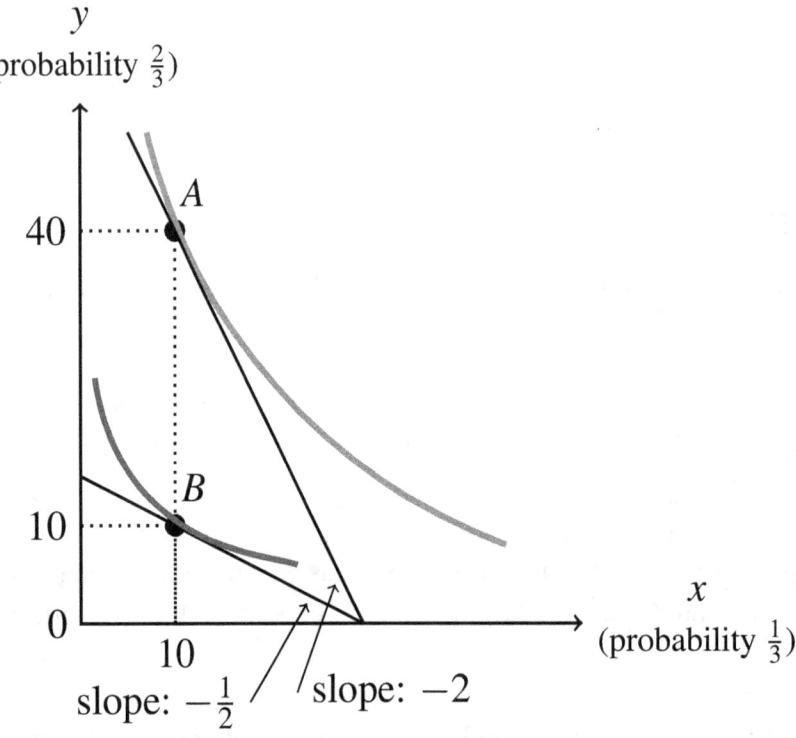

Figure 5.18: The graph for Part (e) of Exercise 5.2.

Solution to Exercise 5.3

Since the individual is risk neutral, we can take his/her utility-of-money function to be the identity function $U(m) = m$. Thus the expected utility of a lottery coincides with the expected value.

(a) The expected utility (= value) of lottery $A = \begin{pmatrix} \$10 & \$40 \\ \frac{1}{3} & \frac{2}{3} \end{pmatrix}$ is $\frac{1}{3}10 + \frac{2}{3}40 = 30$.

(b) The expected utility of lottery $B = \begin{pmatrix} \$10 & \$10 \\ \frac{1}{3} & \frac{2}{3} \end{pmatrix}$ is $\frac{1}{3}10 + \frac{2}{3}10 = 10$.

(c) The indifference curve that goes through $A = (10, 40)$ is the set of lotteries that yield an expected utility (= value) of 30. It is a straight line because of risk neutrality. The slope of the indifference curve at point A is equal to

$$-\frac{p}{1-p}\left(\frac{U'(10)}{U'(40)}\right) = -\frac{\frac{1}{3}}{\frac{2}{3}}\left(\frac{1}{1}\right) = -\frac{1}{2}.$$

(d) Similarly, the indifference curve that goes through $B = (10, 10)$ is the set of lotteries that yield an expected utility (= value) of 10. It is a straight line because of risk neutrality. The slope of the indifference curve at point B is equal to

$$-\frac{p}{1-p}\left(\frac{U'(10)}{U'(10)}\right) = -\frac{\frac{1}{3}}{\frac{2}{3}}1 = -\frac{1}{2}.$$

(e) The two indifference curves are shown in Figure 5.19.   □

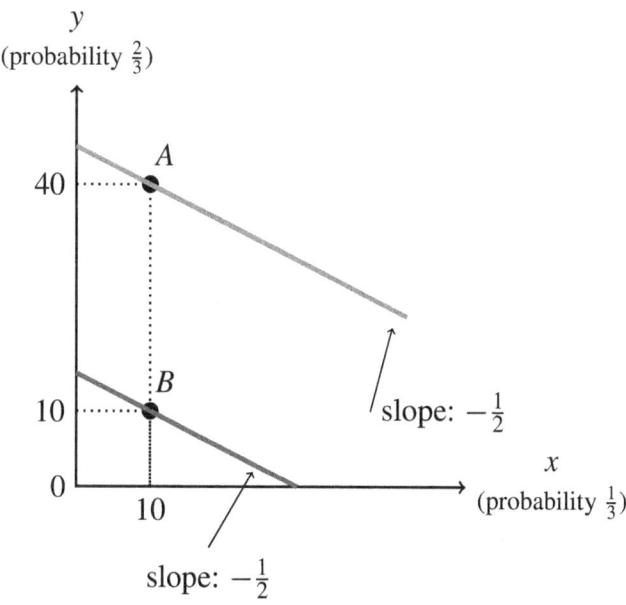

Figure 5.19: The graph for Part (e) of Exercise 5.3.

Solution to Exercise 5.4

(a) $\frac{2}{3}\ln(x) + \frac{1}{3}\ln(y) = \ln(4)$.

(b) First of all, rewrite the above equation as $2\ln(x) + \ln(y) = 3\ln(4)$, from which we get that $e^{(2\ln(x)+\ln(y))} = e^{3\ln(4)}$. Now, $e^{(2\ln(x)+\ln(y))} = e^{2\ln(x)}\,e^{\ln(y)} = \left(e^{\ln(x)}\right)^2 y = x^2 y$. Similarly, $e^{3\ln(4)} = 4^3 = 64$. Thus the equation becomes $x^2 y = 64$ from which we get $\boxed{y = \dfrac{64}{x^2}}$.

(c) $\frac{2}{3}\ln(x) + \frac{1}{3}\ln(y) = \frac{2}{3}\ln(9) + \frac{1}{3}\ln(4)$.

(d) Repeating the steps of Part (b): from $2\ln(x) + \ln(y) = 2\ln(9) + \ln(4)$ we get $e^{(2\ln(x)+\ln(y))} = e^{(2\ln(9)+\ln(4))}$, which becomes $x^2 y = 9^2 4$ which yields $\boxed{y = \dfrac{324}{x^2}}$.

(e) The slope of the indifference curve at point $A = (4,4)$ is equal to[11]

$$-\frac{p}{1-p}\left(\frac{U'(4)}{U'(4)}\right) = -\frac{\frac{2}{3}}{\frac{1}{3}}1 = -2.$$

(f) The slope of the indifference curve at point $B = (9,4)$ is equal to[12]

$$-\frac{p}{1-p}\left(\frac{U'(9)}{U'(4)}\right) = -\frac{\frac{2}{3}}{\frac{1}{3}}\left(\frac{\frac{1}{9}}{\frac{1}{4}}\right) = -\frac{8}{9}.$$

$\square$

---

[11] Alternatively, using the function $f(x) = \frac{64}{x^2}$ of Part (b), $f'(x) = -\frac{128}{x^3}$ so that $f'(4) = -\frac{128}{4^3} = -2$.

[12] Alternatively, using the function $g(x) = \frac{324}{x^2}$ of Part (d), $g'(x) = -\frac{648}{x^3}$ so that $g'(9) = -\frac{648}{9^3} = -\frac{8}{9}$.

Solution to Exercise 5.5

(a) $\mathbb{E}[U(A)] = \frac{1}{5}\sqrt{100} + \frac{4}{5}\sqrt{25} = 2+4 = 6$ and $\mathbb{E}[U(B)] = \frac{1}{5}\sqrt{4} + \frac{4}{5}\sqrt{49} = 6$. Thus A and B lie on the same indifference curve. On the other hand, $\mathbb{E}[U(C)] = \sqrt{40} = 6.3246$. Thus C lies on a higher indifference curve. See Figure 5.20.[13]

(b) The expected value of A, B and C is the same, namely 40. Thus the three points lie on the same indifference curve, which is a straight line with slope $-\frac{1}{4}$. □

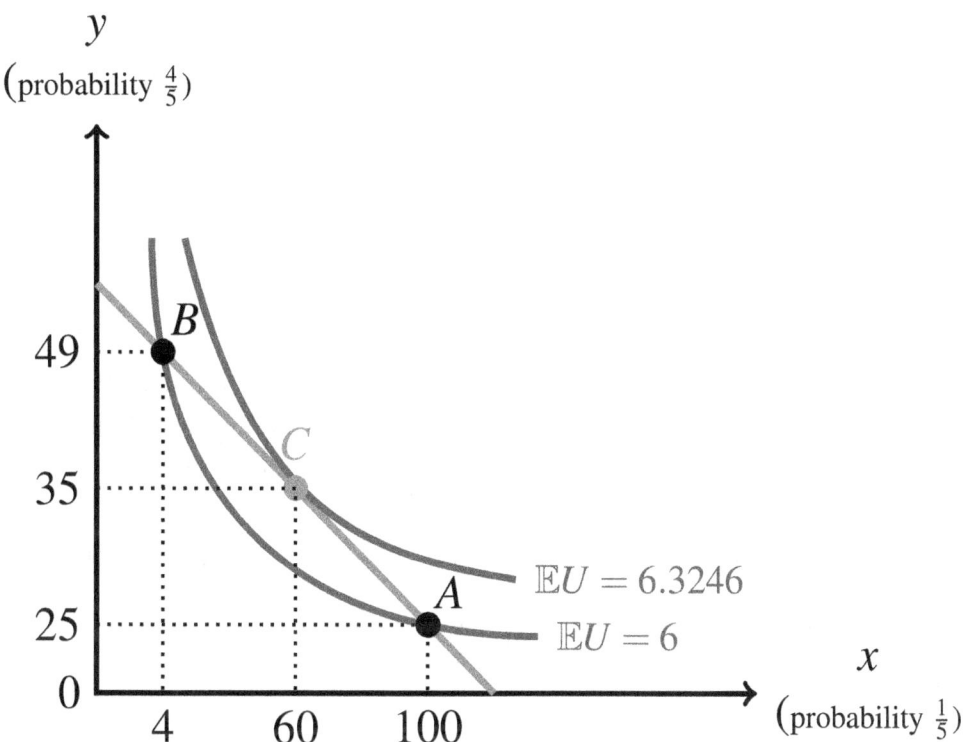

Figure 5.20: The graph for Exercise 5.5.

---

[13] Note that the scale of the axes has been distorted to make the qualitative properties of the graph easier to see.

Solution to Exercise 5.6

(a) $NI = (50000, 80000)$ and $\frac{d}{dm}\ln(m) = \frac{1}{m}$. Thus the slope of the reservation indifference curve at NI is

$$-\frac{\frac{1}{20}}{\frac{19}{20}}\left(\frac{\frac{1}{50,000}}{\frac{1}{80,000}}\right) = -\frac{8}{95} = -0.0842.$$

(b) The slope of *every* isoprofit line is $-\frac{\frac{1}{20}}{\frac{19}{20}} = -\frac{1}{19} = 0.0526$.

(c) The maximum premium that Adam is willing to pay for full insurance is given by the solution to the equation

$$\ln(80,000 - h) = \frac{1}{20}\ln(50,000) + \frac{19}{20}\ln(80,000)$$

which is $h_{max} = \$1,858.10$

(d) The fair premium is equal to $\frac{1}{20}(30,000) = 1,500$. If Adam does not insure, his expected utility is $\frac{1}{20}\ln(50,000) + \frac{19}{20}\ln(80,000) = 11.2663$. If Adam obtains full insurance at premium $\$1,500$, his utility is $\ln(80,000 - 1,500) = 11.2709$. Thus the increase in utility is $11.2709 - 11.2663 = 0.0046$.

(e) The slope of *any* indifference curve at *any* point on the 45° line is equal to the slope of any isoprofit line, namely $-\frac{\frac{1}{20}}{\frac{19}{20}} = -\frac{1}{19} = 0.0526$.   □

Solution to Exercise 5.7

(a) If Frank does not buy insurance he faces the lottery $\begin{pmatrix} W_0 & W_0 - \ell \\ \frac{9}{10} & \frac{1}{10} \end{pmatrix}$ whose expected value is $W_0 - \frac{1}{10}\ell$. If h_{max} is the maximum premium that he is willing to pay for full insurance [that is, h_{max} is the solution to the equation $U(W_0 - h) = \frac{9}{10}U(W_0) + \frac{1}{10}U(W_0 - \ell)$] and R_{NI} is the risk premium associated with the no-insurance lottery [that is, R_{NI} is the solution to the equation $U(W_0 - \frac{1}{10}\ell - R) = \frac{9}{10}U(W_0) + \frac{1}{10}U(W_0 - \ell)$], then $h_{max} = \frac{1}{10}\ell + R_{NI}$. Thus we have the following equation

$$800 = \frac{1}{10}\ell + 500,$$

whose solution is $\ell = 3,000$.

(b) The monopolist would sell Frank the full-insurance contract with premium $\$800$ and thus make an expected profit equal to $800 - \frac{1}{10}3,000 = \$500$.   □

Solution to Exercise 5.8

(a) Bob's expected loss is $\frac{5}{100}110,000 = \$5,500$.

(b) Bob's expected wealth if he does not insure is $195,000 - 5,500 = \$189,500$.

(c) Bob's expected utility if he does not insure is

$$\frac{5}{100}\left[800 - (20 - 8.5)^2\right] + \frac{95}{100}\left[800 - (20 - 19.5)^2\right] = 793.15.$$

(d) The insurance contract with premium $\$1,200$ and deductible $\$20,000$ corresponds to the following point in the wealth diagram: $(173{,}800,\ 193{,}800)$. The corresponding expected utility is

$$\frac{5}{100}\left[800 - (20 - 17.38)^2\right] + \frac{95}{100}\left[800 - (20 - 19.38)^2\right] = 799.29.$$

(e) $U'(m) = 40 - 2m$. Thus the slope of Bob's reservation indifference curve at the no-insurance point is

$$-\frac{\frac{5}{100}}{\frac{95}{100}}\left(\frac{40 - 2(8.5)}{40 - 2(19.5)}\right) = -1.2105.$$

(f) From Part (d) we have that $A = (173{,}800,\ 193{,}800)$. The slope, at point A, of Bob's indifference curve that goes through point A is

$$-\frac{5}{95}\left(\frac{40 - 2(17.38)}{40 - 2(19.38)}\right) = -0.2224.$$

(g) Since $\mathbb{E}[U(A)] = 799.29 > 793.15 = \mathbb{E}[U(NI)]$, the indifference curve that goes through point A lies above reservation indifference curve.

(h) The maximum premium that Bob would be willing to pay for full insurance is given by the solution to the equation $U(W_0 - h) = \mathbb{E}[U(NI)]$, that is, $800 - [20 - (19.5 - h)]^2 = 793.15$, which is 2.1173, that is, $\$21,173$ (slightly less than four times the expected loss).   □

Solution to Exercise 5.9

(a) $U'(m) = \beta e^{-m} > 0$ and $U''(m) = -\beta e^{-m} < 0$, thus Beth is risk averse.

(b) $A(m) = -\frac{U''(m)}{U'(m)} = 1$, a constant.

(c) The maximum premium h_{max} is determined by the solution to

$$U(W_0 - h) = pU(W_0 - \ell) + (1-p)U(W_0), \quad \text{that is,}$$

$$
\begin{aligned}
\alpha - \beta e^{(-W_0 + h)} &= p\left(\alpha - \beta e^{(-W_0 + \ell)}\right) + (1-p)\left(\alpha - \beta e^{-W_0}\right) \\
&= p\alpha + (1-p)\alpha - \beta\left[pe^{(-W_0 + \ell)} + (1-p)e^{-W_0}\right] \\
&= \alpha - \beta\left[pe^{-W_0}e^{\ell} + (1-p)e^{-W_0}\right] \\
&= \alpha - \beta e^{-W_0}\left[pe^{\ell} + 1 - p\right].
\end{aligned}
$$

Subtracting α from both sides and multiplying by $-\frac{1}{\beta}$ we get

$$e^{-W_0}e^{h} = e^{-W_0}\left[pe^{\ell} + 1 - p\right],$$

and multiplying both sides by e^{W_0}, we are left with

$$e^{h} = pe^{\ell} + 1 - p.$$

Thus $h_{max} = \ln(pe^{\ell} + 1 - p)$, independent of W_0. $\qquad\square$

Solution to Exercise 5.10

(a) Barbara's expected utility if she does not insure is: $0.9\sqrt{80,000} + 0.1\sqrt{60,000} = 279.053$.

(b) Barbara's expected utility from a contract with premium h and deductible d is $0.1\sqrt{80,000 - h - d} + 0.9\sqrt{80,000 - h}$. Thus,

	premium	deductible	expected utility
Contract 1:	2,340	500	$0.1\sqrt{77,160} + 0.9\sqrt{77,660} = 278.5856$
Contract 2:	2,280	1,000	$0.1\sqrt{76,720} + 0.9\sqrt{77,720} = 278.6031$
Contract 3:	2,220	1,500	$0.1\sqrt{76,280} + 0.9\sqrt{77,780} = 278.6204$
Contract 4:	2,160	2,000	$0.1\sqrt{75,840} + 0.9\sqrt{77,840} = 278.6375$.

None of the contracts gives her higher expected utility than no insurance. Hence she will not buy insurance. $\qquad\square$

Solution to Exercise 5.11

(a) Letting $h = 10,000 - W_2$ and $d = W_2 - W_1$ we get $10,000 - W_2 = 800 - 0.2(W_2 - W_1)$, that is

$$W_2 = 11,500 - \frac{1}{4}W_1.$$

(b) From Part (a) we have that the slope of the insurance budget line is $-\frac{1}{4}$. The slope of the reservation indifference curve at $NI = (6000, 10000)$ is

$$-\frac{\frac{1}{6}}{\frac{5}{6}}\left(\frac{\frac{1}{6,000}}{\frac{1}{10,000}}\right) = -\frac{1}{3}.$$

Thus the reservation indifference curve is steeper, at NI, than the insurance budget line and, therefore, there are contracts that are better than no insurance.

(c) Since the slope of any indifference curve at any point on the 45° line is equal to $-\frac{\frac{1}{6}}{\frac{5}{6}} = -\frac{1}{5}$, the indifference curve that goes through the point at the intersection of the insurance budget line and the 45° line is less steep than the insurance budget line and thus we are in Case 3 of Section 5.3.2 and the optimal contract is given by the solution to the following two equations:

$$W_2 = 11,500 - \frac{1}{4}W_1 \quad \text{and} \quad -\frac{\frac{1}{6}}{\frac{5}{6}}\left(\frac{\frac{1}{W_1}}{\frac{1}{W_2}}\right) = -\frac{1}{4}$$

which is $W_1 = 7,666.67$ and $W_2 = 9,583.33$. Thus the chosen deductible is

$$d = 9,583.33 - 7,666.67 = \$1,916.66$$

and the corresponding premium is

$$h = 10,000 - 9,583.33 = \$416.67.$$

(d) Expected utility from no insurance is $\frac{1}{6}\ln(6,000) + \frac{5}{6}\ln(10,000) = 9.1252$, while expected utility from the contract of Part (c) is $\frac{1}{6}\ln(7,666.67) + \frac{5}{6}\ln(9,583.33) = 9.1306$.

(e) Expected profits from the contract of Part (c) is $416.67 - \frac{1}{6}(4,000 - 1,916.66) = \$69.45$.

(f) Expected utility from contract (h,d) is: $\frac{1}{6}\ln(10,000 - h - d) + \frac{5}{6}\ln(10,000 - h)$. Replacing h with $800 - 0.2d$ we get the following function:

$$f(d) = \frac{1}{6}\ln(10,000 - 800 + 0.2d - d) + \frac{5}{6}\ln(10,000 - 800 + 0.2d)$$

$$= \frac{1}{6}\ln(9,200 - 0.8d) + \frac{5}{6}\ln(9,200 + 0.2d).$$

To maximize this function we must solve the equation $f'(d) = 0$, that is

$$\frac{1}{6}\left(\frac{1}{9,200 - 0.8d}\right)(-0.8) + \frac{5}{6}\left(\frac{1}{9,200 + 0.2d}\right)0.2 = 0$$

The solution is $d = \frac{5,750}{3} = 1,916.66$ with corresponding premium $h = 800 - 0.2(1,916.67) = 416.67$, confirming the conclusion of Part (c). $\square$

Solution to Exercise 5.12

(a) Letting $h = 576 - W_2$ and $d = W_2 - W_1$ we get $576 - W_2 = \frac{1}{9}(176 - W_2 + W_1)$, that is

$$W_2 = 626 - \frac{1}{8}W_1.$$

(b) From Part (a) we have that the slope of the insurance budget line is $-\frac{1}{8}$. The slope of the reservation indifference curve at $NI = (400, 576)$ is

$$-\frac{\frac{1}{16}}{\frac{15}{16}}\left(\frac{\frac{1}{2\sqrt{400}}}{\frac{1}{2\sqrt{576}}}\right) = -\frac{2}{25}.$$

Thus the reservation indifference curve is less steep, at NI, than the insurance budget line and, therefore, the insurance budget line lies below the reservation indifference curve, that is, there are no contracts that are better than no insurance. Thus we are in Case 1 of Section 5.3.2 and your best decision is not to insure.   □

Solution to Exercise 5.13

(a) The answer is, of course, the same as in Exercise 5.12: $W_2 = 626 - \frac{1}{8}W_1$.

(b) The slope of the insurance budget line is $-\frac{1}{8}$. The slope of the reservation indifference curve at $NI = (400, 576)$ is

$$-\frac{\frac{1}{7}}{\frac{6}{7}}\left(\frac{\frac{1}{2\sqrt{400}}}{\frac{1}{2\sqrt{576}}}\right) = -\frac{1}{5}.$$

Thus the reservation indifference curve is steeper, at NI, than the insurance budget line and, therefore, there are contracts that are better than no insurance.

(c) Since the slope of any indifference curve at any point on the 45° line is equal to $-\frac{\frac{1}{7}}{\frac{6}{7}} = -\frac{1}{6}$, the indifference curve that goes through the point at the intersection of the insurance budget line and the 45° line is steeper than the insurance budget line and thus we are in Case 2 of Section 5.3.2 and the optimal contract is given by the full-insurance contract (the point of intersection between the insurance budget line and the 45° line), that is, by the solution to the following two equations:

$$W_2 = 626 - \frac{1}{8}W_1 \quad \text{and} \quad W_2 = W_1$$

which is $W_1 = W_2 = \frac{5{,}008}{9} = 556.44$. Thus the chosen deductible is zero and the premium is $h = 576 - 556.44 = \$19.56$.

(d) Expected utility from no insurance is $\frac{1}{7}\sqrt{400} + \frac{6}{7}\sqrt{576} = 23.4286$, while expected utility from the contract of Part (c) is $\sqrt{556.44} = 23.589$.

(e) Expected profits from the contract of Part (c) is $19.56 - \frac{1}{7}400 = -\$37.58$, thus a loss.

(f) Expected utility from contract (h,d) is: $\frac{1}{7}\sqrt{576-h-d}+\frac{6}{7}\sqrt{576-h}$. Replacing h with $\frac{1}{9}(176-d)$ we get the following function:

$$f(d) = \frac{1}{7}\sqrt{576 - \frac{176}{9} + \frac{1}{9}d - d} + \frac{6}{7}\sqrt{576 - \frac{176}{9} + \frac{1}{9}d}$$

$$= \frac{1}{7}\sqrt{556.44 - \frac{8}{9}d} + \frac{6}{7}\sqrt{556.44 + \frac{1}{9}d}.$$

We know from Part (c) that the maximum of the function $f(d)$ is achieved at a corner (that is, not in the interior of the interval $[0,400]$) and thus it cannot be found by solving the equation $f'(d) = 0$ (indeed, the solution to this equation is -398.36 which is outside the interval $[0,400]$). Another way to see that the solution is at a corner, is to calculate the value $f'(d)$ at $d = 0$: $f'(0) = -0.0007 < 0$, indicating that increasing the deductible from 0 reduces expected utility. $\quad\square$

Solution to Exercise 5.14

(a) The utility function is $U(m) = 1 - \frac{1}{m+1}$. Thus $U'(m) = \frac{1}{(m+1)^2}$ and $U''(m) = -\frac{2}{(m+1)^3}$. Since $U''(m) < 0$ (given that $m \geq 0$), David is risk averse.

(b) The Arrow-Pratt measure of risk aversion is $A_U(m) = -\frac{U''(m)}{U'(m)} = \frac{2}{m+1}$.

(c) Since coverage = loss − deductible, the equation is $h = \gamma(\ell - d) = \gamma(3000 - d)$.

(d) Replacing h with $W_0 - W_2 = 8,000 - W_2$ and $d = (W_2 - W_1)$ in the equation of Part (c) we get

$$W_2 = \frac{8,000 - 3,000\gamma}{1-\gamma} - \frac{\gamma}{1-\gamma}W_1.$$

(e) Yes: replacing W_1 with $5,000$ ($= W_0 - \ell = 8,000 - 3,000$, the horizontal coordinate of NI) in the above equation we get $W_2 = 8,000$ (the vertical coordinate of NI).

(f) David will choose not to insure when the insurance budget line is steeper than the reservation indifference curve at the NI point, that is, when (recall that money is measure in thousands of dollars)

$$\frac{\gamma}{1-\gamma} > \frac{p}{1-p}\left(\frac{U'(5)}{U'(8)}\right) = \frac{1}{9}\left(\frac{(8+1)^2}{(5+1)^2}\right) = \frac{9}{25}.$$

Solving $\frac{\gamma}{1-\gamma} > \frac{9}{25}$ we get $\gamma > \frac{9}{34}$.

(g) David will choose full insurance when the slope of the indifference curve at the offered full-insurance contract (which is $-\frac{p}{1-p} = -\frac{1}{9}$) is, in absolute value, greater than or equal to the slope of the budget line (which is $-\frac{\gamma}{1-\gamma}$). Solving $\frac{1}{9} \geq \frac{\gamma}{1-\gamma}$ we get $\gamma \leq \frac{1}{10}$.

(h) David will choose partial insurance when

1. he prefers insurance to no insurance (that is, as seen in Part (f), when $\gamma < \frac{9}{34}$) and
2. the slope of the indifference curve at the offered full-insurance contract is, in absolute value, less than the slope of the budget line (that is, as seen in Part (g), when $\gamma > \frac{1}{10}$).

Thus David will choose partial insurance when

$$\frac{1}{10} < \gamma < \frac{9}{34}.$$

Assume that $\frac{1}{10} < \gamma < \frac{9}{34}$. Then David will choose that contract $C = \left(W_1^C, W_2^C\right)$ at which there is a tangency between the budget line and the indifference curve through C, that is, C must satisfy the following equations (recall that wealth levels are expressed in dollars while the argument of the utility function is expressed in thousands of dollars):

$$W_2 = \frac{8,000 - 3,000\gamma}{1-\gamma} - \frac{\gamma}{1-\gamma}W_1 \quad \text{and} \quad \frac{1}{9}\left[\frac{\left(\frac{W_2^C}{1,000}+1\right)^2}{\left(\frac{W_1^C}{1,000}+1\right)^2}\right] = \frac{\gamma}{1-\gamma}.$$

□

Solution to Exercise 5.15

(a) Replacing h with $W_0 - W_2 = 3,600 - W_2$ and d with $(W_2 - W_1)$ in the equation $h = 810 - \frac{3}{10}d$ we get

$$W_2 = \frac{27,900}{7} - \frac{3}{7}W_1.$$

(b) No, because the slope of an isoprofit line is $-\frac{p}{1-p} = -\frac{\frac{1}{4}}{\frac{3}{4}} = -\frac{1}{3} \neq -\frac{3}{7}$.

(c) Yes: replacing W_1 in the equation of Part (a) with 900 ($= W_0 - \ell = 3,600 - 2,700$, the horizontal coordinate of NI) we get $W_2 = 3,600$ ($= W_0$, the vertical coordinate of NI).

(d) Yes, because the absolute value of the slope of the reservation indifference curve at NI, namely $\frac{1}{3}\frac{3,600}{900} = \frac{4}{3}$ (recall that $U(m) = \ln(m)$ and $U'(m) = \frac{1}{m}$) is greater than the absolute value of the slope of the insurance budget line, namely $\frac{3}{7}$.

(e) Since the slope of the indifference curve at the full-insurance contract is $-\frac{1}{3}$, which is less – in absolute value – than the slope of the budget line (in absolute value), the best contract is a partial-insurance contract. It is found by solving the following equations:

$$W_2 = \frac{27,900}{7} - \frac{3}{7}W_1 \quad \text{and} \quad \frac{1}{3}\left(\frac{W_2}{W_1}\right) = \frac{3}{7}.$$

The solution is: $W_1 = 2,325$ and $W_2 = \frac{20,925}{7} = 2,989.29$. Thus the premium is $h = 3,600 - 2,989.29 = 610.71$ and the deductible is $d = 2,989.29 - 2,325 = 664.29$.

(f) Let F be the full-insurance contract (obtained by solving the equation $W_1 = \frac{27,900}{7} - \frac{3}{7}W_1$) and B the contract of Part (e). Then

$$NI = (900, 3600), \qquad F = (2790, 2790) \qquad \text{and} \qquad B = (2325, 2989.29)$$

Thus

- $\mathbb{E}[U(NI)] = \frac{1}{4}\ln(900) + \frac{3}{4}\ln(3,600) = 7.8421.$
- $\mathbb{E}[U(F)] = \ln(2,790) = 7.9338.$
- $\mathbb{E}[U(B)] = \frac{1}{4}\ln(2,325) + \frac{3}{4}\ln(2989.29) = 7.94.$

(g) Expected utility from contract (h,d) is: $\frac{1}{4}\ln(3,600 - h - d) + \frac{3}{4}\ln(3,600 - h)$. Replacing h with $810 - \frac{3}{10}d$ we get the following function:

$$f(d) = \frac{1}{4}\ln(3,600 - 810 + 0.3d - d) + \frac{3}{4}\ln(3,600 - 810 + 0.3d)$$
$$= \frac{1}{4}\ln(2,790 - 0.7d) + \frac{3}{4}\ln(2,790 + 0.3d).$$

To maximize this function we must solve the equation $f'(d) = 0$, that is

$$\frac{0.225}{2,790 + 0.3d} - \frac{0.175}{2,790 - 0.7d} = 0$$

The solution is $d = 664.29$ with corresponding premium $h = 610.71$, confirming the conclusion of Part (e). $\qquad\qquad\square$

Solution to Exercise 5.16

Contract A is the following point in the (W_1, W_2) space: $W_2^A = 1,600 - 44 = 1,556$, $W_1^A = 1,556 - 360 = 1,196$, that is, $A = (1196, 1556)$.

(a) Replacing h with $(1,600 - W_2)$ and d with $(W_2 - W_1)$ in the equation $h = 152 - \frac{3}{10}d$ we get

$$W_2 = \frac{14,480}{7} - \frac{3}{7}W_1.$$

(b) $\mathbb{E}[U(NI)] = \frac{1}{5}\sqrt{1,024} + \frac{4}{5}\sqrt{1600} = 38.4$ and $\mathbb{E}[U(A)] = \frac{1}{5}\sqrt{1,196} + \frac{4}{5}\sqrt{1,556} = 38.4736$. Thus point A lies above the reservation indifference curve.

(c) The slope of the indifference curve that goes through point A is, at point A, equal to

$$-\frac{p}{1-p}\left(\frac{U'(1,196)}{U'(1,556)}\right) = \frac{1}{4}\left(\frac{\sqrt{1,556}}{\sqrt{1,196}}\right) = -0.2852.$$

Since $0.2852 < \frac{3}{7} = 0.4286$, the indifference curve is less steep, at point A, than the insurance budget line; thus the insurance budget line lies below the indifference curve that goes through point A and, therefore, the best contract on the budget line is contract A. $\qquad\qquad\square$

Solution to Exercise 5.17

For both Carla and Don, no insurance corresponds to the lottery

$$NI = \begin{pmatrix} \$14,400 & \$32,400 \\ \frac{1}{5} & \frac{4}{5} \end{pmatrix}$$

whose expected utility is:

for Carla: $\frac{1}{5}\sqrt{14,400} + \frac{4}{5}\sqrt{32,400} = 168$

for Don: $\frac{1}{5}\left(1 - \frac{1}{1.44+1}\right) + \frac{4}{5}\left(1 - \frac{1}{3.24+1}\right) = 0.7294.$

Mutual insurance corresponds to the lottery

$$MI = \begin{pmatrix} \$14,400 & \$23,400 & \$32,400 \\ \frac{1}{25} & \frac{8}{25} & \frac{16}{25} \end{pmatrix}$$

whose expected utility is:

for Carla: $\frac{1}{25}\sqrt{14,400} + \frac{8}{25}\sqrt{23,400} + \frac{16}{25}\sqrt{32,400} = 168.9506$

for Don: $\frac{1}{25}\left(1 - \frac{1}{1.44+1}\right) + \frac{8}{25}\left(1 - \frac{1}{2.34+1}\right) + \frac{16}{25}\left(1 - \frac{1}{3.24+1}\right) = 0.7369.$

Thus they are both better off with mutual insurance than with no insurance. $\qquad\square$

Solution to Exercise 5.18

(a) The probabilities are as follows:

3 losses	2 losses	1 loss	no losses
$\left(\frac{1}{5}\right)^3 = \frac{1}{125}$	$3\left(\frac{1}{5}\right)^2\frac{4}{5} = \frac{12}{125}$	$3\frac{1}{25}\left(\frac{4}{5}\right)^2 = \frac{48}{125}$	$\left(\frac{4}{5}\right)^3 = \frac{64}{125}$

(b) Expected utility from no insurance is

$$\mathbb{E}[U(NI)] = \frac{1}{5}\sqrt{10,000} + \frac{4}{5}\sqrt{40,000} = 180$$

while expected utility from mutual insurance is

$$\mathbb{E}[U(MI)] = \frac{1}{125}\sqrt{10,000} + \frac{12}{125}\sqrt{40,000 - \frac{1}{3}60,000}$$

$$+ \frac{48}{125}\sqrt{40,000 - \frac{1}{3}30,000} + \frac{64}{125}\sqrt{40,000}$$

$$= 183.29.$$

Thus mutual insurance is better than no insurance for each of them.

$\qquad\square$

Solution to Exercise 5.19

Expected utility from no insurance is

$$\mathbb{E}[U(NI)] = \frac{1}{5}\sqrt{10,000} + \frac{4}{5}\sqrt{40,000} = 180.$$

Expected utility form a mutual insurance (*MI*) agreement is

$$\mathbb{E}[U(MI)] = \frac{3}{30}\sqrt{10,000} + \frac{7}{30}\sqrt{40,000 - \frac{1}{2}30,000} + \frac{20}{30}\sqrt{40,000} = 180.23.$$

Thus mutual insurance would still be preferred by both to no insurance. □

6. Insurance and moral hazard

6.1 Moral hazard or hidden action

So far we have assumed that the probability of loss p is constant and the individual's decision is merely whether or not to insure and which contract to choose from a given menu. When we say that "the probability of loss is constant" we mean that it cannot be affected by the individual's behavior.

In some cases this is a reasonable assumption: for example, there is nothing that a shopkeeper can do to make it less likely that there will be a riot, or an earthquake, or a meteorite strike.

In other cases, however, there is a causal link between the behavior of the insured person and the probability that she will suffer a loss: for example, the probability that her bicycle will be stolen is higher if she leaves it unattended and unlocked, and lower if she locks it to a permanent fixture with a sturdy cable and padlock.

In cases where the probability of loss can be affected by the individual's actions we say that the insurance company faces a situation of *moral hazard* or *hidden action*. Below are a few more examples of possible actions that the individual can take to reduce the probability of loss:

- Install a home security alarm, to make a robbery less likely.

- Always lock the door(s) to one's house, to make a robbery less likely.

- Clear the brush around the house, to make it less likely that a brush fire will reach the building.

- Drive carefully and below the speed limit, to make it less likely that one will be involved in a car accident.

- Exercise regularly and eat healthy food to reduce the probability of vascular or cardiac disease.

As the above examples illustrate, what an individual can do to reduce the probability of loss can be either

- taking an action involving extra effort, or
- incurring an extra expense.

We shall refer to both of the above as *making extra effort*. The crucial element of both is that they involve "disutility", that is, they make the individual worse off, *ceteris paribus*. Because of this, the insurance company realizes that the individual will prefer to avoid the extra effort if she is protected from the consequences of not exerting it. For example, if the individual has full insurance, then she has no incentive to incur extra expenses or exert extra effort in order to reduce the probability of suffering a loss: if the loss occurs, she will be fully reimbursed by the insurance company. On the other hand, the insurance company cares very much about the behavior of its customers, because the more careless they are, the more likely it is that the insurance company will have to cover their losses. In order to incentivize the customer to exert extra effort, the insurance company might want to make it more costly for the insured to suffer a loss, by requiring a substantial deductible.

If the customer's behavior can be observed by the insurance company and verified by a court of law, then the insurance company can specify it in the contract and make any payments conditional on the customer's actions. For example, the insurance company could require the customer to install a security system in her house and make any reimbursements due to theft conditional on proof that the security system was in fact installed. However, in most cases it is impossible, or prohibitively expensive, for the insurer to monitor the behavior of its customers. For example, no insurance company will find it worthwhile to have an insurance agent follow the customer around to make sure that she always locks her bicycle, when left unattended!

We will assume that the customer's behavior cannot be observed by the insurance company; however, the insurance company can try to figure out what the potential customer would do under different insurance contract.

6.2 Two levels of unobserved effort

We will limit ourselves to the binary case, where the individual has only two choices in terms of effort: either *exert effort*, denoted by E, or exert *no effort*, denoted by N. The individual's choice affects the probability of loss: it will be lower in she exerts effort, that is, letting p_E be the probability of loss in the case of effort and p_N the probability of loss in the case of no effort,

$$0 < p_E < p_N < 1. \tag{6.1}$$

As in previous chapters, we denote the individual's initial wealth by W_0 and the potential loss by ℓ (with $0 < \ell \leq W_0$). We continue to assume that the individual has vNM preferences; however, the outcomes of the lotteries now include not only wealth levels but also the "inconvenience" or "cost" of exerting effort. Thus we can think of the individual as having two utility-of-money functions: one if she exerts effort, denoted by $U_E(m)$ and the other if she exerts no effort, denoted by $U_N(m)$.[1]

---

[1] Equivalently, the vNM utility function has two arguments: money and level of effort.

The fact that effort is costly (either in a psychological or in a monetary sense) is captured by the following assumption:

$$U_N(m) > U_E(m), \quad \text{for every } m \geq 0.$$

To simplify the analysis we will consider the following special case: let $U(m)$ be a strictly increasing and concave function then

$$U_N(m) = U(m) \tag{6.2}$$

$$U_E(m) = U(m) - c, \quad \text{with } c > 0. \tag{6.3}$$

Note that, since $p_E < p_N$,[2]

$$\frac{p_E}{1 - p_E} < \frac{p_N}{1 - p_N}. \tag{6.4}$$

It follows from (6.2) and (6.3) that, for any point (W_1, W_2) in the wealth space,

- with No-effort, the slope of the indifference curve at point (W_1, W_2) is

$$-\frac{p_N}{1 - p_N} \left(\frac{U'(W_1)}{U'(W_2)} \right) \tag{6.5}$$

- with Effort, the slope of the indifference curve at point (W_1, W_2) is

$$-\frac{p_E}{1 - p_E} \left(\frac{U'(W_1)}{U'(W_2)} \right). \tag{6.6}$$

Thus, for any point $A = (W_1^A, W_2^A)$ in the wealth space, we deduce from (6.4), (6.5) and (6.6) that

the indifference curve (through point A) corresponding to **Effort**

is, at point A, **less steep than**,

the indifference curve (through point A) corresponding to **No-effort**.

---

[2] This can be seen as follows:

(1) $\frac{p_E}{1-p_E} < \frac{p_N}{1-p_E}$ because the denominator is the same and $p_E < p_N$, and

(2) $\frac{p_N}{1-p_E} < \frac{p_N}{1-p_N}$ because the numerator is the same and $(1 - p_E) > (1 - p_N)$ (since $p_E < p_N$).

Figure 6.1 shows two sets of indifference curves: one corresponding to Effort (the less steep ones) and one corresponding to No-effort (the steeper ones).

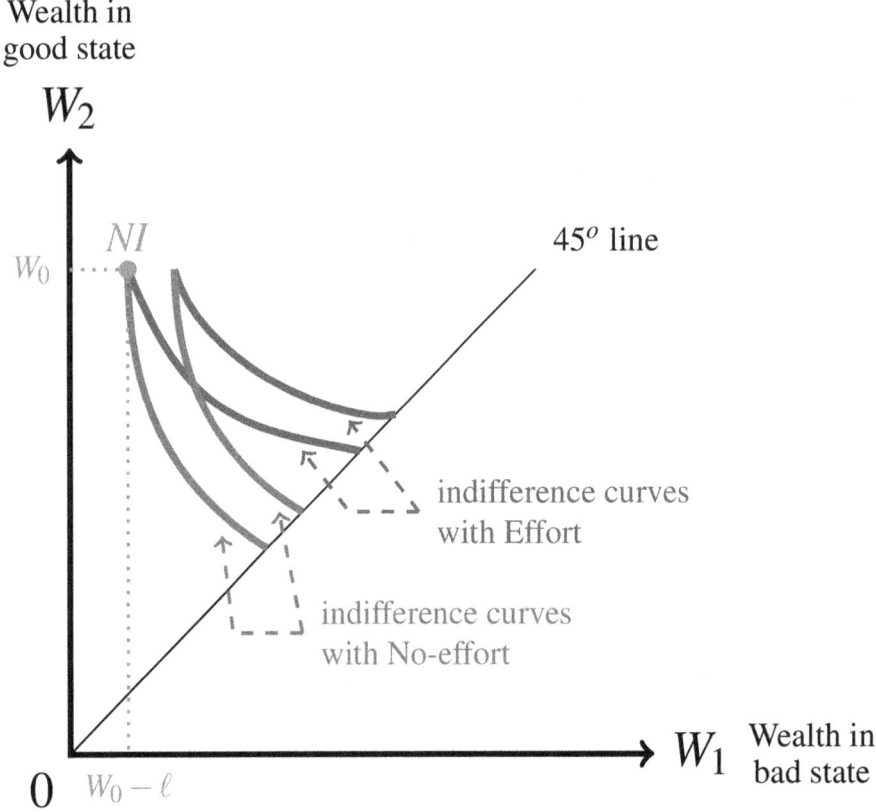

Figure 6.1: Indifference curves corresponding to Effort are less steep than those corresponding to No-effort.

When offered an insurance contract, the individual will have four possible choices:

1. remain uninsured and choose Effort,

2. remain uninsured and choose No-effort,

3. purchase the insurance contract and choose Effort,

4. purchase the insurance contract and choose No-effort,

and she will choose the option that yields the highest expected utility.

In general, the individual's decision problem can be framed as follows:

○ first determine the best effort level if uninsured,

○ then, for each offered insurance contract, determine the best effort level if that contract is purchased,

○ compare the expected utility from the best choice of effort under each option and choose that option that yields the largest expected utility.

For example, consider an individual who has an initial wealth of $50,000 and faces a potential loss of $30,000 with the following probability:

$$\text{probability of loss} = \begin{cases} p_E = \frac{1}{10} & \text{if she chooses Effort} \\ p_N = \frac{1}{5} & \text{if she chooses No-effort} \end{cases}$$

Her vNM preferences are represented the following vNM utility-of-money function (for $m > 0$):[3]

$$U(m) = \begin{cases} 10 - \left(\frac{m}{10,000}\right)^{-1} & \text{if she chooses Effort} \\ 10.01 - \left(\frac{m}{10,000}\right)^{-1} & \text{if she chooses No-effort} \end{cases}$$

Suppose that she is offered the following menu of insurance contracts:

	premium	deductible
Contract 1:	$1,000	$5,000
Contract 2:	$500	$8,000
Contract 3:	$100	$12,000

Will she insure and, if so, which contract will she choose?

Step 1. Determine the best effort level in case of no insurance $NI = (20000, 50000)$:

Effort: $\mathbb{E}[U_E(NI)] = \frac{1}{10}\left(10 - 2^{-1}\right) + \frac{9}{10}\left(10 - 5^{-1}\right) = \boxed{9.77}$.

No-effort: $\mathbb{E}[U_N(NI)] = \frac{1}{5}\left(10.01 - 2^{-1}\right) + \frac{4}{5}\left(10.01 - 5^{-1}\right) = 9.75$.

Thus, if uninsured, the individual will choose Effort.

Step 2. Determine the best effort level for Contract 1, namely $C_1 = (44000, 49000)$:

Effort: $\mathbb{E}[U_E(C_1)] = \frac{1}{10}\left[10 - (4.4)^{-1}\right] + \frac{9}{10}\left[10 - (4.9)^{-1}\right] = 9.7936$.

No-effort: $\mathbb{E}[U_N(C_1)] = \frac{1}{5}\left[10.01 - (4.4)^{-1}\right] + \frac{4}{5}\left[10.01 - (4.9)^{-1}\right] = \boxed{9.8013}$.

Thus, under Contract 1, the individual will choose No-effort.

Step 3. Determine the best effort level for Contract 2, namely $C_2 = (41500, 49500)$:

Effort: $\mathbb{E}[U_E(C_2)] = \frac{1}{10}\left[10 - (4.15)^{-1}\right] + \frac{9}{10}\left[10 - (4.95)^{-1}\right] = 9.7941$.

No-effort: $\mathbb{E}[U_N(C_2)] = \frac{1}{5}\left[10.01 - (4.15)^{-1}\right] + \frac{4}{5}\left[10.01 - (4.95)^{-1}\right] = \boxed{9.8002}$.

Thus, under Contract 2, the individual will choose No-effort.

Step 4. Determine the best effort level for Contract 3, namely $C_3 = (37900, 49900)$:

Effort: $\mathbb{E}[U_E(C_3)] = \frac{1}{10}\left[10 - (3.79)^{-1}\right] + \frac{9}{10}\left[10 - (4.99)^{-1}\right] = 9.7933$.

No-effort: $\mathbb{E}[U_N(C_3)] = \frac{1}{5}\left[10.01 - (3.79)^{-1}\right] + \frac{4}{5}\left[10.01 - (4.99)^{-1}\right] = \boxed{9.7969}$.

Thus, under Contract 3, the individual will choose No-effort.

---

[3] This is an instance of (6.2) and (6.3) with $c = 0.01$.

Of all these options, the one that gives the highest expected utility is Contract 2 with No-effort. Thus the individual would purchase Contract 2 and choose No-effort. The insurer's expected profit from Contract 2 is thus $h - p_N(\ell - d) = 500 - \frac{1}{5}(30,000 - 8,000) = \$-3,900$: a loss! Hence the insurance company would **not** want to offer Contract 2 (or any of the other two contracts, since they all involve a loss). Before we address the issue of what contract(s) would be offered by an insurer, we need to re-examine the notion of "reservation indifference curve" in the context of moral hazard.

> Test your understanding of the concepts introduced in this section, by going through the exercises in Section 6.5.1 at the end of this chapter.

6.3 The reservation utility locus

In previous chapters we defined the reservation indifference curve as the indifference curve that goes through the no-insurance point *NI*. We can no longer do so in the present context, because, for every point in the wealth space, there are now **two** indifference curves, one corresponding to Effort and the other to No-effort. Since a reservation indifference curve is supposed to contain all the contracts that yield the same expected utility as no insurance, we first need to determine the "reservation utility" of the individual, that is, the maximum utility that she can obtain if she does not insure. Letting $\mathbb{E}[U_E(NI)]$ be the expected utility under no insurance if the individual chooses Effort and $\mathbb{E}[U_N(NI)]$ be the expected utility under no insurance if the individual chooses No-effort, the reservation utility is:

$$EU_{NI} = max\left\{\mathbb{E}[U_E(NI)], \mathbb{E}[U_N(NI)]\right\}. \tag{6.7}$$

The interesting case is where under no insurance the individual will choose Effort; it is interesting because insurance might provide an incentive for the individual no switch to No-effort. Thus in this section and the next we will assume that $\mathbb{E}[U_E(NI)] > \mathbb{E}[U_N(NI)]$ so that, by (6.7),

$$EU_{NI} = \mathbb{E}[U_E(NI)]. \tag{6.8}$$

The individual will reject any contract which, with the best choice of effort, will yield a utility which is less than $\mathbb{E}[U_E(NI)]$, that is, $\mathbb{E}[U_E(NI)]$ provides the *reservation level of utility*. Does this mean that the indifference curve corresponding to Effort that goes through *NI* can be taken to be the reservation indifference curve, that is, the set of contracts that give an expected utility equal to $\mathbb{E}[U_E(NI)]$? The answer is negative, because the fact that the individual prefers to choose Effort if uninsured does not imply that she will continue to choose Effort when insured. For example, *if fully insured then she will be better off by choosing No-effort*.

Figure 6.2 shows the two indifference curves that go through the *NI* point: the less steep one corresponds to Effort and a utility level of $\bar{u} = \mathbb{E}[U_E(NI)]$ and the steeper one to No-effort and a utility level of $\hat{u} = \mathbb{E}[U_N(NI)]$. In accordance with (6.8) we assume that $\bar{u} > \hat{u}$, that is, that when uninsured the individual chooses Effort. Let $F = \left(W_1^F, W_1^F\right)$ be the point at the intersection of the 45° line and the indifference curve corresponding to Effort that goes through *NI*; then $\mathbb{E}[U_E(F)] = U_E(W_1^F)$. By definition of indifference curve, $U_E(W_1^F) = \mathbb{E}[U_E(NI)] = \bar{u}$; however, if offered the full-insurance contract F the individual can achieve a higher level of utility by purchasing the contract and switching to No-effort. In fact, by (6.2) and (6.3),

$$U_N(W_1^F) = U_E(W_1^F) + c = \bar{u} + c > \bar{u}.$$

Let us use the expression *reservation utility locus*[4] to denote the set of points (contracts) in the wealth plane that give an expected utility equal to $\bar{u}$, when the individual makes the best choice of effort; then, while *NI* belongs to it, point F does not. *Thus the reservation utility locus does not coincide with the indifference curve corresponding to Effort that goes through NI.*

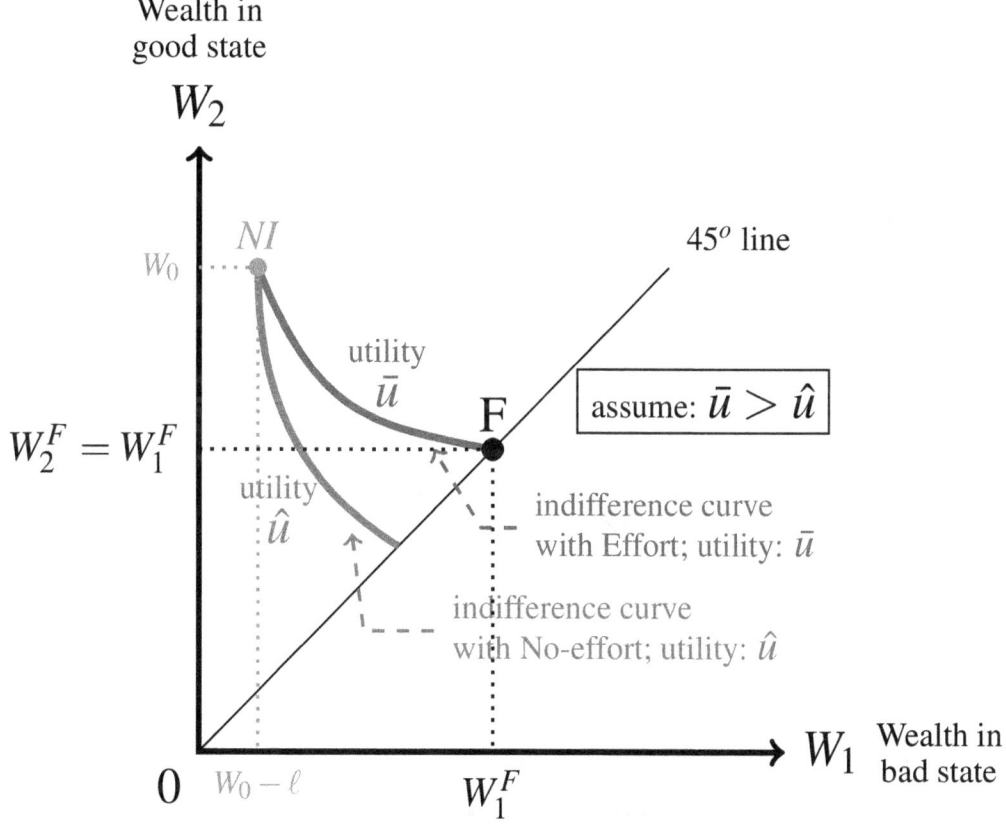

Figure 6.2: The two indifference curves through *NI*.

---

[4]Instead of 'reservation indifference curve', since it does not coincide with an indifference curve.

How do we determine the reservation utility locus?

Continue to denote by $\bar{u}$ the individual's expected utility when uninsured and choosing Effort. We need to consider the expected utility from choosing No-effort. By hypothesis,

$$\mathbb{E}[U_N(NI)] < \bar{u}$$

and, as shown above,

$$U_N(F) > \bar{u}.$$

Thus, by continuity, there must be a point, call it $A = \left(W_1^A, W_2^A\right)$, on the indifference curve corresponding to Effort that goes through NI, such that

$$\mathbb{E}[U_N(A)] = \bar{u}$$

as shown in Figure 6.3.

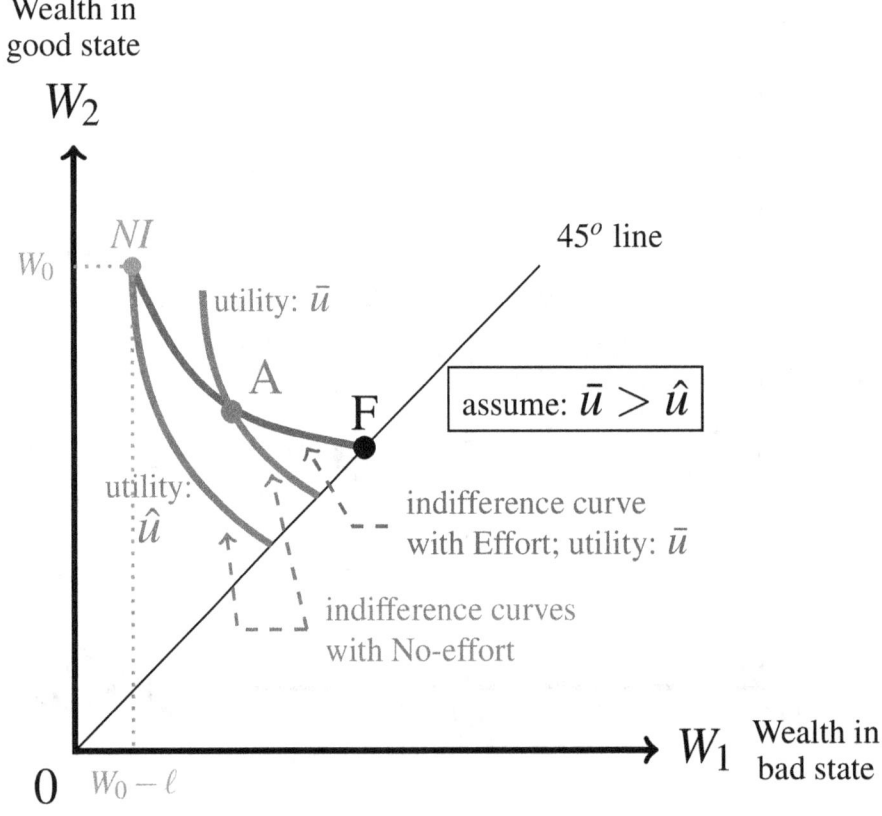

Figure 6.3: Point A is such that $\mathbb{E}[U_N(A)] = \mathbb{E}[U_E(A)] = \bar{u}$.

Thus, since the reservation utility level (that is, the maximum utility that the individual can achieve if not insured) is $\bar{u}$ $(= \mathbb{E}[U_E(NI)])$, the reservation utility locus is a *kinked curve* consisting of the initial segment from NI to point A of the indifference curve through NI corresponding to Effort and the segment from point A to the 45° line of the indifference curve through A corresponding to No-effort, where point A is such that $\mathbb{E}[U_N(A)] = \mathbb{E}[U_E(A)] = \mathbb{E}[U_E(NI)]$.

The reservation utility locus is shown as a thick continuous line in Figure 6.4.

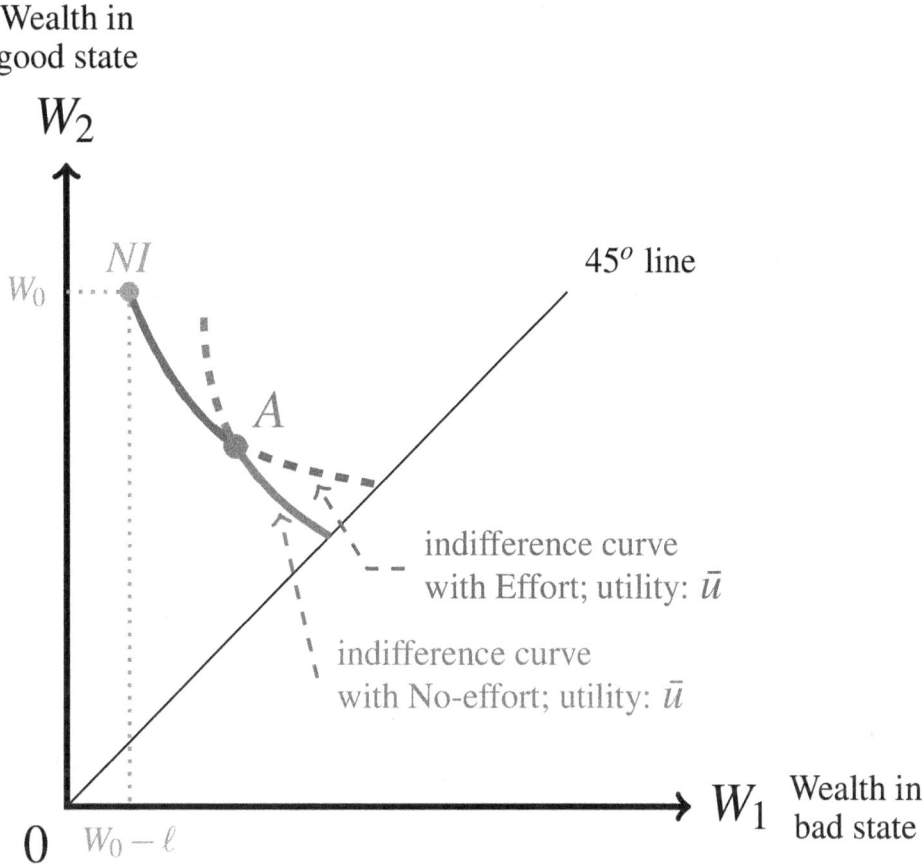

Figure 6.4: The reservation utility locus is the union of the thick continuous lines.

Let us illustrate all of the above in an example.

Consider an individual whose vNM utility-of-money function is

$$\begin{cases} U_N(m) = \sqrt{m} & \text{if she chooses No-effort} \\ U_E(m) = \sqrt{m} - c & \text{if she chooses Effort} \end{cases} \quad \text{with } c > 0.$$

The individual's initial wealth is W_0 and she faces a potential loss of ℓ. The probability of her incurring a loss is p_E if she chooses Effort and p_N if she chooses No-effort, with $0 < p_E < p_N < 1$.

◆ Let us first determine for what values of c she will choose Effort when not insured.

Her expected utility if she has no insurance and chooses No-effort is

$$\mathbb{E}[U_N(NI)] = p_N \sqrt{W_0 - \ell} + (1 - p_N)\sqrt{W_0}$$

and her expected utility if she has no insurance and chooses Effort is

$$\mathbb{E}[U_E(NI)] = p_E\left(\sqrt{W_0 - \ell} - c\right) + (1 - p_E)\left(\sqrt{W_0} - c\right)$$
$$= p_E\sqrt{W_0 - \ell} + (1 - p_E)\sqrt{W_0} - c.$$

Then it must be that

$$c < \left(p_E\sqrt{W_0 - \ell} + (1 - p_E)\sqrt{W_0}\right) - \left(p_N\sqrt{W_0 - \ell} + (1 - p_N)\sqrt{W_0}\right),$$

that is,

$$c < (p_N - p_E)\left(\sqrt{W_0} - \sqrt{W_0 - \ell}\right) \tag{6.9}$$

For the rest of this section let us fix the following values of the parameters, which satisfy (6.9):[5]

$W_0 = 2,500$	$\ell = 1,600$	$p_E = \dfrac{1}{20}$	$p_N = \dfrac{1}{10}$	$c = \dfrac{15}{16}$

◆ What is the individual's reservation utility level?

Since (6.9) is satisfied, the individual – if uninsured – will choose Effort and thus her reservation utility is:

$$\mathbb{E}[U_E(NI)] = \frac{1}{20}\sqrt{900} + \frac{19}{20}\sqrt{2,500} - \frac{15}{16} = \frac{769}{16} = 48.0625.$$

◆ Let us find the contract, call it A, that would make the individual indifferent between

1. not insuring and choosing Effort,
2. purchasing contract A and choosing Effort,
3. purchasing contract A and choosing No-effort.

---

[5] In fact, with these values, the right-hand side of (6.9) is equal to 1.

Let $A = \left(W_1^A, W_2^A \right)$. Then it must be that $\mathbb{E}[U_E(NI)] = \mathbb{E}[U_E(A)]$ and $\mathbb{E}[U_E(A)] = \mathbb{E}[U_N(A)]$, that is,

$$48.0625 = \frac{1}{20}\sqrt{W_1^A} + \frac{19}{20}\sqrt{W_2^A} - \frac{15}{16} \quad \text{and} \qquad (6.10)$$

$$\frac{1}{20}\sqrt{W_1^A} + \frac{19}{20}\sqrt{W_2^A} - \frac{15}{16} = \frac{1}{10}\sqrt{W_1^A} + \frac{9}{10}\sqrt{W_2^A}. \qquad (6.11)$$

The solution is $W_1^A = 972.66$ and $W_2^A = 2,493.75$; thus A is the contract with premium $2,500 - 2,493.75 = \$6.25$ and deductible $2,493.75 - 972.66 = \$1,521.09$.

♦ Suppose that the individual is offered contract A and she breaks her indifference by purchasing the contract. What is the insurer's expected profit from this contract?

With contract A the individual is indifferent between Effort and No-effort. Thus expected profit will be

- $h - p_E(\ell - d) = 6.25 - \frac{1}{20}(1,600 - 1,521.09) = \$2.31$ if the individual chooses Effort.
- $h - p_N(\ell - d) = 6.25 - \frac{1}{10}(1,600 - 1,521.09) = \$ -1.641$ if the individual chooses No-effort.

♦ Let us find the full-insurance contract, call it F, that makes the individual indifferent between purchasing the contract and not insuring.

We saw above that, without insurance, the individual can achieve a level of utility of 48.0625 (by opting for Effort). On the other hand, with any full-insurance contract, the individual will maximize her utility by choosing No-effort. Thus we are looking for a level of wealth W such that $\sqrt{W} = 48.0625$. The solution is $W = 2,310$. Thus $F = (2310, 2310)$, that is, a contract with premium $2,500 - 2,310 = \$190$ and zero deductible.

♦ Suppose that the individual is offered contract F and she breaks her indifference by purchasing the contract. What is the insurer's expected profit from this contract?

Expected profit will be $\quad h - p_N \ell = 190 - \frac{1}{10}1600 = \$30$.

♦ What is the reservation utility locus for this individual?

It is the union of the following two curves: (1) the portion of the indifference curve through NI corresponding to Effort, from NI to point A, followed by (2) the portion of the indifference curve through A corresponding to No-effort from point A to point F.

In the above example, an insurer would be better off offering contract F than contract A. We now turn to the issue of what contract(s) would be offered by a monopolist.

> Test your understanding of the concepts introduced in this section, by going through the exercises in Section 6.5.2 at the end of this chapter.

6.4 **The profit-maximizing contract for a monopolist**

In Chapter 5 (Section 5.2.1) we showed that – in the case where the probability of loss p is fixed and thus there is no issue of moral hazard – a monopolist would offer only one contract, namely the full-insurance contract with the maximum premium that the individual is willing to pay for full insurance, namely $h_{max} = p\ell + R_{NI}$, where $p\ell$ is expected loss and R_{NI} is the risk premium associated with the no-insurance lottery. Such contract is determine by the intersection of the reservation indifference curve and the 45° line.

In the case of moral hazard, the situation is somewhat more complicated. First of all, there are now two sets of isoprofit lines: one set corresponds to the case where the individual chooses Effort (so that the probability of loss is p_E and the slope of each isoprofit line is $-\frac{p_E}{1-p_E}$) and the other set corresponds to the case where the individual chooses No-effort (so that the probability of loss is p_N and the slope of each isoprofit line is $-\frac{p_N}{1-p_N}$). Since $p_E < p_N$, $\frac{p_E}{1-p_E} < \frac{p_N}{1-p_N}$ and thus the isoprofit lines in the former set are less steep than the ones in the latter set. In order to use the correct isoprofit lines, the monopolist must first figure out what choice of effort the individual will make.

As in the case considered in Chapter 5, the monopolist will want to offer a contract that extracts the maximum surplus from the individual, that is, the contract that leaves the individual just indifferent between insuring and not insuring.

As in the previous section, we will continue to assume that, if uninsured, the individual will choose Effort, that is,

$$\mathbb{E}[U_E(NI)] > \mathbb{E}[U_N(NI)].$$

Then the monopolist's problem is to find that contract on the reservation utility locus that maximizes its profits. Figure 6.5 (which reproduces Figure 6.4) shows the reservation utility locus (it is the union of the two thick, continuous curves).

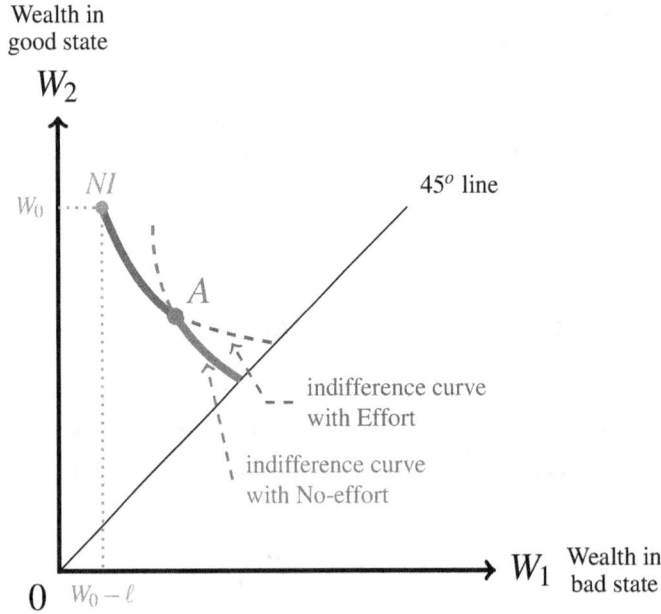

Figure 6.5: The reservation utility locus is the union of the two thick, continuous curves.

Let us begin by considering the first segment of the reservation utility locus, namely the portion of the indifference curve through *NI* corresponding to Effort, from point *NI* to point *A* (where, as before, *A* is the contract that yields the reservation utility no matter whether the individual chooses Effort or No-effort). It is shown in Figure 6.6.

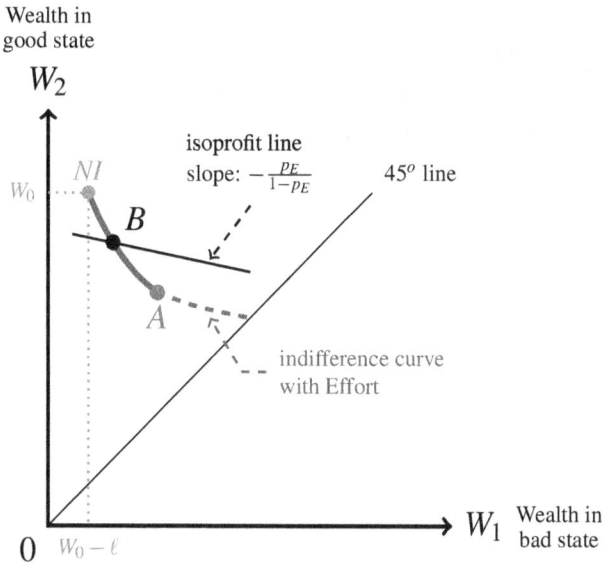

Figure 6.6: Point *A* is such that $\mathbb{E}[U_N(A)] = \mathbb{E}[U_E(A)]$.

If the insurance company wants to offer a contract that

1. leaves the customer with no surplus (that is, her expected utility with the offered contract is her reservation utility, call it $\bar{u}$) and

2. induces the customer to choose Effort,

then the insurance company has to offer a contract on this portion of the reservation utility locus. Note that if the individual purchases a contract that lies on this portion of the reservation utility locus then she will indeed choose Effort. In fact, since contract *A* is such that the individual is indifferent between choosing Effort and No-effort, that is, $\mathbb{E}[U_E(A)] = \mathbb{E}[U_N(A)] = \bar{u}$, any point *B* to the left of point *A* on this portion of the reservation utility locus is such that $\mathbb{E}[U_N(B)] < \bar{u}$ (since it lies on a lower *N*-indifference curve than the *N*-indifference curve that goes through *A*). On the other hand, if offered contract *A* the individual is indifferent between choosing Effort and No-effort; **we will assume that in this case she will choose Effort.**[6]

Since, for any of the contracts being considered, the individual will choose Effort, the relevant probability of loss is p_E and thus the relevant isoprofit lines are those with slope $-\frac{p_E}{1-p_E}$. Figure 6.6 shows one such isoprofit line, namely the one that goes through point *B*. Recall from Chapter 5 (Section 5.1.4) that at any point above the 45^0 line the Effort-indifference curve through that point is steeper than the p_E-isoprofit-line. Thus

---

[6] Without this assumption, instead of contract *A* the insurance company would offer a contract slightly to the left of point *A* (on the portion of the curve under consideration) in order to provide the customer with an incentive to choose Effort (and thus reduce the probability of loss). To simplify the exposition we assume that, with contract *A*, the individual would choose Effort.

contract B cannot be profit-maximizing for the insurer, since there are points on this portion of the reservation utility locus that lie below the isoprofit line through B and thus yield higher profits than B.

Thus we conclude that of all the points on the portion of the reservation utility locus considered so far, point A represents the profit-maximizing contract.

Let us now turn to the other portion of the reservation utility locus, namely the segment from point A to the 45° line of the indifference curve through A corresponding to No-effort, shown in Figure 6.7, where the point of intersection between the indifference curve and the 45° line is denoted by F.

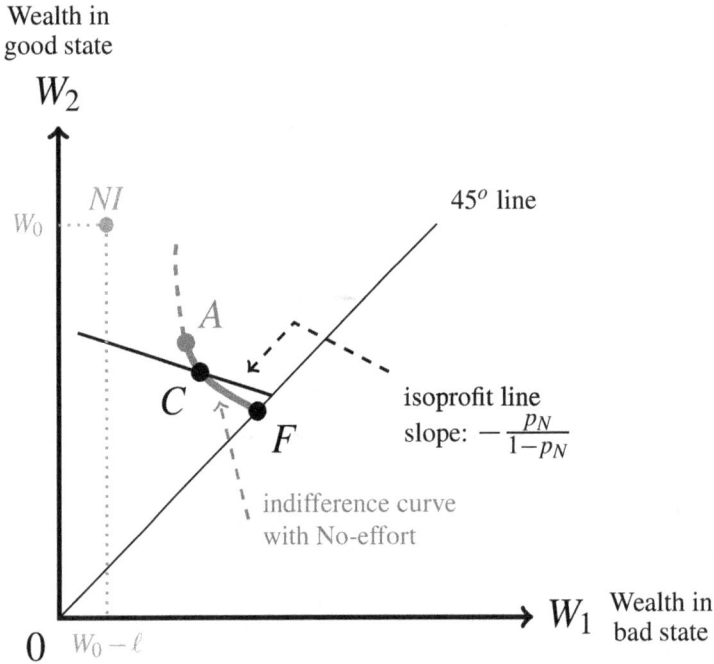

Figure 6.7: Point A is such that $\mathbb{E}[U_N(A)] = \mathbb{E}[U_E(A)]$.

Note that if the individual purchases a contract that lies on this portion of the reservation utility locus then she will choose No-effort. In fact, since contract A lies on the indifference curve corresponding to Effort and utility level $\bar{u} = \mathbb{E}[U_E(NI)]$, any point to the right of A on this portion of the reservation utility locus will be lie on an Effort-indifference curve corresponding to a utility level less than $\bar{u}$ (while it lies on the No-effort-indifference curve corresponding to $\bar{u}$).[7]

Since, for any of the contracts being considered, the individual will choose No-effort, the relevant probability of loss is p_N and thus the relevant isoprofit lines are those with slope $-\frac{p_N}{1-p_N}$. Figure 6.7 shows one such isoprofit line, namely the one that goes through point C. Recall from Chapter 5 (Section 5.1.4) that at any point above the 45° line the No-effort-indifference curve through that point is steeper than the p_N-isoprofit-line. Thus contract C cannot be profit-maximizing for the insurer, since there are points on this portion of the reservation utility locus that lie below the isoprofit line through C and thus yield

---

[7]As for point A we continue to assume that the individual would choose Effort.

higher profits than C.

Thus we conclude that of all the points on the portion of the reservation utility locus under consideration, point F represents the profit-maximizing contract.

Let $A = \left(W_1^A, W_2^A\right)$ and $F = \left(W^F, W^F\right)$ so that the corresponding premia and deductibles are

	premium	deductible
Contract A :	$h_A = W_0 - W_2^A$	$d_A = W_2^A - W_1^A$
Contract F :	$h_F = W_0 - W^F$	$d_A = 0$

Furthermore, let π_A be the expected profit from contract A and π_F be the expected profit from contract F, that is,

$$\pi_A = h_A - p_E(\ell - d_A)$$

$$\pi_F = h_F - p_N \ell.$$

Then we can conclude from the above analysis that the monopolist will offer

- contract A if $\pi_A > \pi_F$,

- contract F if $\pi_F > \pi_A$

and be indifferent between the two contracts if $\pi_A = \pi_F$.

In the numerical example considered at the end of the previous section, the monopolist would opt for the full-insurance contract F, since $\pi_F = 30$ and $\pi_A = 2.31$ (as shown on page 165).

Now we give an example where the monopolist prefers to offer the partial-insurance contract A. Let us keep the same data as in the example considered at the end of the previous section, but change the value of p_E from $\frac{1}{20}$ to $\frac{1}{40}$. Thus we have that the vNM utility-of-money function is

$$\begin{cases} U_N(m) = \sqrt{m} & \text{if she chooses No-effort} \\ U_E(m) = \sqrt{m} - \frac{15}{16} & \text{if she chooses Effort} \end{cases}$$

$W_0 = 2,500$	$\ell = 1,600$	$p_E = \dfrac{1}{40}$	$p_N = \dfrac{1}{10}$

Note that, if uninsured, the individual would choose Effort, since

$$\mathbb{E}[U_E(NI)] = \frac{1}{40}\sqrt{900} + \frac{39}{40}\sqrt{2,500} - \frac{15}{16} = 48.5625$$

and

$$\mathbb{E}[U_N(NI)] = \frac{1}{10}\sqrt{900} + \frac{9}{10}\sqrt{2,500} = 48.$$

Contract A is given by the solution to

$$\begin{cases} 48.5625 = \frac{1}{40}\sqrt{W_1^A} + \frac{39}{40}\sqrt{W_2^A} - \frac{15}{16} \\ \\ 48.5625 = \frac{1}{10}\sqrt{W_1^A} + \frac{9}{10}\sqrt{W_2^A} \end{cases}$$

The solution is $W_1^A = 1,392.22$ and $W_2^A = 2,481.29$, that is, $A = (1392.22, 2481.29)$. Thus $h_A = 2,500 - 2,481.29 = 18.71$ and $d_A = 2,481.29 - 1,392.22 = 1,089.07$.

Contract F is given by the solution to $\sqrt{W^F} = 48.5625$, which is $W^F = 2,358.32$ so that $F = (2358.32, 2358.32)$ and $h_F = 2,500 - 2,358.32 = 141.68$. Hence[8]

$$\pi_A = 18.71 - \frac{1}{40}(1,600 - 1,089.07) = \$5.94$$

$$\pi_F = 141.68 - \frac{1}{10}(1,600) = \$-18.32$$

so that the monopolist would offer contract A, thereby inducing the individual to reduce the probability of loss by choosing Effort.

What would the monopolist's profit be if it offered the full-insurance contract G which is given by the intersection of the 45° line and the indifference curve corresponding to Effort that goes through the NI point? In this example contract G is obtained by solving $\sqrt{W^F} - \frac{15}{16} = 48.5625$, that is, $G = (2450.25, 2450.25)$ with corresponding premium $h_G = 2,500 - 2450.25 = 49.75$. Thus one might be tempted to answer that the monopolist's profit would be $49.75 - \frac{1}{40}(1,600) = \$9.75$, but this answer is wrong! The individual would be very happy to purchase contract G because her best choice would then be No-effort, with an expected utility of $\sqrt{2,450.25} = 49.5$ (instead of 48.5625) and thus, as a matter of fact, the monopolist's profits would turn out to be $\pi_G = 49.75 - \frac{1}{10}(1,600) = \$-110.25$!

> Test your understanding of the concepts introduced in this section, by going through the exercises in Section 6.5.3 at the end of this chapter.

---

[8] Recall the assumption that, with contract A, the individual would choose Effort: see Footnote 6 on page 167.

6.5 Exercises

The solutions to the following exercises are given in Section 6.6 at the end of this chapter.

6.5.1 Exercises for Section 6.2: Two levels of unobserved effort

Exercise 6.1 Emily has an initial wealth of $80,000 and faces a potential loss of $36,000. The probability of loss depends on the amount of effort she puts into trying to avoid the loss. If she puts a high level of effort, then the probability is 5%, while if she exerts low effort the probability is 15%. Her vNM utility-of-money function is

$$U(m) = \begin{cases} \sqrt{m} & \text{if low effort} \\ \sqrt{m} - 1 & \text{if high effort} \end{cases}$$

(a) If Emily remains uninsured, what level of effort will she choose?

(b) If Emily is offered a full insurance contract with premium $2,250 and she accepts it, what level of effort will she choose?

(c) If Emily is offered a full insurance contract with premium $2,250 will she accept it?

(d) What is the insurance company's expected profit from a full insurance contract with premium $2,250?

Exercise 6.2 Susan has an initial wealth of $10,000 and faces a potential loss of $1,900. The probability of loss depends on the amount of effort she puts into trying to avoid the loss. If she puts a high level of effort, then the probability is $\frac{1}{10}$, while if she exerts low effort the probability is $\frac{4}{10}$. Her vNM utility-of-money function is

$$U(m) = \begin{cases} \sqrt{m} & \text{if low effort} \\ \sqrt{m} - 2 & \text{if high effort} \end{cases}$$

(a) If Susan remains uninsured, what level of effort will she choose?

(b) If Susan is offered a partial insurance contract with premium $800 and deductible $200 and she accepts it, what level of effort will she choose?

(c) If Susan is offered the contract of Part (b) will she accept it?

Exercise 6.3 Bob owns a house near Lake Tahoe. The house is worth $949,000. He also has $1,000 in his bank account, so that his entire wealth is $950,000. The probability that there will be a forest fire next year is $\frac{1}{10}$. If a forest fire occurs then the house will incur damages equal to $400,000. However, by spending $\$x$ on protective measures Bob can reduce the probability that the fire will reach the house from $\frac{1}{10}$ to $\frac{1}{10} - \frac{x}{15,000}$. Thus the more he spends, the lower the probability. The most he can spend is $1,000. Bob's vNM utility of money function is $U(m) = 10 \ln(m)$.

(a) If Bob is not insured, which of the following four options will he choose (assuming that these are the only options)?

(1) $x = 0$,

(2) $x = \$400$,

(3) $x = \$750$,

(4) $x = \$1,000$.

(b) If Bob is offered a full-insurance contract with premium h, what value of x will he choose?

(c) Suppose that Bob is offered a full insurance contract at premium $h = \$40,000$. Will he purchase it?

Exercise 6.4 In this exercise we consider the case where the individual's effort has an effect not on the probability of loss but on the *size* of the loss.

Mike's initial wealth is $6,400 and he faces a potential loss with probability $\frac{1}{4}$. The size of the loss depends on his choice of effort: it he chooses Effort then the loss is $\ell_E = \$471$, while if he chooses No-effort then the loss is $\ell_N = \$1,216$. Mike's vNM utility-of-money function is

$$\begin{cases} U_N(m) = \sqrt{m} & \text{if he chooses No-effort} \\ U_E(m) = \sqrt{m} - 1 & \text{if he chooses Effort} \end{cases}$$

(a) If Mike is uninsured, will he choose Effort or No-effort?

(b) If Mike purchases a full-insurance contract with premium h, will he choose Effort or No-effort?

(c) Suppose that Mike is offered an insurance contract with premium $h = \$80$ and deductible $d = \$471$. Will he purchase it?

6.5.2 Exercises for Section 6.3: The reservation utility locus

Exercise 6.5 Consider again the information given in Exercise 6.2: Susan has an initial wealth of $10,000 and faces a potential loss of $1,900; the probability of loss depends on the amount of effort she puts into trying to avoid the loss; if she puts a high level of effort, then the probability is $\frac{1}{10}$, while if she exerts low effort the probability is $\frac{4}{10}$; her vNM utility-of-money function is

$$U(m) = \begin{cases} \sqrt{m} & \text{if low effort} \\ \sqrt{m} - 2 & \text{if high effort} \end{cases}$$

(a) What is Susan's reservation level of utility?

(b) Write two equations whose solution gives that point, call it A, on the indifference curve through NI that corresponds to high effort such that Susan's expected utility at A if she chooses low effort is equal to her reservation level of utility.

(c) Find a full-insurance contract, call it F, that yields Susan the same expected utility, when she chooses low effort, as contract A of Part (b). Calculate the premium of contract F

(d) Describe in words how you would draw the reservation utility locus for Susan.

Exercise 6.6 In this exercise we consider a slightly different type of vNM utility-of-money function, where instead of $U_E(m) = U_N(m) - c$ we have that $U_E(m) = \alpha U_N(m)$ with $0 < \alpha < 1$.

Tom has an initial wealth of $4,900 and faces a potential loss of $1,300; the probability of loss depends on the amount of effort he puts into trying to avoid the loss; if he puts a high level of effort, then the probability is $\frac{1}{8}$, while if he exerts low effort the probability is $\frac{3}{8}$; his vNM utility-of-money function is

$$U(m) = \begin{cases} \sqrt{m} & \text{if low effort} \\ \alpha\sqrt{m} & \text{if high effort} \end{cases} \quad \text{with } 0 < \alpha < 1.$$

(a) For what values of α would Tom choose high effort if uninsured?

(b) Let $\alpha = 0.9$. What is Tom's reservation level of utility?

(c) Let $\alpha = 0.98$. What is Tom's reservation level of utility?

(d) Assume that $\alpha = 0.98$. Write two equations whose solution gives that insurance contract, call it A, such that if Tom purchases this contract he gets his reservation level of utility, no matter whether he chooses low effort or high effort.

(e) Continue to assume that $\alpha = 0.98$. Find a full-insurance contract, call if F, such that Tom is indifferent between not insuring and purchasing contract F.

(f) Continue to assume that $\alpha = 0.98$. Describe in words how you would draw the reservation utility locus for Tom.

6.5.3 Exercises for Section 6.4: The profit-maximizing contract for a monopolist

Exercise 6.7 Carol has an initial wealth of $10,000 and faces a potential loss of $4,000; the probability of loss depends on the amount of effort she puts into trying to avoid the loss; if she puts a high level of effort, then the probability is $\frac{1}{10}$, while if she exerts low effort the probability is $\frac{1}{2}$; her vNM utility-of-money function is

$$U(m) = \begin{cases} 10\ln(\frac{m}{1,000}) & \text{if low effort} \\ 10\ln(\frac{m}{1,000}) - c & \text{if high effort} \end{cases} \quad \text{with } c > 0.$$

(a) For what values of c would Carol choose high effort if uninsured?

(b) Assume that $c = 1.8$. What insurance contract would a monopolist offer to Carol?

(c) Assume that $c = 1.5$. What insurance contract would a monopolist offer to Carol?

6.6 Solutions to Exercises

Solution to Exercise 6.1

(a) If Emily chooses low effort, her expected utility is

$$0.15\sqrt{80,000 - 36,000} + 0.85\sqrt{80,000} = 271.881$$

and if she chooses high effort, her expected utility is

$$0.05\left(\sqrt{80,000 - 36,000} - 1\right) + 0.95\left(\sqrt{80,000} - 1\right) = 278.189.$$

Thus she will choose high effort.

(b) Emily will choose low effort, because her utility will be $\sqrt{80,000 - 2,250}$ while with high effort it would be less, namely $\sqrt{80,000 - 2,250} - 1$.

(c) She will accept the contract, because her utility if she accepts it is $\sqrt{80,000 - 2,250} = 278.837$, while her best alternative would be to remain uninsured and choose high effort with an expected utility of 278.189.

(d) Since Emily will indeed buy insurance (and exert low effort), expected profits will be $2,250 - 0.15(36,000) = \$-3,150$, that is, a loss. Thus it would not be a good idea for the insurance company to offer this contract. $\square$

Solution to Exercise 6.2

(a) If Susan is uninsured and chooses high effort, her expected utility is

$$0.1\left(\sqrt{10,000-1,900}-2\right)+0.9\left(\sqrt{10,000}-2\right)=97$$

while if she chooses low effort, her expected utility is

$$0.4\sqrt{10,000-1,900}+0.6\sqrt{10,000}=96.$$

Thus she will choose high effort.

(b) The contract under consideration (premium of \$800, deductible of \$200) corresponds to the following point in the wealth space: $C=(9000,9200)$. If Susan purchases this contract and chooses high effort, then her expected utility is

$$0.1\left(\sqrt{9,000}-2\right)+0.9\left(\sqrt{9,200}-2\right)=93.81$$

while if she chooses low effort, her expected utility is

$$0.4\sqrt{9,000}+0.6\sqrt{9,200}=95.5.$$

Thus, under this contract, she would choose low effort.

(c) She will **not** accept the contract, because her highest utility if she accepts it is 95.5, while her best alternative would be to remain uninsured and choose high effort with an expected utility of 97.   □

Solution to Exercise 6.3

(a) If Bob chooses to spend \$x on preventive measures his expected utility – when not insured – is

$$NI(x)=\left(\frac{1}{10}-\frac{x}{15,000}\right)10\ln\left(950,000-400,000-x\right)$$
$$+\left[1-\left(\frac{1}{10}-\frac{x}{15,000}\right)\right]10\ln\left(950,000-x\right).$$

Since $NI(0)=137.096$, $NI(400)=137.237$, $NI(750)=137.361$ and $NI(1,000)=137.449$, of the four options he will choose $x=\$1,000$.

(b) If he is fully insured at premium h then his utility, if he does not spend any money on preventive measures, is $10\ln(950,000-h)$, while if he spends \$x (with $x>0$) then his utility is less, namely $10\ln(950,000-h-x)$. Thus he will choose $x=0$.

(c) As determined in Part (b), if he buys the full insurance contract with premium \$40,000 then he will choose $x=0$, so that his utility will be $10\ln(950,000-40,000)=10\ln(910,000)=137.21$. This is less than his expected utility if he remains uninsured and spends \$1,000 on preventive measures, which is 137.449 as calculated in Part (a). Thus he will **not** accept the contract.   □

Solution to Exercise 6.4

(a) If Mike is uninsured and chooses No-effort then his expected utility is

$$\mathbb{E}[U_N(NI)] = \frac{1}{4}\sqrt{6,400 - 1,216} + \frac{3}{4}\sqrt{6,400} = 78$$

while if he chooses Effort his expected utility is

$$\mathbb{E}[U_E(NI)] = \frac{1}{4}\sqrt{6,400 - 471} + \frac{3}{4}\sqrt{6,400} - 1 = 78.25.$$

Thus he will choose Effort, if not insured.

(b) With a full-insurance contract with premium h his utility if he chooses Effort is $\sqrt{6,400 - h} - 1$ while his utility if he chooses No-effort is higher, namely $\sqrt{6,400 - h}$. Thus he would choose No-effort (he does not care about the size of the loss, since he gets fully reimbursed from the insurance company if the loss occurs).

(c) When the deductible is \$471 ($= \ell_E$, loss with Effort) it would not make sense for Mike to purchase the contract and choose Effort, because he would be better off by not insuring and choosing Effort (his wealth would be larger by an amount equal to the premium). Thus he would compare expected utility from no insurance with Effort (which was calculated to be 78.25 in Part (a)) with expected utility with the contract and No-effort which is (recall that the premium is \$80)

$$\frac{1}{4}\sqrt{6,400 - 80 - 471} + \frac{3}{4}\sqrt{6,400 - 80} = 78.74.$$

Thus Mike would purchase the contract and choose No-effort.   □

Solution to Exercise 6.5

(a) We saw in Part (a) of Exercise 6.2 that if Susan is uninsured and chooses low effort, her expected utility is 96 and if she chooses high effort her expected utility is 97. Thus her reservation level of utility is 97: she would not accept a contract that did not give her an expected utility of at least 97.

(b) Let $A = (W_1^A, W_2^A)$. The first equation says that A should lie on the indifference curve through NI corresponding to high effort. Since, as computed in Part (a) of Exercise 6.2, $\mathbb{E}[U_E(NI)] = 97$, the first equation is

$$0.1\left(\sqrt{W_1^A} - 2\right) + 0.9\left(\sqrt{W_2^A} - 2\right) = 97.$$

The second equation says that contract A gives the same expected utility whether Susan chooses high effort or low effort:

$$0.4\sqrt{W_1^A} + 0.9\sqrt{W_2^A} = 0.1\left(\sqrt{W_1^A} - 2\right) + 0.9\left(\sqrt{W_2^A} - 2\right).$$

The solution of these two equations is: $W_1^A = 8,649$ and $W_2^A = 9,933.44$. Thus A is the contract with premium $10,000 - 9,933.44 = \$66.56$ and deductible $9,933.44 - 8,649 = \$1,284.44$.

(c) We are looking for a level of wealth W such that

$$\sqrt{W} = 0.4\sqrt{W_1^A} + 0.9\sqrt{W_2^A} \quad (= 97).$$

The solution is $W = 9,409$. Thus $F = (9409, 9409)$, that is, a contract with premium $10,000 - 9,409 = \$591$ and zero deductible.

(d) The reservation utility locus for Susan is the union of the following two curves: (1) the portion of the indifference curve through NI corresponding to high effort from NI to point A, followed by (2) the portion of the indifference curve through A corresponding to low effort from point A to point F. □

Solution to Exercise 6.6

(a) When uninsured, Tom's expected utility is:

if low effort: $\quad \dfrac{3}{8}\sqrt{3,600} + \dfrac{5}{8}\sqrt{4900} = \dfrac{265}{4} = 66.25$

if high effort: $\quad \dfrac{1}{8}\alpha\sqrt{3,600} + \dfrac{7}{8}\alpha\sqrt{4900} = \dfrac{275}{4}\alpha = 68.75\alpha.$

Thus, when uninsured, Tom will choose high effort if $68.75\alpha > 66.25$, that is, if $\alpha > \frac{53}{55} = 0.9636$.

(b) The assumption is that $\alpha = 0.9$. Since in this case $\alpha < 0.9636$, Tom – when uninsured – will choose low effort. Thus his reservation level of utility is 66.25, as computed in Part (a).

(c) The assumption is that $\alpha = 0.98$. Since in this case $\alpha > 0.9636$, Tom – when uninsured – will choose high effort. Thus his reservation level of utility is 68.75(0.98) = 67.375, as computed in Part (a).

(d) Let the contract be $A = \left(W_1^A, W_2^A\right)$. The equations are:

$$\frac{1}{8}(0.98)\sqrt{W_1^A} + \frac{7}{8}(0.98)\sqrt{W_2^A} = \frac{3}{8}\sqrt{W_1^A} + \frac{5}{8}\sqrt{W_2^A}$$

$$\frac{1}{8}(0.98)\sqrt{W_1^A} + \frac{7}{8}(0.98)\sqrt{W_2^A} = 67.375.$$

The solution is $W_1^A = 4,088$ and $W_2^A = 4,821.57$.

(e) The assumption is that $\alpha = 0.98$. Contract F is given by the solution to: $\sqrt{W} = 67.375$ which is $W = 4,539.39$. Thus $F = (4539.39, 4539.39)$.

(f) The reservation utility locus for Tom is the union of the following two curves: (1) the portion, from point NI to point A, of the indifference curve through NI corresponding to high effort followed by (2) the portion, from point A to point F, of the indifference curve through A corresponding to low effort. □

Solution to Exercise 6.7

(a) If Carol is uninsured and exerts low effort, her expected utility is:

$$\frac{1}{2}10\ln(6) + \frac{1}{2}10\ln(10) = 20.4717$$

while with high effort her expected utility is

$$\frac{1}{10}(10\ln(6) - c) + \frac{9}{10}(10\ln(10) - c) = 22.515 - c.$$

Thus she will choose high effort if $20.4717 < 22.515 - c$, that is, if $c < 2.0433$.

(b) The assumption is that $c = 1.8$, so that – if uninsured – Carol would choose high effort and her expected utility would be $22.515 - 1.8 = 20.715$. The monopolist would only consider two options:

- the partial-insurance contract A given by the intersection of the low-effort indifference curve corresponding to a utility of 20.715 and the high-effort indifference curve corresponding to a utility of 20.715, and

- the full-insurance contract F that makes Carol indifferent between (1) purchasing F and exerting low effort and (2) not insuring and exerting high effort.

Contract A is given by the solution to the following two equations:

$$\frac{1}{2}10\ln\left(\frac{W_1}{1,000}\right) + \frac{1}{2}10\ln\left(\frac{W_2}{1,000}\right) = \frac{1}{10}\ln\left(\frac{W_1}{1,000}\right) + \frac{9}{10}\ln\left(\frac{W_2}{1,000}\right) - 1.8$$

$$\frac{1}{2}10\ln\left(\frac{W_1}{1,000}\right) + \frac{1}{2}10\ln\left(\frac{W_2}{1,000}\right) = 20.715$$

which is $W_1 = 6,337.6$ and $W_2 = 9,939.33$, so that $A = (6337.6, 9939.33)$ with corresponding premium $h_A = 10,000 - 9,939.33 = \$60.67$ and deductible $d_A = 9.939.33 - 6,337.6 = 3,601.73$.

Contract F is given by the solution to $10\ln\left(\frac{W}{1,000}\right) = 20.715$, which is $W = 7,936.72$; thus $F = (7936.72, 7936.72)$ with corresponding premium $h_F = 10,000 - 7,936.72 = \$2,063.28$

Assuming that with contract A Carol would choose high effort, the expected profit with contract A is $h_A - \frac{1}{10}(\ell - d_A) = 60.66 - \frac{1}{10}(4,000 - 3,601.73) = \$20.84$. On the other hand, expected profit from Contract F is $h_F - \frac{1}{2}\ell = 2,063.26 - \frac{1}{2}(4,000) = 63.28$. Thus the monopolist would offer the full-insurance contract F.

(c) The assumption is that $c = 1.5$, so that – if uninsured – Carol would choose high effort and her expected utility would be $22.515 - 1.5 = 21.015$. The monopolist would only consider two options:

- the partial-insurance contract A given by the intersection of the low-effort indifference curve corresponding to a utility of 21.015 and the high-effort indifference curve corresponding to a utility of 21.015, and

- the full-insurance contract F that makes Carol indifferent between (1) purchasing F and exerting low effort and (2) not insuring and exerting high effort.

Contract A is given by the solution to the following two equations:

$$\frac{1}{2}10\ln\left(\frac{W_1}{1,000}\right) + \frac{1}{2}10\ln\left(\frac{W_2}{1,000}\right) = \frac{1}{10}\ln\left(\frac{W_1}{1,000}\right) + \frac{9}{10}\ln\left(\frac{W_2}{1,000}\right) - 1.5$$

$$\frac{1}{2}10\ln\left(\frac{W_1}{1,000}\right) + \frac{1}{2}10\ln\left(\frac{W_2}{1,000}\right) = 21.015$$

which is $W_1 = 6,780.16$ and $W_2 = 9,865.07$, so that $A = (6780.16, 9,865.07)$ with corresponding premium $h_A = 10,000 - 9,865.07 = \$134.93$ and deductible $d_A = 9,865.07 - 6,780.16 = 3,084.91$.

Contract F is given by the solution to $10\ln\left(\frac{W}{1,000}\right) = 21.015$, which is $W = 8,178.43$; thus $F = (8178.43, 8178.43)$ with corresponding premium $h_F = 10,000 - 8,178.43 = \$1,821.57$

Assuming that with contract A Carol would choose high effort, the expected profit with contract A is $h_A - \frac{1}{10}(\ell - d_A) = 134.93 - \frac{1}{10}(4,000 - 3,084.91) = \$43.42$. On the other hand, expected profit from Contract F is $h_F - \frac{1}{2}\ell = 1,821.57 - \frac{1}{2}(4,000) = \$-178.43$, a loss. Thus the monopolist would offer the partial-insurance contract A.

□

7. Insurance and adverse selection

7.1 Adverse selection or hidden type

The expression 'adverse selection', or 'hidden type', refers to any situation in which one party to a contract (e.g. a buyer) possesses information relevant to the contract that is not available to the opposing party (e.g. a seller). Thus it is a situation of *asymmetric information*.

For example, in the context of health insurance, the insurance company (the seller of insurance) is typically aware of the fact that there are individuals who – because of their family history – are at a higher risk of developing a condition that requires extensive medical services, while other individuals represent a lower risk. If the insurance company offers a contract that would, on average, cover its expected costs *if everybody (high-risk and low-risk individuals) were to purchase that contract*, it might discover that its costs are much higher than expected, because only the high-risk individuals ended up purchasing the contract.[1]

As in Chapter 6, we will consider two different probabilities of loss: one higher than the other. In the context studied in Chapter 6, we had only one (type of) individual and the probability of loss was determined by the individual's behavior. On the other hand, in this chapter we will assume that, *for each individual, the probability of loss is constant* (thus not affected by the individual's behavior) and the different probabilities are associated with *different types of individuals*: the high-risk individuals have a higher probability of loss than the low-risk individuals. Thus there is no moral hazard issue here: *the uncertainty on the part of the insurance company has to do with its inability to tell high-risk from low-risk individuals apart* (while being fully aware that it faces two different types of potential customers).

---

[1] This was the rationale behind the original provision of the Affordable Care Act that established a mandate for individuals to purchase health insurance.

7.2   **Two types of customers**

Suppose that there are two types of individuals. They are all identical in terms of initial wealth, denoted by W_0, and in terms of the potential loss that they face, denoted by ℓ (with $0 < \ell \le W_0$). They also have the same vNM utility-of-money function $U(m)$. What they differ in is the probability of loss: it is p_H for type-H (= high-risk) individuals and p_L for type-L (= low-risk) individuals, with

$$0 < p_L < p_H < 1.$$

It follows that type-H individuals have steeper indifference curves than type-L individuals, as shown in Figure 7.1. In fact, fix an arbitrary point $C = (W_1^C, W_2^C)$ in the wealth plane. The slope of the indifference curve going through this point is

$$-\frac{p_H}{1 - p_H} \frac{U'(W_1^C)}{U'(W_2^C)} \qquad \text{for type-H individuals}$$

and

$$-\frac{p_L}{1 - p_L} \frac{U'(W_1^C)}{U'(W_2^C)} \qquad \text{for type-L individuals.}$$

Since $p_L < p_H$,

$$\frac{p_L}{1 - p_L} < \frac{p_H}{1 - p_H}.$$

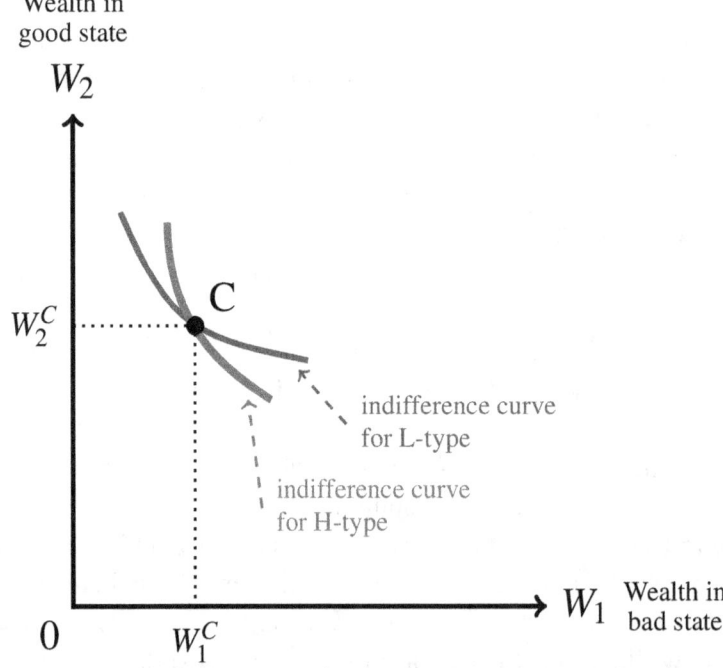

Figure 7.1: The indifference curve through point C for type-H is steeper than the indifference curve through point C for type-L.

Since the H-type indifference curve is steeper than the L-type indifference curve at any point, this must be true also at the no-insurance point, that is, the reservation indifference curve for the H-type is steeper than the reservation indifference curve for the L-type, as shown in Figure 7.2.[2]

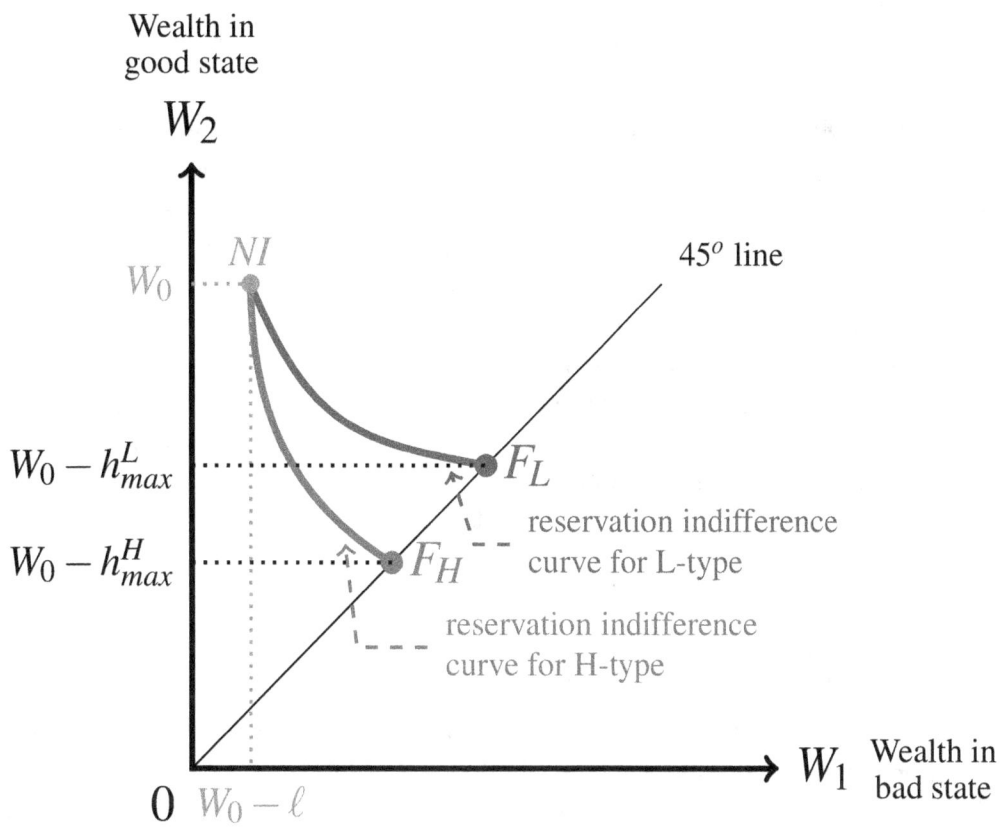

Figure 7.2: The reservation indifference curve of an H-type is steeper than the reservation indifference curve of an L-type.

It follows that the maximum premium that the L-type individuals are willing to pay for full insurance, denoted by h^L_{max}, is smaller than the maximum premium that the H-type individuals are willing to pay for full insurance, denoted by h^H_{max}: $h^L_{max} < h^H_{max}$, as shown in Figure 7.2. Letting F_L be the full-insurance contract that the L-type individuals consider to be just as good as no insurance and F_H the full-insurance contract that the H-type individuals consider to be just as good as no insurance, we have that $F_L = \left(W_0 - h^L_{max}, W_0 - h^L_{max}\right)$ and $F_H = \left(W_0 - h^H_{max}, W_0 - h^H_{max}\right)$, with $W_0 - h^L_{max} > W_0 - h^H_{max}$.

---

[2]Recall that the reservation indifference curve is the indifference curve that goes through the no-insurance point NI.

Let $N_H > 0$ be the number of H-type individuals in the population and $N_L > 0$ be the number of L-type individuals and define

$$q_H = \frac{N_H}{N_H + N_L} \quad \text{so that} \quad 1 - q_H = \frac{N_L}{N_H + N_L}. \tag{7.1}$$

Then $0 < q_H < 1$ and $0 < 1 - q_H < 1$.

7.2.1 The contracts offered by a monopolist who can tell individuals apart

As a benchmark, we shall first consider the case of a monopolist who is able to tell whether an individual who applies for insurance is an H-type or and L-type. For example, a health insurance company might be legally allowed to require applicants to submit to a DNA test that reveals whether a defective gene is present, in which case the individual is more likely to develop a particular disease requiring extensive medical care.

In the perfect-information case, from the point of view of the monopolist there are effectively two separate insurance markets: one for the H-types and one for the L-types. Then we can apply the analysis of Chapter 5 (Section 5.2.1) and conclude that the monopolist would offer the full-insurance contract F_L to type-L individuals and the full-insurance contract F_H to type-H individuals so that its expected profits would be[3]

$$\text{total profits:} \quad \left(h_{max}^H - p_H \ell \right) N_H + \left(h_{max}^L - p_L \ell \right) N_L \tag{7.2}$$

$$\text{profit per customer:} \quad \left(h_{max}^H - p_H \ell \right) q_H + \left(h_{max}^L - p_L \ell \right) (1 - q_H). \tag{7.3}$$

Which type of individual is "better" for the insurance company, that is, which type yields higher profits? The H-type is better in that she is willing to pay a higher premium for full insurance, but on the other hand she will submit a claim with higher probability, that is, the H-type yields higher revenue but also higher cost. Thus, in principle, either type could be more profitable. The answer depends on the specific values of the parameters.

For example, suppose that initial wealth is $W_0 = 3,600$, potential loss is $\ell = 2,000$ and the utility-of-money function is $U(m) = \sqrt{m}$.

- Let $p_L = \frac{1}{10}$ and $p_H = \frac{4}{10}$. To find h_{max}^L solve the equation

$$\frac{1}{10}\sqrt{1,600} + \frac{9}{10}\sqrt{3,600} = \sqrt{W}.$$

The solution is $W = 3,364$ so that $h_{max}^L = 3,600 - 3,364 = \$236$ and thus the expected profit from an L-type is

$$236 - \frac{1}{10}(2,000) = \$36.$$

To find h_{max}^H solve the equation

$$\frac{4}{10}\sqrt{1,600} + \frac{6}{10}\sqrt{3,600} = \sqrt{W}.$$

---

[3]To obtain profit per customer from total profits, divide by $(N_H + N_L)$ and use (7.1).

The solution is $W = 2,704$ so that $h_{max}^H = 3,600 - 2,704 = \$896$ and thus the expected profit from an H-type is

$$896 - \frac{4}{10}(2,000) = \$96.$$

Thus in this case insuring an H-type is more profitable than insuring an L-type.

- Let $p_L = \frac{3}{10}$ and $p_H = \frac{8}{10}$. To find h_{max}^L solve the equation

$$\frac{3}{10}\sqrt{1,600} + \frac{7}{10}\sqrt{3,600} = \sqrt{W}.$$

The solution is $W = 2,916$ so that $h_{max}^L = 3,600 - 2,916 = \$684$ and thus the expected profit from an L-type is

$$684 - \frac{3}{10}(2,000) = \$84.$$

To find h_{max}^H solve the equation

$$\frac{8}{10}\sqrt{1,600} + \frac{2}{10}\sqrt{3,600} = \sqrt{W}.$$

The solution is $W = 1,936$ so that $h_{max}^H = 3,600 - 1,936 = \$1,664$ and thus the expected profit from an H-type is

$$1,664 - \frac{8}{10}(2,000) = \$64.$$

Thus in this case insuring an L-type is more profitable than insuring an H-type.

Test your understanding of the concepts introduced in this section, by going through the exercises in Section 7.5.1 at the end of this chapter.

7.3 The monopolist under asymmetric information

We now turn to the case of asymmetric information, where each individual knows her own probability of loss, but the monopolist only knows that there are N_H high-risk individuals with probability of loss p_H and N_L low-risk individuals with probability of loss p_L.

We will consider three options for the monopolist:

Option 1. Cater only for the high-risk individuals by offering one insurance contract, designed in such a way that only the H-type will purchase it.

Option 2. Cater for both types of individuals, by offering one insurance contract that is attractive to both the L-type and the H-type.

Option 3. Offer a menu of two contracts: one – call it C_H – targeted to the H-type and the other – call it C_L – targeted to the L-type.

The shaded area in left pane of Figure 7.3 shows the set of insurance contracts that are attractive to the H-type, in that they yield at least the reservation utility to this type of individuals, while the shaded area in right pane shows the set of insurance contracts that are attractive to the L-type, in that they yield at least the reservation utility to this type of individuals. It is clear from Figure 7.3 that if an insurance contract is attractive to an L-type then it is also attractive to an H-type.

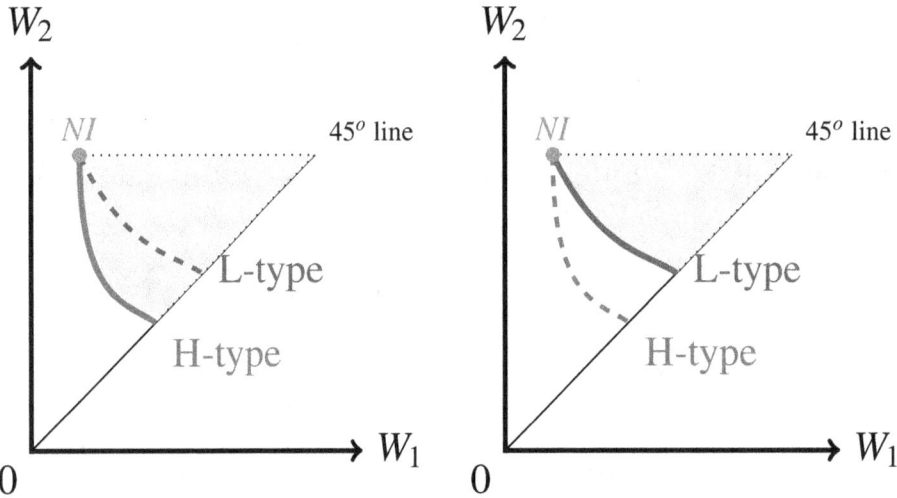

Figure 7.3: The shaded area in the left pane shows the set of insurance contracts that are acceptable to the H-type; the shaded area in the right pane shows the set of insurance contracts that are acceptable to the L-type.

7.3.1 The monopolist's profit under Option 1

If the monopolist chooses Option 1 then it will offer a contract that lies in the shaded area shown in Figure 7.4: the area between the two reservation indifference curves.

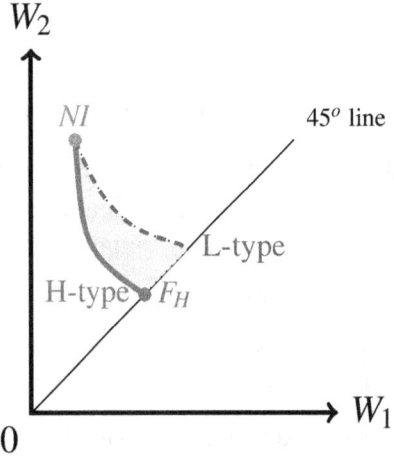

Figure 7.4: Contracts in the shaded area are acceptable to the H-type but not to the L-type.

Under Option 1, the monopolist caters only for one type of individuals, namely the H-type, and thus we can use the analysis of Chapter 5 (Section 5.2.1) and conclude that, in order to maximize its profits, it will offer the full-insurance contract that leaves the H-type indifferent between insuring and not insuring (shown as point F_H in Figure 7.4). Let h_{max}^H be the premium of this contract. Then the monopolist's total profits under Option 1, denoted by π_1, will be

$$\pi_1 = N_H \left(h_{max}^H - p_H \ell \right). \tag{7.4}$$

For example, if the individuals' initial wealth is $W_0 = 3,600$, the potential loss is $\ell = 2,000$, the utility-of-money function is $U(m) = \sqrt{m}$ and $p_H = \frac{8}{10}$, then, as calculated at the end of the previous section, $h_{max}^H = \$1,664$ and the expected profit from a single contract would be $1,664 - \frac{8}{10}(2,000) = \$64$, so that total profits would be $\$64 N_H$.

7.3.2 The monopolist's profit under Option 2

If the monopolist chooses Option 2 then it will offer a contract that lies in the shaded area shown in the right pane of Figure 7.3: the area on and above the reservation indifference curve of the L-type. Which of these contracts maximizes the monopolist's profits?

One might be tempted to infer from the analysis of Chapter 5 that the monopolist would offer the full-insurance contract at the intersection of the reservation indifference curve of the L-type and the 45° line. However this conclusion is not correct: the monopolist – under Option 2 – would prefer to offer (to everybody) a *partial*-insurance contract.

To see this, recall the reasoning developed in Chapter 5: the crucial step in that reasoning was to note that, at any point *not* on the 45° line, the reservation indifference curve of the L-type is steeper than the isoprofit line with slope $-\frac{p_L}{1-p_L}$, so that there are points to the right of the point under consideration which represent contracts that are acceptable to the L-type and yield higher profit to the insurer *if sold only to the L-types*. In other words, the line with slope $-\frac{p_L}{1-p_L}$ is a relevant isoprofit line only under the assumption that the insurer is dealing only with L-type individuals. However, as remarked above, *any contract that is acceptable to an L-type is also acceptable to an H-type* and thus offering such a contract implies that the expected profit from this contract is **not** $[h - p_L(\ell - d)]$ (where h is the premium and d the deductible), because the probability of receiving a claim from a customer should reflect the fact that some customers are L-types and others are H-types.

This is the essence of the notion of adverse selection: the contract that is offered determines the composition of the pool of applicants: if the insurer offers the full insurance contract with premium h_{max}^H determined in Section 7.3.1, the pool of applicants will consist entirely of H-types, while if the insurer offers a contract that is acceptable to the L-types then the pool of applicants will consist of all the individuals, L-types and H-types.

What is the probability of receiving a claim from a customer if an insurance contract is purchased by both types? Recall that q_H is the fraction of individuals in the population who are H-types (and $(1 - q_H)$ is the fraction of L-types; see (7.1) on page 184). Thus we can take q_H as the probability that any particular customer taken from the set of customers who submit a claim is an H-type (and $(1 - q_H)$ as the probability that she is an L-type). Thus the expected profit from a contract with premium h and deductible d which is purchased by both types is:

$$h - [q_H p_H (\ell - d) + (1 - q_H) p_L (\ell - d)] = h - [q_H p_H + (1 - q_H) p_L] (\ell - d). \quad (7.5)$$

We call the number $[q_H p_H + (1 - q_H) p_L]$ the *average probability of loss* and denote it by $\bar{p}$:

average probability of loss: $\bar{p} = q_H p_H + (1 - q_H) p_L.$ (7.6)

Note that, since $p_L < p_H$ and $0 < q_H < 1$,

$$p_L < \bar{p} < p_H. \quad (7.7)$$

Thus when both types are insured with the same contract, the relevant isoprofit line is a straight line with slope $-\frac{\bar{p}}{1-\bar{p}}$; we call isoprofit lines with this slope *average isoprofit lines*. It follows from (7.7) that

$$\frac{p_L}{1 - p_L} < \frac{\bar{p}}{1 - \bar{p}} < \frac{p_H}{1 - p_H}. \quad (7.8)$$

Of course, it is still true that at a point on the 45° line the slope of the L-type indifference curve is $-\frac{p_L}{1-p_L}$; however the straight line with this slope is no longer a relevant isoprofit line: the relevant isoprofit line has a slope of $-\frac{\bar{p}}{1-\bar{p}}$ and is thus steeper than the L-type indifference curve at that point. Figure 7.5 shows this for the reservation indifference curve of the L-type.

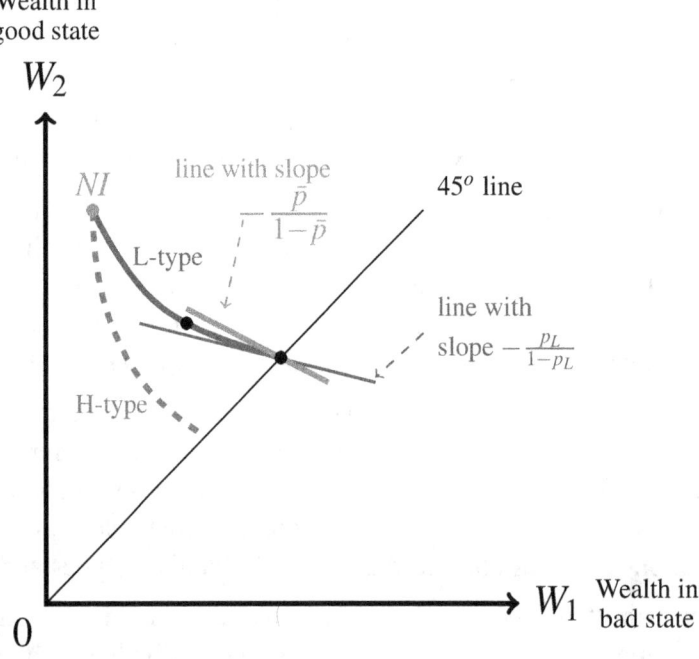

Figure 7.5: The reservation indifference curve of the L-type is less steep, at a point on the 45° line, than the average isoprofit line, whose slope is $-\frac{\bar{p}}{1-\bar{p}}$.

Given the relative slope of the L-type reservation indifference curve and the average isoprofit line at a full-insurance contract, such a contract cannot be profit-maximizing under Option 2: there will be contracts to the left of it (thus partial-insurance contracts) that are acceptable to the L-type (and thus to both types) and are below that average isoprofit line (and thus yield higher expected profits). Of course, this argument applies to any contract where the average isoprofit line is steeper than the L-type reservation indifference curve. Hence, the profit-maximizing choice for the monopolist under Option 2 is that contract on the L-type reservation indifference curve where there is a tangency between the indifference curve and the average isoprofit line, as shown in Figure 7.6.

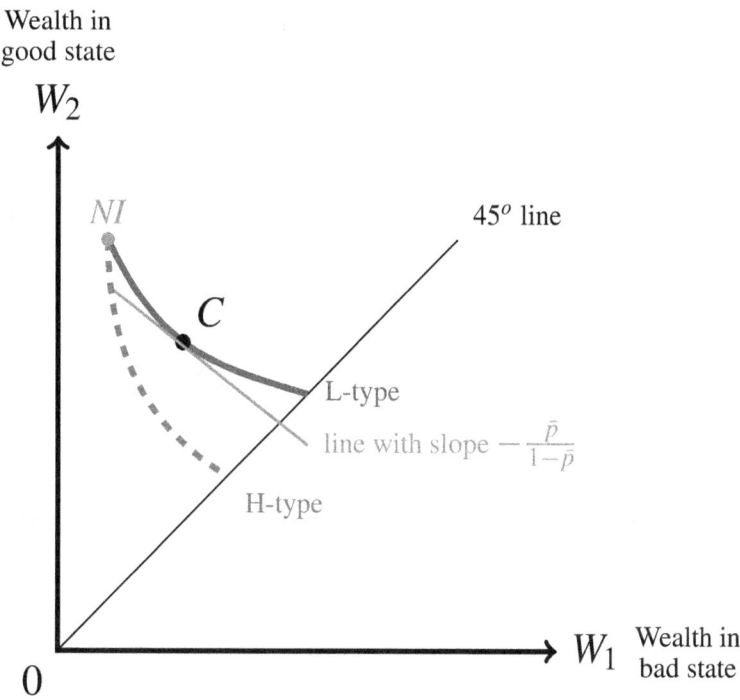

Figure 7.6: C is the profit-maximizing contract for the monopolist under Option 2.

The existence of such a contract is guaranteed if and only if the slope of the L-type reservation indifference curve at the no-insurance point is, in absolute value, greater than $\frac{\bar{p}}{1-\bar{p}}$.[4] On the other hand, if the slope of the L-type reservation indifference curve at the no-insurance point is, in absolute value, less than $\frac{\bar{p}}{1-\bar{p}}$, then Option 2 cannot yield positive profits. The reason for this is that the average isoprofit line that goes through the no-insurance point is the zero-profit line and thus every contract that is acceptable to the L-types will be above the zero profit line, which means that it would yield negative profits.

---

[4] If this condition is satisfied, then at NI the slope of the indifference curve is larger than $\frac{\bar{p}}{1-\bar{p}}$ and at a point on the 45° line it is smaller than $\frac{\bar{p}}{1-\bar{p}}$; thus, by the Intermediate Value Theorem, there must be a point along the curve where it is equal.

If Option 2 is profitable, the profit-maximizing contract under this option, let us denote it by $C = (W_1^C, W_2^C)$, is given by the solution to the following equations:

$$p_L U(W_1^C) + (1 - p_L) U(W_2^C) = p_L U(W_0 - \ell) + (1 - p_L) U(W_0) \tag{7.9}$$

$$\frac{p_L}{1 - p_L} \left(\frac{U'(W_1^C)}{U'(W_2^C)} \right) = \frac{\bar{p}}{1 - \bar{p}}. \tag{7.10}$$

Equation (7.9) states that an L-type individual is indifferent between contract C and no insurance, that is, contract C lies on the reservation indifference curve for the L-type; equation (7.10) states that, at point C, the reservation indifference curve of the L-type is tangent to (has the same slope as) the average isoprofit line.

As an example, let us revisit the case considered at the end of Section 7.2.1 where the individuals' initial wealth is $W_0 = 3,600$, potential loss is $\ell = 2,000$, the utility-of-money function is $U(m) = \sqrt{m}$, $p_L = \frac{3}{10}$ and $p_H = \frac{8}{10}$; furthermore, let $N_H = 2,400$ and $N_L = 3,900$, so that $q_H = \frac{8}{21}$. Thus the average probability of loss is

$$\bar{p} = \frac{8}{21} \left(\frac{8}{10} \right) + \frac{13}{21} \left(\frac{3}{10} \right) = \frac{103}{210}.$$

To see if Option 2 is profitable, we check if the L-type reservation indifference curve is steeper, at the no-insurance point $NI = (1600, 3600)$, than the average isoprofit line; that is, we check if

$$\frac{p_L}{1 - p_L} \left(\frac{U'(1,600)}{U'(3,600)} \right) > \frac{\bar{p}}{1 - \bar{p}}. \tag{7.11}$$

Since

$$\frac{p_L}{1 - p_L} \left(\frac{U'(1,600)}{U'(3,600)} \right) = \frac{\frac{3}{10}}{\frac{7}{10}} \left(\frac{\frac{1}{80}}{\frac{1}{120}} \right) = \frac{9}{14} = 0.6429$$

and

$$\frac{\bar{p}}{1 - \bar{p}} = \frac{\frac{103}{210}}{\frac{107}{210}} = 0.9626,$$

inequality (7.11) is not satisfied and thus Option 2 is **not** profitable.

Let us now change the value of N_L from 3,900 to 44,000: $N_L = 44,000$ (while everything else remains as above). Then $q_H = \frac{2,400}{2,400+44,000} = \frac{3}{58}$ so that

$$\bar{p} = \frac{3}{58} \left(\frac{8}{10} \right) + \frac{55}{58} \left(\frac{3}{10} \right) = \frac{189}{580} = 0.3259$$

and thus inequality (7.11) is satisfied and Option 2 is profitable. The profit-maximizing contract under Option 2, denoted by $C = (W_1^C, W_2^C)$, is given by the solution to the following equations (which correspond to equations (7.9) and (7.10)):

$$\frac{3}{10}\sqrt{W_1^C} + \frac{7}{10}\sqrt{W_2^C} = \frac{3}{10}\sqrt{1,600} + \frac{7}{10}\sqrt{3,600}$$

$$\frac{\frac{3}{10}}{\frac{7}{10}}\left(\frac{\frac{1}{2\sqrt{W_1^C}}}{\frac{1}{2\sqrt{W_2^C}}}\right) = \frac{\frac{189}{580}}{\frac{391}{580}}.$$

The solution is $W_1^C = 2,456.53$ and $W_2^C = 3,124.97$, that is, $C = (2456.53, 3124.97)$; the corresponding premium is $3,600 - 3,124.97 = \$475.03$ and the deductible is $3,124.97 - 2,456.53 = \$668.44$ so that the expected profit from a single contract is

$$475.03 - \bar{p}(2,000 - 668.44) = 475.03 - \frac{189}{580}(1,331.56) = \$41.13$$

and total expected profits are

$$41.13\,(N_L + N_H) = 41.13(2,400 + 44,000) = \$1,908,432.$$

7.3.3 The monopolist's profit under Option 3

If the monopolist chooses Option 3 then it will offer two contracts: one contract– call it C_H – targeted to the H-type and the other contract – call it C_L – targeted to the L-type. Let us express these contracts in terms of premium and deductible and denote them by

$$C_H = (h_H, d_H) \qquad \text{and} \qquad C_L = (h_L, d_L).$$

We shall use the following abbreviations:

$\mathbb{E}_H[U(NI)]$ H-type's expected utility from no insurance
$\mathbb{E}_L[U(NI)]$ L-type's expected utility from no insurance
$\mathbb{E}_H[U(C_H)]$ H-type's expected utility from contract C_H
$\mathbb{E}_L[U(C_H)]$ L-type's expected utility from contract C_H
$\mathbb{E}_H[U(C_L)]$ H-type's expected utility from contract C_L
$\mathbb{E}_L[U(C_L)]$ L-type's expected utility from contract C_L.

Thus

$$\begin{aligned}
\mathbb{E}_H[U(NI)] &= p_H U(W_0 - \ell) + (1 - p_H)U(W_0) \\
\mathbb{E}_L[U(NI)] &= p_L U(W_0 - \ell) + (1 - p_L)U(W_0) \\
\mathbb{E}_H[U(C_H)] &= p_H U(W_0 - h_H - d_H) + (1 - p_H)U(W_0 - h_H) \\
\mathbb{E}_L[U(C_H)] &= p_L U(W_0 - h_H - d_H) + (1 - p_L)U(W_0 - h_H) \\
\mathbb{E}_H[U(C_L)] &= p_H U(W_0 - h_L - d_L) + (1 - p_H)U(W_0 - h_L) \\
\mathbb{E}_L[U(C_L)] &= p_L U(W_0 - h_L - d_L) + (1 - p_L)U(W_0 - h_L).
\end{aligned}$$

In order for contract C_H to be chosen by H-type individuals two conditions must be satisfied:

$$\mathbb{E}_H[U(C_H)] \geq \mathbb{E}_H[U(NI)] \qquad\qquad\qquad (IR_H)$$

$$\mathbb{E}_H[U(C_H)] \geq \mathbb{E}_H[U(C_L)] \qquad\qquad\qquad (IC_H)$$

The first condition, (IR_H), is called the *Individual Rationality constraint for type H* and says that the H-types must consider the contract targeted to them to be at least as good as no insurance. The second condition, (IC_H), is called the *Incentive Compatibility constraint for type H* and says that the H-types must consider the contract targeted to them to be at least as good as the other contract that is offered (namely C_L).

Similarly, in order for contract C_L to be chosen by L-type individuals two conditions must be satisfied:

$$\mathbb{E}_L[U(C_L)] \geq \mathbb{E}_L[U(NI)] \tag{IR_L}$$

$$\mathbb{E}_L[U(C_L)] \geq \mathbb{E}_L[U(C_H)] \tag{IC_L}$$

The first condition, (IR_L), is the *Individual Rationality constraint for type L*: it says that the L-types must consider the contract targeted to them to be at least as good as no insurance. The second condition, (IC_L), is he *Incentive Compatibility constraint for type L*: it says that the L-types must consider the contract targeted to them to be at least as good as the other contract that is offered (namely C_H).

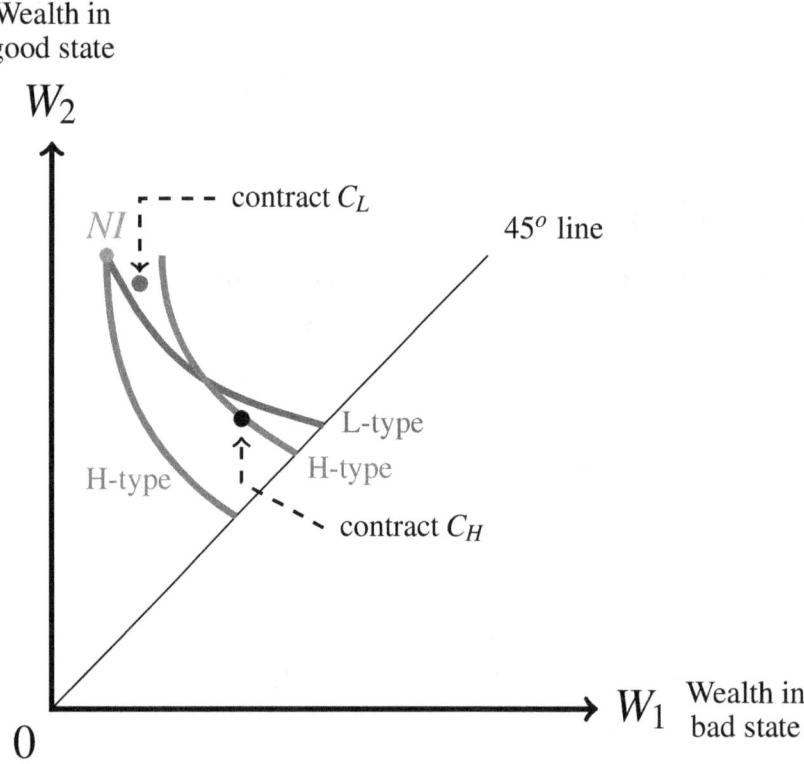

Figure 7.7: Two contracts that satisfy the four constraints.

Figure 7.7 shows a pair of contracts that satisfy all four constraints as strict inequalities: (1) contract C_H is strictly above the H-type reservation indifference curve and thus (IR_H) is satisfied as a strict inequality, (2) contract C_L is to the left of the H-type indifference curve that goes through contract C_H and thus (IC_H) is satisfied as a strict inequality, (3) contract C_L is strictly above the L-type reservation indifference curve and thus (IR_L) is satisfied as a strict inequality and (4) contract C_H is worse than contract C_L for the L-type (indeed, it is even worse than no insurance).

On the other hand, Figure 7.8 shows a pair of contracts where the (IC_H) and (IR_L) constraints are satisfied as equalities while the other two constraints are satisfied as strict inequalities.

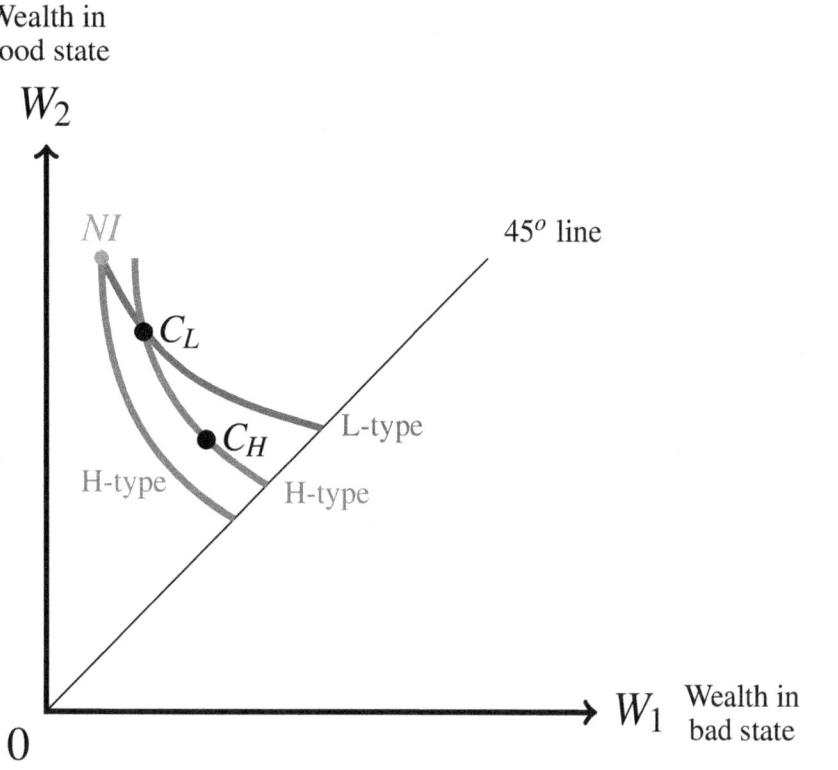

Figure 7.8: Another pair of contracts that satisfy the four constraints.

From now on, *we will assume that, if indifferent between contract C_H and contract C_L the H-types will choose contract C_H.* Furthermore, we will continue to assume that, if indifferent between insuring and not insuring, each individual will choose to insure.

If the monopolist offers a menu of two contracts, C_H and C_L, that satisfy the four constraints, then the H-types will purchase contract $C_H = (h_H, d_H)$ and the L-types will purchase contract $C_L = (h_L, d_L)$ and thus the monopolist's expected total profits will be

$$\pi_3 = N_H \left[h_H - p_H \left(\ell - d_H \right) \right] + N_L \left[h_L - p_L \left(\ell - d_L \right) \right].$$

Thus the monopolist, under Option 3, faces the following maximization problem:

$$\underset{h_H, d_H, h_L, d_L}{Max} \quad \pi_3 = N_H \left[h_H - p_H \left(\ell - d_H \right) \right] + N_L \left[h_L - p_L \left(\ell - d_L \right) \right]$$

subject to

$(IR_H) \quad \mathbb{E}_H [U(C_H)] \geq \mathbb{E}_H [U(NI)]$

$(IC_H) \quad \mathbb{E}_H [U(C_H)] \geq \mathbb{E}_H [U(C_L)]$

$(IR_L) \quad \mathbb{E}_L [U(C_L)] \geq \mathbb{E}_L [U(NI)]$

$(IC_L) \quad \mathbb{E}_L [U(C_L)] \geq \mathbb{E}_L [U(C_H)]$

Let us study this maximization problem.

We showed at the beginning of this section (see Figure 7.3) that, if an insurance contract is acceptable to the L-type (in that it lies on or above the L-type's reservation indifference curve), then it is acceptable to the H-type too (that is, it lies on or above the H-type's reservation indifference curve); thus

$$\mathbb{E}_L[U(C_L)] \geq \mathbb{E}_L[U(NI)] \quad \text{implies that} \quad \mathbb{E}_H[U(C_L)] \geq \mathbb{E}_H[U(NI)]. \quad (7.12)$$

It follows that the (IR_H) constraint can be derived from the (IR_L) and (IC_H) constraints:

- by (IR_L), $\mathbb{E}_L[U(C_L)] \geq \mathbb{E}_L[U(NI)]$, which, by (7.12) implies

$$\mathbb{E}_H[U(C_L)] \geq \mathbb{E}_H[U(NI)]; \quad (7.13)$$

- by (IC_H), $\mathbb{E}_H[U(C_H)] \geq \mathbb{E}_H[U(C_L)]$ and this, together with (7.13) yields the (IR_H) constraint: $\mathbb{E}_H[U(C_H)] \geq \mathbb{E}_H[U(NI)]$.

Thus:

♦ **First observation:** the (IR_H) constraint is redundant.

Hence the monopolist's maximization problem can be simplified to:

$$\underset{h_H, d_H, h_L, d_L}{Max} \quad \pi_3 = N_H \left[h_H - p_H (\ell - d_H)\right] + N_L \left[h_L - p_L (\ell - d_L)\right]$$

subject to:

$$(IC_H) \quad \overbrace{p_H U (W_0 - h_H - d_H) + (1 - p_H) U (W_0 - h_H)}^{\mathbb{E}_H[U(C_H)]}$$

$$\geq \underbrace{p_H U (W_0 - h_L - d_L) + (1 - p_H) U (W_0 - h_L)}_{\mathbb{E}_H[U(C_L)]}$$

$$(IR_L) \quad \overbrace{p_L U (W_0 - h_L - d_L) + (1 - p_L) U (W_0 - h_L)}^{\mathbb{E}_L[U(C_L)]} \quad (7.14)$$

$$\geq \underbrace{p_L U (W_0 - \ell) + (1 - p_L) U (W_0)}_{\mathbb{E}_L[U(NI)]}$$

$$(IC_L) \quad \overbrace{p_L U (W_0 - h_L - d_L) + (1 - p_L) U (W_0 - h_L)}^{\mathbb{E}_L[U(C_L)]}$$

$$\geq \underbrace{p_L U (W_0 - h_H - d_H) + (1 - p_L) U (W_0 - h_H)}_{\mathbb{E}_L[U(C_H)]}$$

♦ **Second observation:** at a solution of the above maximization problem, the (IC_H) constraint must be satisfied as an equality, that is, contracts C_H and C_L must be on the same indifference curve for the H-type (as illustrated in Figure 7.8 on page 193).

To see this, start with two contracts (C_H) and (C_L) that satisfy the above three constraints and suppose that $\mathbb{E}_H[U(C_H)] > \mathbb{E}_H[U(C_L)]$. Modify contract C_H by increasing the premium h_H up to the point where (IC_H) is satisfied as an equality, that is, up to the point where $\mathbb{E}_H[U(C_H)] = \mathbb{E}_H[U(C_L)]$.[5] Then profits will increase, since π_3 is increasing in h_H, and thus the initial pair $\{C_H, C_L\}$ could not have been a solution to the maximization problem.[6]

So far we have concluded that the solution to the initial constrained optimization problem requires that the two contracts C_H and C_L must be on the same indifference curve for the H-type.

- ♦ **Third observation:** at a solution of the maximization problem (7.14), contract C_L – which, by the second observation, must be on the same H-type indifference curve as contract C_H – must be above contract C_H.

To see this, suppose that contract C_H were above contract C_L, as shown in Figure 7.9.

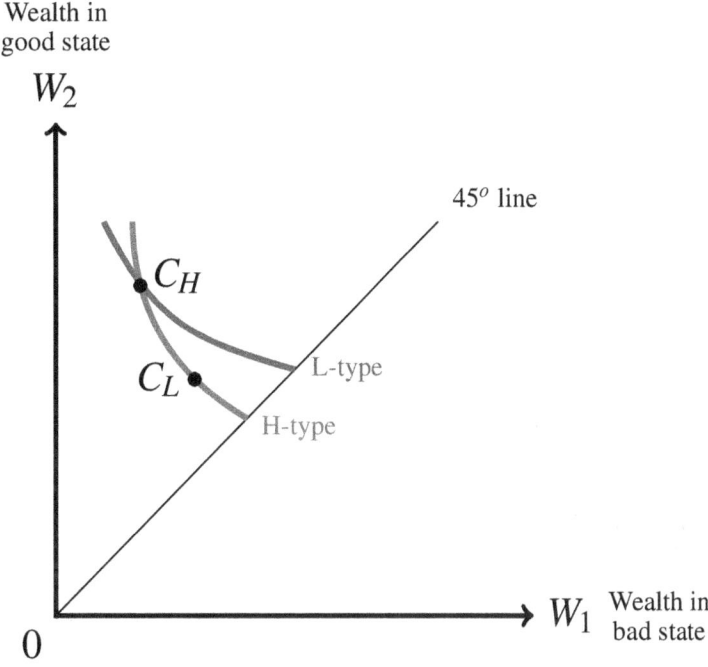

Figure 7.9: Contract C_H – which, by the second observation, must be on the same H-type indifference curve as contract C_L – cannot be above contract C_L.

Then we can draw the indifference curve of the L-type that goes through contract C_H: it will be less steep than the indifference curve of the H-type and thus contract C_L will be below this L-type indifference curve, implying the the L-type would strictly prefer contract C_H to contact C_L, contradicting the incentive compatibility constraint for the L-type, (IC_L).

---

[5]The right-hand side of (IC_H) is independent of h_H while the left-hand side is decreasing in h_H.

[6]Note that an increase in h_H does not affect the (IR_L) constraint (both sides of it are independent of h_H), while it reinforces the (IC_L) constraint, since the left-hand side of (IC_L) is independent of h_H, while the right-hand side is decreasing in h_H; thus if the (IC_L) constraint was satisfied to start with, then it will continue to be satisfied after the increase in h_H.

Thus, by the second and third observation, the two contracts C_H and C_L must be on the same H-type indifference curve, with C_L above C_H, as shown in Figure 7.10.[7]

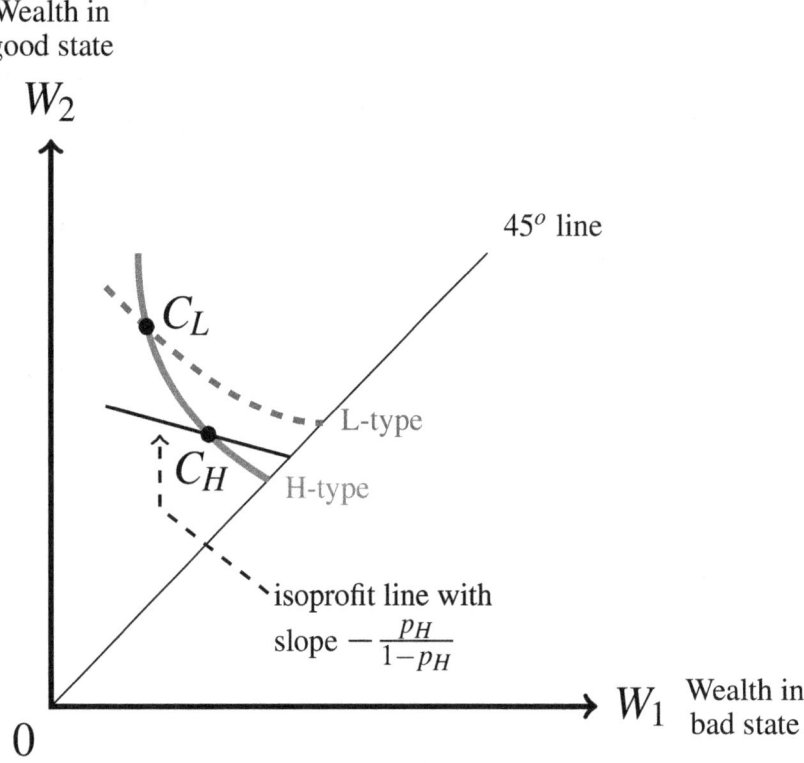

Figure 7.10: Contract C_H cannot be above the 45° line.

♦ **Fourth observation:** at a solution of the maximization problem (7.14), contract C_H must be a full-insurance contract.

To see this, suppose that C_H is not a full-insurance contract, that is, suppose that it lies above the 45° line. Then, as we know from Chapter 5, the H-type indifference curve is steeper at point C_H than the isoprofit line with slope $-\frac{p_H}{1-p_H}$, as shown in Figure 7.10. This is indeed a relevant isoprofit line, because – by the (IC_L) constraint – contract C_H will be purchased only by the H-types. Hence there are points below contract C_H, on the H-type indifference curve, that will yield higher profits to the monopolist, since any such contract would still be bought only by the H-types.[8]

---

[7]To reach this conclusion one also needs to rule out the possibility that $C_H = C_L$. This is a consequence of the fourth observation below: starting from $C_H = C_L$ above the 45° line, the monopolist could increase its profits by separating C_H from C_L and moving it, along the H-type indifference curve, towards the 45° line; on the other hand, if – to start with – $C_H = C_L$ is already on the 45° line, then, by the (IC_L) constraint it must be on or above the reservation indifference curve for the L-type and we know from the analysis of Option 2 that this is not a profit-maximizing configuration.

[8]Moving contract C_H towards the 45° line, along the H-type indifference curve, will not alter the (IR_L) constraint (which is independent of h_H and d_H) and will make contract C_H even less attractive than contract C_L for the L-type, that is, the (IC_L) constraint will still hold.

◆ **Fifth observation:** at a solution of the maximization problem (7.14), the (IR_L) constraint must be satisfied as an equality, that is, contract C_L must be on the reservation indifference curve of the L-type.

To see this, consider the situation depicted in Figure 7.11 where contract C_L is above the reservation indifference curve of the L-type (and – in accordance with the previous observations – C_L and C_H lie on the same indifference curve of the H-type; furthermore, C_H is a full-insurance contract, that is, it lies on the 45° line). Draw the isoprofit line with slope $-\frac{p_L}{1-p_L}$ that goes through contract C_L. We know from Chapter 5 that the H-type indifference curve at point C_L is steeper than the line with slope $-\frac{p_H}{1-p_H}$ which, in turn, is steeper than the line with slope $-\frac{p_L}{1-p_L}$. Thus there are points on the H-type indifference curve (to which both C_L and C_H belong) that are below this isoprofit line. Modify C_L contract by moving it along the H-type indifference curve up to the point where it intersects the reservation indifference curve of the L-type, that is, until the (IR_L) constraint is satisfied as an equality. Then the (IC_H) constraint is not affected (it is still satisfied as an equality) and the (IC_L) constraint is also not affected, since contract C_H is still worse, for the L-type, than the modified contract C_L. Thus the new C_L contract is still purchased only by the L-types and hence yields higher profits to the monopolist than the original C_L contract (since the new contract is below the isoprofit line with slope $-\frac{p_L}{1-p_L}$ that goes through the original contract).

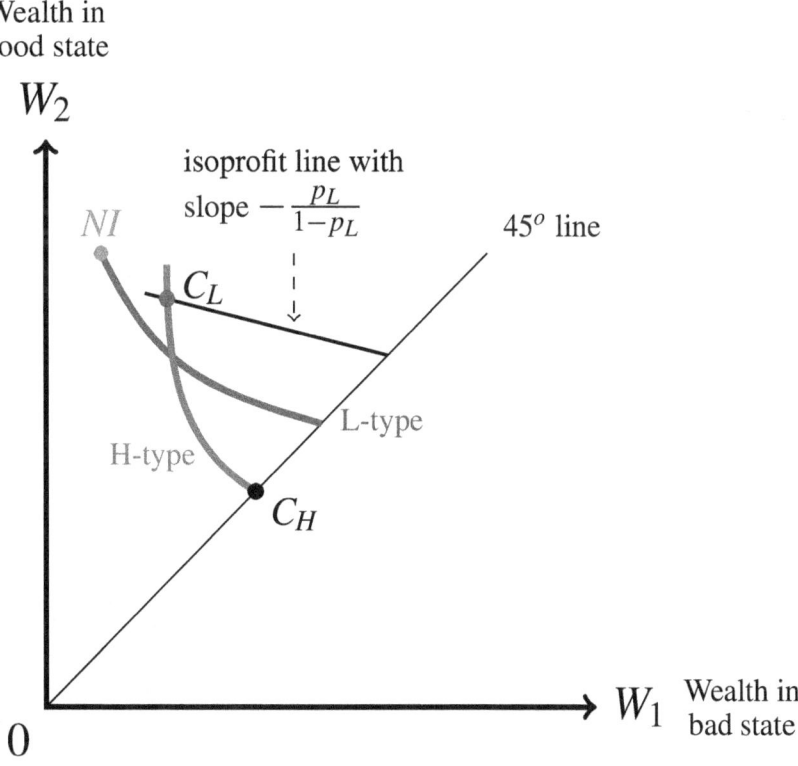

Figure 7.11: Contract C_L cannot be above the L-type reservation indifference curve.

We conclude from the above five observations that

> The pair of contracts (C_H, C_L)
> is a solution of the maximization problem (7.14) only if
> - C_H is on the 45° line and
> - C_L lies at the intersection of
>   (1) the indifference curve of the H-type that goes through C_H and
>   (2) the indifference curve of the L-type that goes through NI.

Fix an arbitrary premium h_H for the full-insurance contract C_H (thus $d_H = 0$), such that C_H lies on the segment of the 45° line between F_H and F_L, where F_H is the point of intersection of the reservation indifference curve of the H-type and the 45° line and F_L is the point of intersection of the reservation indifference curve of the L-type and the 45° line: see Figure 7.12. Then the contract C_L at the intersection of the reservation indifference curve of the L-type and the indifference curve of the H-type that goes through contract C_H is uniquely determined; hence we can think of this contract C_L as a function of h_H:

$$C_L(h_H) = (h_L(h_H), d_L(h_H)). \qquad (7.15)$$

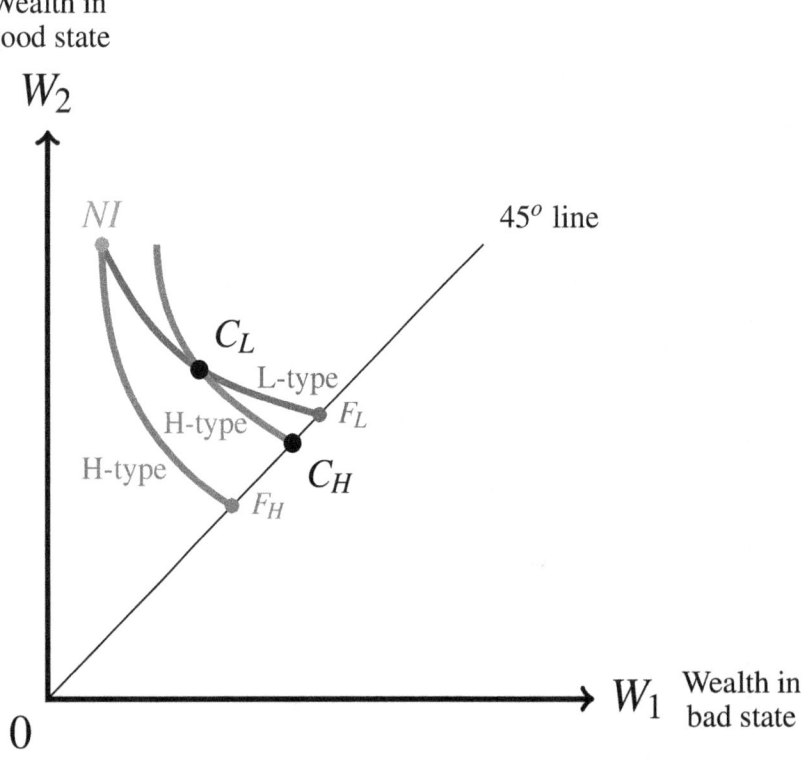

Figure 7.12: Contract C_L is uniquely determined by the choice of contract C_H on the segment of the 45° line between points F_H and F_L.

Then the constrained maximization problem (7.14) can be reduced to the following unconstrained maximization problem:

$$\underset{h_H \in [h_{max}^L, h_{max}^H]}{Max} \pi_3(h_H) = N_H(h_H - p_H \ell) + N_L[h_L(h_H) - p_L(\ell - d_L(h_H))] \quad (7.16)$$

where h_{max}^L is the maximum premium that the L-type is willing to pay for full insurance (the premium of contract F_L in Figure 7.12) and h_{max}^H is the maximum premium that the H-type is willing to pay for full insurance (the premium of contract F_H in Figure 7.12).

ⓡ Note that one possible choice under Option 3 is to set $h_H = h_{max}^H$, that is, to choose $C_H = F_H$ (see Figure 7.12), in which case the corresponding contract for the L-type is the trivial contract with $h_L = 0$ and $d_L = \ell$, that is, $C_L = NI$. This amounts to insuring only the H-types, with the full-insurance contract that was obtained as the profit-maximizing contract under Option 1. Thus *Option 1 is a special case of Option 3*.

Before we discuss the solution to (7.16) in general, let us consider a numerical example.

Let the following be common to all individuals: initial wealth $W_0 = 1,600$, potential loss $\ell = 700$ and vNM utility-of-money function $U(m) = \sqrt{m}$. The H-types face a probability of loss $p_H = \frac{1}{5}$ while the L-types face a probability of loss $p_L = \frac{1}{10}$.

- To find h_{max}^L solve the equation

$$\frac{1}{10}\sqrt{900} + \frac{9}{10}\sqrt{1,600} = \sqrt{1,600 - h}.$$

  The solution is $h_{max}^L = 79$.

- To find h_{max}^H solve the equation

$$\frac{1}{5}\sqrt{900} + \frac{4}{5}\sqrt{1,600} = \sqrt{1,600 - h}.$$

  The solution is $h_{max}^H = 156$.

Given $h_H \in [79, 156]$, contract C_L is given by the solution to the following pair of equations:

$$\frac{1}{10}\sqrt{900} + \frac{9}{10}\sqrt{1,600} = \frac{1}{10}\sqrt{1,600 - h_L - d_L} + \frac{9}{10}\sqrt{1,600 - h_L}$$

$$(7.17)$$

$$\frac{1}{5}\sqrt{1,600 - h_L - d_L} + \frac{4}{5}\sqrt{1,600 - h_L} = \sqrt{1,600 - h_H}.$$

The first equation states that C_L lies on the reservation indifference curve of the L-type and the second equation states that C_L lies on the indifference curve of the H-type that goes through the full-insurance contract C_H with premium h_H. The solution to (7.17) is

$$h_L(h_H) = h_H + 156\sqrt{1,600 - h_H} - 6,084 \quad (7.18)$$

$$d_L(h_H) = 80 h_H + 5,460\sqrt{1,600 - h_H} - 219,260. \quad (7.19)$$

Let there be a total of N individuals and let q_H be the fraction of type-H individuals (thus $N_H = q_H N$), so that $(1 - q_H)$ is the fraction of type-L individuals (thus $N_L = (1 - q_H)N$). Then the monopolist's objective is to choose that value of $h_H \in [79, 156]$ that maximizes the function

$$\pi_3(h_H) = N \left[q_H \left(h_H - p_H \, 700 \right) + (1 - q_H) \left[h_L(h_H) - p_L(700 - d_L(h_H)) \right] \right] \quad (7.20)$$

where $h_L(h_H)$ and $d_L(h_H)$ are given by (7.18) and (7.19), respectively. The solution of this maximization problem depends on the value of q_H, that is, on how many H-types there are relative to the L-types.

For example, if $q_H = \frac{1}{20}$ then the graph of the profit function (7.20) is shown in Figure 7.13. The profit-maximizing value of h_H is an interior point of the interval $[79, 156]$, namely 96.64. Replacing this value in (7.18) and (7.19) we obtain $h_L = 61.26$ and $d_L = 172.80$. Thus the monopolist offers a full-insurance contract $C_H = (h_H = 96.64, d_H = 0)$ and a partial-insurance contract $C_L = (h_L = 61.26, d_L = 172.80)$ and the H-types purchase contract C_H while the L-types purchase contract C_L. We call such a situation a *separating equilibrium*, since the monopolist – through the menu of contracts it offers – is able to induce a separation of the types: all the individuals of one type purchase one contract and all the individuals of the other type purchase the other contract.

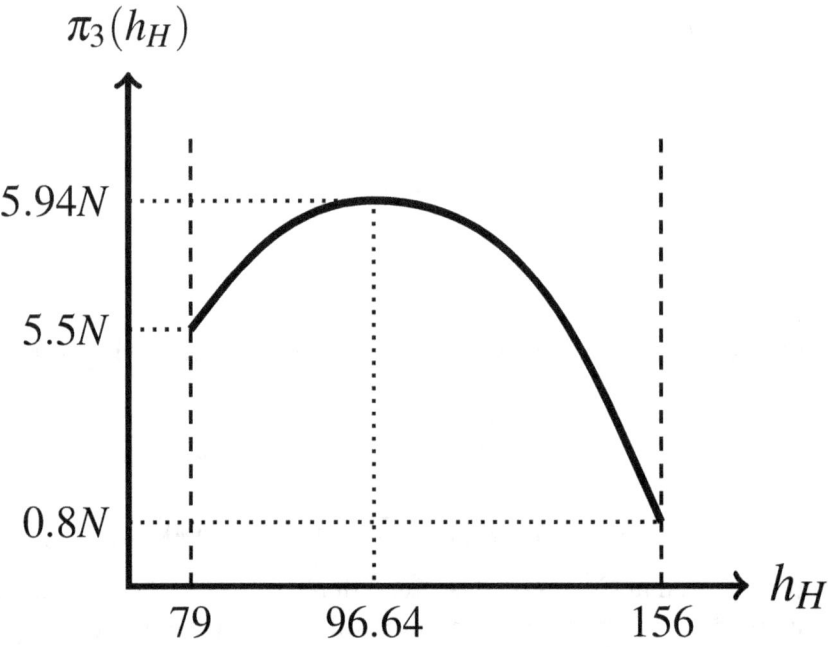

Figure 7.13: The graph of the profit function (7.20) when $q_H = \frac{1}{20}$.

Now consider the case where $q_H = \frac{1}{5}$. For this case the graph of the profit function (7.20) is shown in Figure 7.14. It is clear from the graph that in this case the solution of the profit-maximizing problem is a corner solution at $h_H = h^H_{max} = 156$ and only the H-types insure (the contract targeted to the L-types is the trivial contract with $h_L = 0$ and $d_L = 700$: see the remark on page 199).

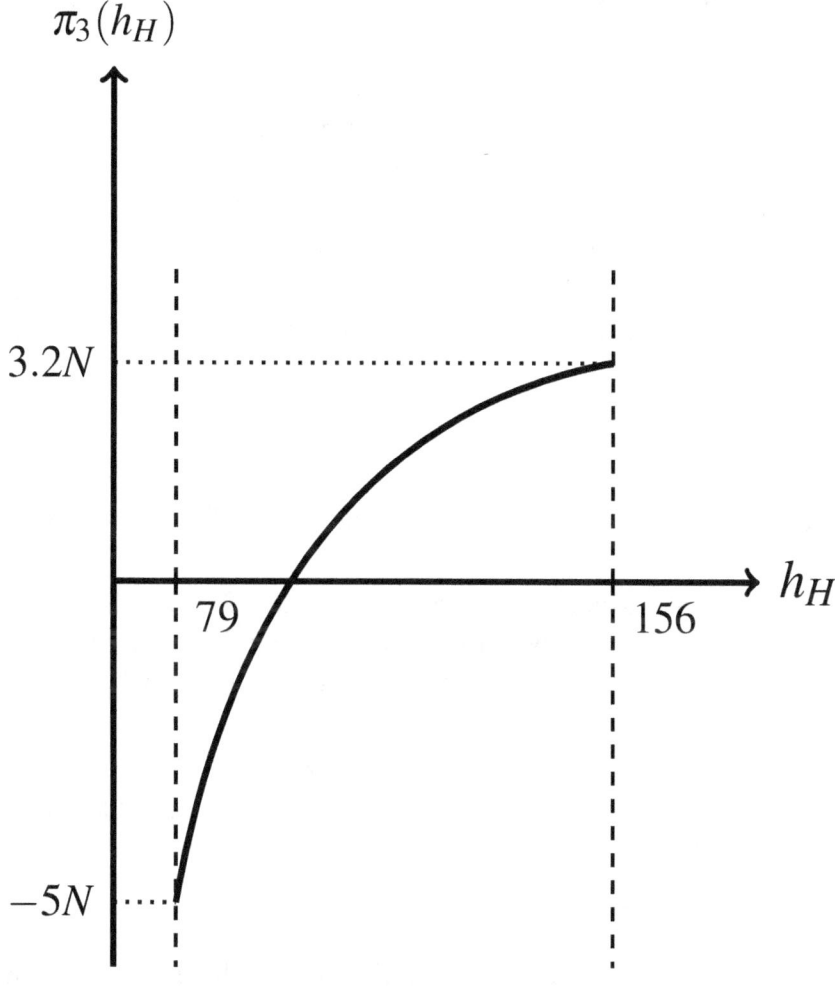

Figure 7.14: The graph of the profit function (7.20) when $q_H = \frac{1}{5}$.

The above example illustrates a general feature of the profit-maximization under Option 3:

⊛ When q_H is "sufficiently close to 1" (that is, when the number of H-types is large relative to the entire population of potential customers), the monopolist will choose to insure only the H-types by offering the full-insurance contract with premium h_{max}^H (that is, the solution to the profit maximization problem (7.16) given on page 199 is the corner solution, as illustrated in Figure 7.14). As a consequence, the (IR_H) constraint is satisfied as an equality.

⊛ Otherwise the monopolist will offer two contracts:

   (1) a full-insurance contract C_H with premium $h_H < h_{max}^H$, which will be purchased by the H-types, who therefore enjoy a surplus (that is, they are strictly better off than with no insurance or, in other words, the (IR_H) constraint is satisfied as a strict inequality), and

   (2) a partial-insurance contract which will be purchased by the L-types, located at the intersection of the reservation indifference curve of the L-types and the indifference curve of the H-types that goes through contract C_H (thus the (IR_L) and (IC_H) constraints are satisfied as equalities while the (IR_H) and (IC_L) constraints are satisfied as strict inequalities).

The expression "q_H sufficiently close to 1" is rather vague: its exact meaning depends on the specific values of the parameters. For instance, it can be shown that, in the example considered above, "q_H sufficiently close to 1" means $q_H \geq \frac{9}{47} = 0.1915$.[9]

7.3.4 Option 2 revisited

We saw above that Option 1 can be viewed as a subcase of Option 3. Now we compare Option 2 and Option 3.

Recall that the profit-maximizing contract under Option 2 (if it exists) is that contract on the reservation indifference curve of the L-type where the slope of the indifference curve is equal to the slope of the average profit line, which is $-\frac{\bar{p}}{1-\bar{p}}$, where $\bar{p}$ is the average probability of loss, that is,

$$\bar{p} = q_H p_H + (1 - p_H) p_L.$$

Denote the maximum profits that the monopolist can make under Option 2 by π_2^*. If $B = (h_B, d_B)$ is the profit-maximizing contract under Option 2 then

$$\pi_2^* = (N_H + N_L)\left[h_B - \bar{p}\left(\ell - d_B\right)\right],$$

where N_H is the number of individuals of type H and N_L is the number of individuals of type L.

---

[9]Thus, in that example, if $q_H \geq \frac{9}{47}$ then the monopolist will choose to insure only the H-types, while if $q_H < \frac{9}{47}$ then the monopolist will implement a separating two-contract solution. To find this critical value of q_H, first calculate the derivative of the function $\pi_3(h_H)$ given in (7.20) and evaluate it at the corner point $h_H = 156$; this will give an expression in terms of q_H and then set this expression equal to zero and solve for q_H. In this case the solution is $q_H = \frac{9}{47}$; hence if $q_H \geq \frac{9}{47}$ then the function $\pi_3(h_H)$ is increasing or constant at $h_H = 156$ and thus the function is maximized at $h_H = 156$, while if $q_H < \frac{9}{47}$ then the function $\pi_3(h_H)$ is decreasing at $h_H = 156$ and thus the function is maximized at a point to the left of $h_H = 156$.

We want to show that $\pi_2^* < \pi_3^*$, where π_3^* is the maximum profit that the monopolist can make under Option 3.

Figure 7.15 shows the contract, denoted by B, that maximizes profits under Option 2. If the monopolist offers only this contract, then both types of individuals will purchase it. Suppose that the monopolist switches from a one-contract menu containing only contract B to a two-contract menu $\{B, F\}$ obtained by adding to contract B also the full-insurance contract F given by the intersection of the H-type indifference curve that goes through B and the 45° line, as shown in Figure 7.15. Then the L-types will continue to buy contract B (since it is strictly better for them that the newly added contract F), while the H-types will switch to contract F.[10] Thus profits from the L-types will not change, but profits from the H-types will increase.[11] The pair of contracts $\{B, F\}$ satisfies all the constraints considered under Option 3 (namely, IR_H, IC_H, IR_L, IC_L) and yields profits that are larger than π_2^*; thus π_3^* (which may be even larger) is greater than π_2^*.

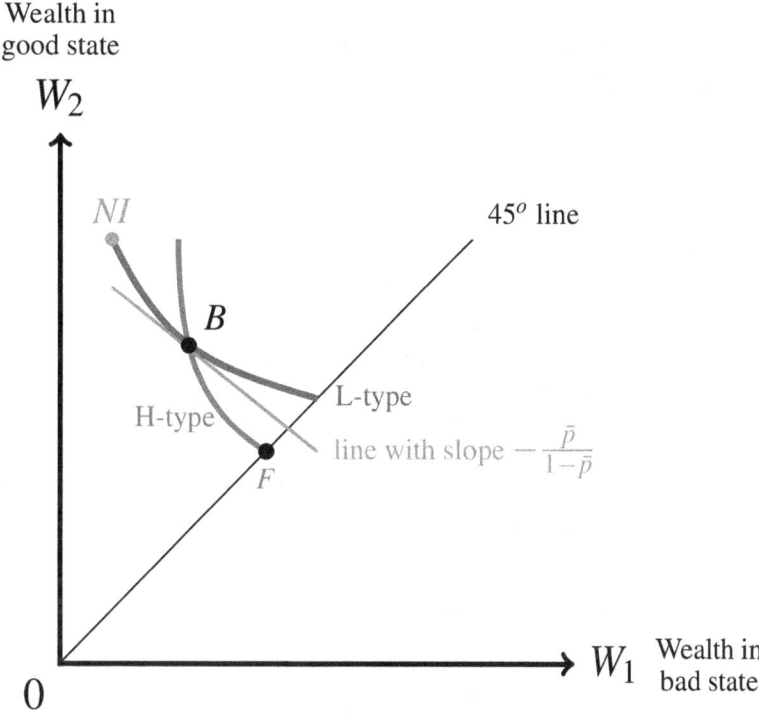

Figure 7.15: Option 2 is inferior to Option 3.

Test your understanding of the concepts introduced in this section, by going through the exercises in Section 7.5.2 at the end of this chapter.

---

[10] As usual, we assume that, if indifferent, the H-types will choose the contract targeted to them. Otherwise the newly offered contract would have to be slightly above contract F on the 45° line.

[11] Because of the usual argument that at a point above the 45° line, such as point B in Figure 7.15, the H-type indifference curve is steeper than the isoprofit line with slope $-\frac{p_H}{1-p_H}$, which is the relevant isoprofit line if we consider contracts on the portion of the H-type indifference curve between point B and point F, since those contracts would be purchased only by the H-types.

7.4   A perfectly competitive insurance industry

In Chapters 2 and 5 (Sections 2.6.4 and 5.2.2) we studied the equilibrium in a perfectly competitive insurance industry with free entry when there is only one type of potential customer. Now we extend the analysis to the case of asymmetric information with two types of individuals. We continue to assume that all the individuals are identical in terms of initial wealth W_0 and potential loss ℓ (with $0 < \ell \leq W_0$); furthermore, hey also have the same vNM utility-of-money function $U(m)$. What they differ in is the probability of loss: it is p_H for type-H (= high-risk) individuals and p_L for type-L (= low-risk) individuals, with $0 < p_L < p_H < 1$.

Recall that a free-entry competitive equilibrium is defined as a situation where

1. each firm in the industry makes zero profits, and

2. there is no unexploited profit opportunity in the industry, that is, there is no currently not offered contract that would yield positive profits to a (existing or new) firm that offered that contract.

In the one-type case we saw that at the free-entry competitive equilibrium every firm offers the full-insurance contract that lies at the intersection of the zero-profit line and the 45° line. Recall that the no-insurance point NI can be thought of as a trivial contract with zero premium and deductible equal to the full loss ℓ: such a "contract" obviously yields zero profits; thus the zero-profit line goes through point NI. In the two-type context the situation is complicated by the fact that there are **three** zero-profit lines:

- a "low-risk" line (through NI) with slope $-\frac{p_L}{1-p_L}$, which is a relevant isoprofit line if and only if the contracts on this line are sold only to the low-risk individuals,

- an "average-risk" line (through NI) with slope $-\frac{\bar{p}}{1-\bar{p}}$, where

$$\bar{p} = q_H p_H + (1 - q_H) p_L,$$

    which is a relevant isoprofit line if and only if the contracts on this line are sold to both types of individuals,

- a "high- risk" line (through NI) with slope $-\frac{p_H}{1-p_H}$, which is a relevant isoprofit line if and only if the contracts on this line are sold only to the hight-risk individuals.

Since $0 < p_L < p_H < 1$ and $0 < q_H < 1$, $p_L < \bar{p} < p_H$ and thus

$$\frac{p_L}{1 - p_L} < \frac{\bar{p}}{1 - \bar{p}} < \frac{p_H}{1 - p_H}. \tag{7.21}$$

Hence the low-risk zero-profit line is less steep that the average risk zero-profit line, which, in turn, is less steep than the high-risk zero-profit line.

Figure 7.16 shows the three zero-profit lines.

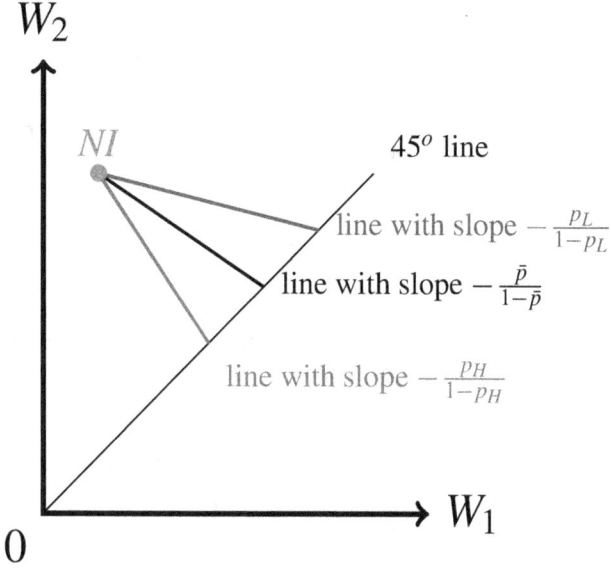

Figure 7.16: Three zero-profit lines in the two-type case.

We also note that, at any insurance contract, the slope of the H-type indifference curve is – in absolute value – greater than or equal to $\frac{p_H}{1-p_H}$ and thus, by (7.21), it is greater than the absolute value of the slope of the average isoprofit line through that point, as shown in Figure 7.17.

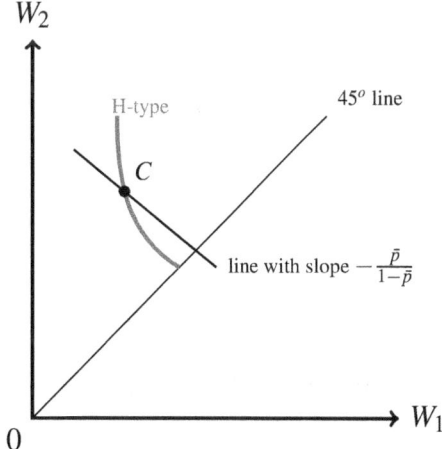

Figure 7.17: At any (full- or partial-) insurance contract the H-type indifference curve is steeper than the average isoprofit line.

In what follows we shall assume that the reservation indifference curve of the L-type is steeper, at the no-insurance point, than the average zero-profit line, that is,

$$\frac{p_L}{1-p_L}\left(\frac{U'(W_0-\ell)}{U'(W_0)}\right) > \frac{\bar{p}}{1-\bar{p}}. \tag{7.22}$$

Inequality (7.22) ensures that it is possible to insure both types of individuals with the same contract, without making a loss.[12]

In principle, a free-entry competitive equilibrium could be one of two types:

- a *pooling equilibrium* where all the firms in the industry offer the same contract, which is bought by both types of individuals, or

- a *separating equilibrium* where two contracts are offered in the industry: one contract, denoted by C_H, which is purchased only by the H-types and the other contract, denoted by C_L, which is purchased only by the L-types.

Let us begin by considering the possibility of a pooling equilibrium. We want to show that such an equilibrium is *not* possible. By Condition 1 of the definition of free-entry competitive equilibrium, the contract in question, call it $B = (h_B, d_B)$ (with $0 \le d_B < \ell$), must be on the average zero profit line, that is,

$$h_B - \bar{p}(\ell - d_B) = 0. \tag{7.23}$$

Consider the function $\pi_L(h,d) = h - p_L(\ell - d)$ that gives, for every insurance contract (h,d) the expected profit from that contract *if it is bought only by the low-risk individuals*, that is, only by the L-types. Since $p_L < \bar{p}$, it follows from (7.23) that $p_L(\ell - d_B) < \bar{p}(\ell - d_B)$ and thus

$$\pi_L(h_B, d_B) = h_B - p_L(\ell - d_B) > 0. \tag{7.24}$$

Since the function $\pi_L(h,d)$ is a continuous function, it follows from (7.24) that, for every insurance contract $A = (h_A, d_A)$,

if A is sufficiently close to B then $\pi_L(h_A, d_A) = h_A - p_L(\ell - d_A) > 0.$ (7.25)

Thus, if we can find a contract, close to B, that would be considered better than B by the L-types, but worse than B by the H-types, then any firm that introduced contract A would attract only the L-types and thus, by (7.25), it would make positive profits, contradicting the second requirement of the definition of a free-entry competitive equilibrium. Does such a contract exist?

---

[12] By (7.22) there are contracts that are above the reservation indifference curve of the L-type (and thus attractive to both types) and below the average zero-profit line (and thus yielding positive profits if purchased by both types).

The answer is affirmative, as shown in Figure 7.18: draw the indifference curves of the two types that go through contract B. The L-type indifference curve is less steep than the H-type indifference curve and thus there are contracts, such as contract A in Figure 7.18, which are below the H-type indifference curve through B and above the L-type indifference curve through B. Thus if such a contract A were to be introduced, the L-types would switch from the original contract B to the new contract A while the H-types would stay with contract B. Hence, by (7.25), the firm that introduced contract A would make positive profits, contradicting the second requirement of the definition of free-entry competitive equilibrium.

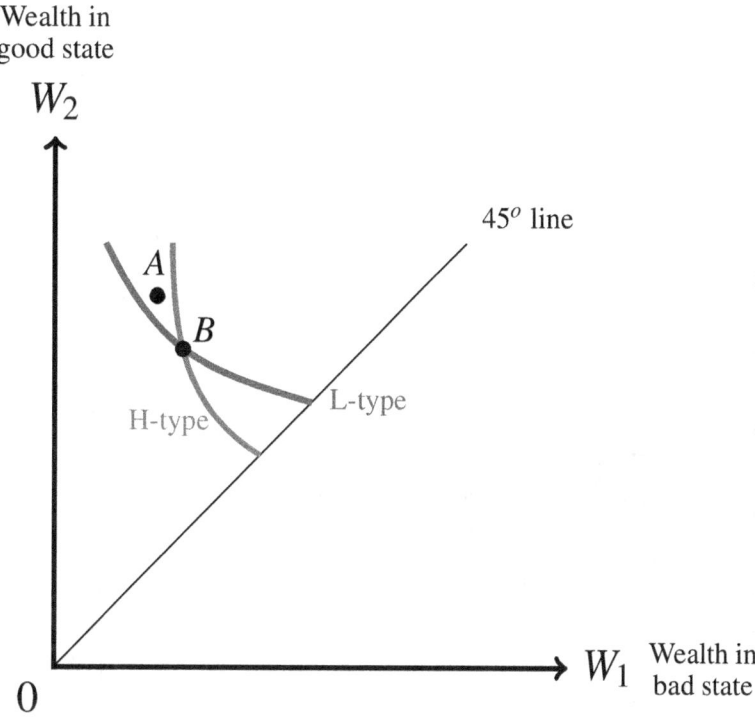

Figure 7.18: If, initially, both types purchase contract B and then contract A is added as an option, then the H-types will not switch to A while the L-types will.

Thus we conclude that, if there is a free-entry competitive equilibrium, then it must be a two-contract separating equilibrium. We now turn to the question of whether a two-contract $\{C_H, C_L\}$ equilibrium exists with all H-types purchasing contract C_H and all L-type purchasing contract C_L.

- By the zero-profit condition (the first requirement of a free-entry competitive equilibrium), contract C_H must be on the high-risk zero-profit line (the line through NI with slope $-\frac{p_H}{1-p_H}$) and contract C_L must be on the low-risk zero-profit line (the line through NI with slope $-\frac{p_L}{1-p_L}$).

- Furthermore, contract C_H must be the full-insurance contract on the high-risk zero-profit line because, if it were above the 45° line, then – by the usual argument based on the observation that at such a point the H-type indifference curve is steeper than the high-risk zero-profit line – there would be contracts below that zero profit line and above that indifference curve that would yield positive profits to a firm that introduced such a contract (which would induce the H-types to switch to it), contradicting the second requirement of a free-entry competitive equilibrium.

It remains to determine where on the low-risk zero-profit line contract C_L should be. Draw the indifference curve of the H-type that goes through contract C_H and call the point at the intersection of this indifference curve and the low-risk zero-profit line contract C, as shown in Figure 7.19.

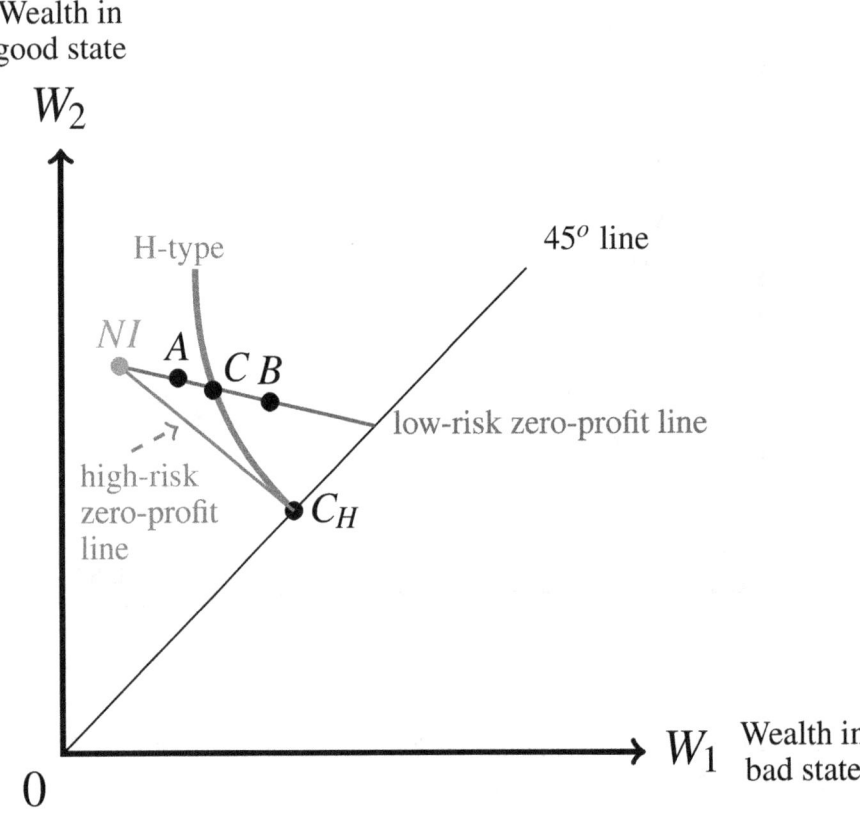

Figure 7.19: Where on the low-risk zero-profit line could contract C_L be?

- Suppose that contract C_L is on the low-risk zero-profit line to the right of point C, such as point B in Figure 7.19. Then such a contract B would be preferred to C_H by both types,[13] giving rise to a situation where all types purchase the same contract, which – as we saw above – cannot be a free-entry competitive equilibrium.

---

[13]B is preferred to C_H by type H because B is to the right of the H-type indifference curve through C_H and B is preferred to C_H by type L because C_H is below the L-type indifference curve through B: this indifference curve is not shown in Figure 7.19, but it is less steep than the indifference curve of the H-type through B (also not shown); hence, since C_H is below the latter, it is also below the former.

- Suppose that contract C_L is on the low-risk zero-profit line to the left of point C, such as point A in Figure 7.19. Then – by the usual argument based on the observation that at such a point the L-type indifference curve is steeper than the low-risk zero-profit line – there would be contracts below that zero profit line and above the indifference curve of the L-type that goes through A that would attract the L-types, and only the L-types, and yield positive profits, contradicting the first requirement of a free-entry competitive equilibrium.

Thus we conclude that contract C_L must be at the intersection of the low-risk zero-profit line and the indifference curve of the H-type that goes through contract C_H, that is, it must coincide with point C in Figure 7.19.

We have determined that necessary conditions for a pair of contracts $\{C_H, C_L\}$ to be a free-entry competitive equilibrium are:

(1) C_H is at the intersection of the high-risk zero-profit line and the 45° line, and

(2) C_L is at the intersection of the low-risk zero-profit line and the H-type indifference curve through C_H.

While necessary, the above two conditions are not sufficient for a free-entry competitive equilibrium. To see this, consider the situation depicted in Figure 7.20.

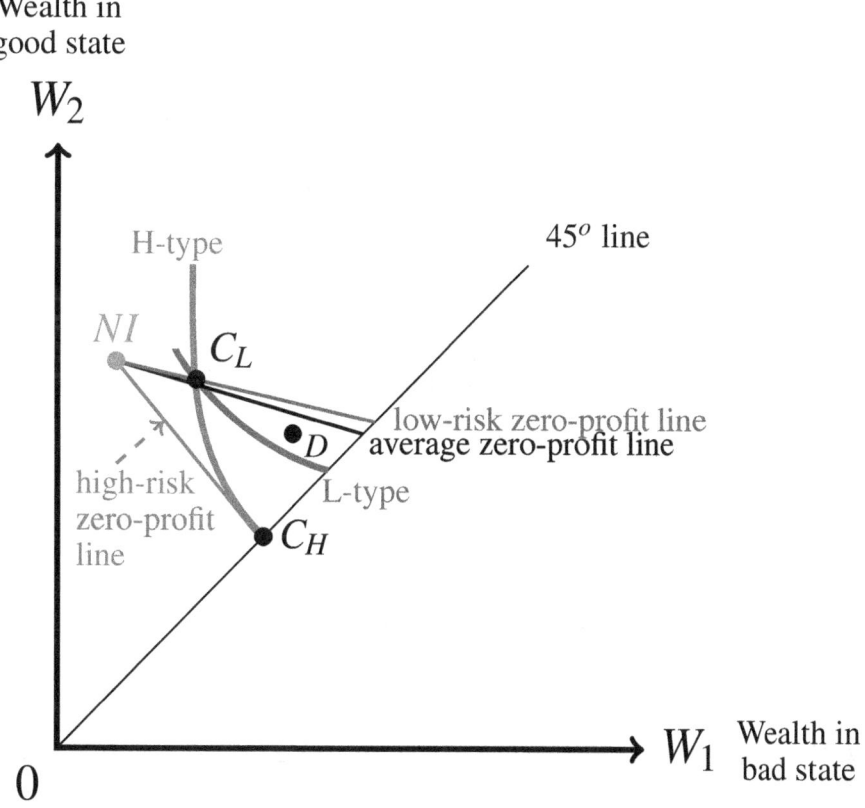

Figure 7.20: A case where the pair of contracts $\{C_H, C_L\}$ is not a free-entry competitive equilibrium because of the existence of contracts like D.

Suppose that the contracts currently offered in the industry are C_H and C_L and one of the existing firms, or a new firm, introduces contract D. The H-types will switch to contract D, since it is better than the contract that they are currently purchasing, namely C_H (D is to the right of the H-type indifference curve through C_H) and the L-types will also switch to D, since it is better than the contract that they are currently purchasing, namely C_L (D is to the right of the L-type indifference curve through C_L). Then, for the firm that introduced contract D, the relevant isoprofit lines are the average isoprofit lines; since contract D is below the average zero-profit line, it yields positive profits to the firm, contradicting the second requirement of a free-entry competitive equilibrium.

Thus, in order for the two-contract configuration $\{C_H, C_L\}$ described above to be a free-entry competitive equilibrium, it is also necessary that there be no contracts such as contract D described above, that is, it must **not** be the case that the average zero-profit line crosses the L-type indifference curve that goes through contract C_L. In other words, the average zero-profit line must be entirely below the L-type indifference curve through C_L, as shown in Figure 7.21.

Since the higher the value of q_H (that is, the larger the number of H-types in the population relative to the number of L-types), the closer the average zero-profit line will be to the high-risk zero-profit line, this additional requirement for the existence of a free-entry competitive equilibrium can be understood in terms of q_H being "sufficiently large".

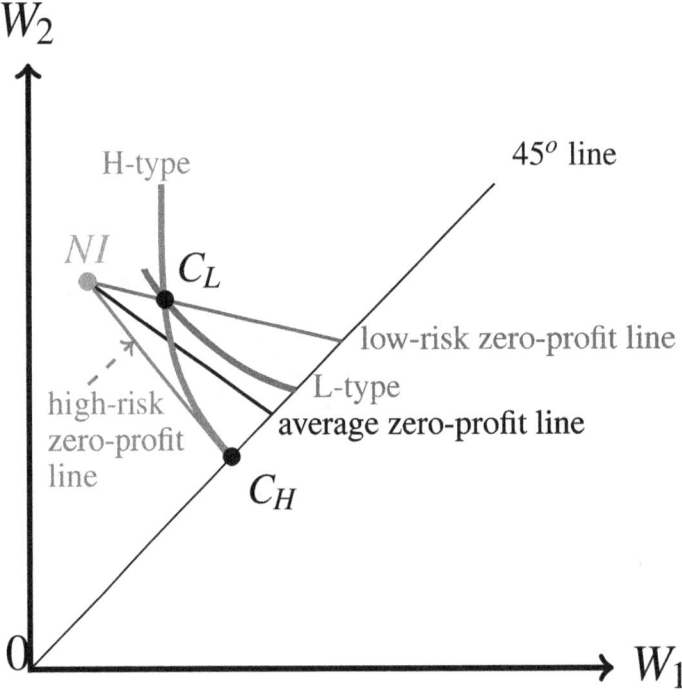

Figure 7.21: The pair of contracts $\{C_H, C_L\}$ is a free-entry competitive equilibrium.

Test your understanding of the concepts introduced in this section, by going through the exercises in Section 7.5.3 at the end of this chapter.

7.5 Exercises

The solutions to the following exercises are given in Section 7.6 at the end of this chapter.

7.5.1 Exercises for Section 7.2: Two types of customers

Exercise 7.1 Sara and Mary have the same initial wealth of \$400 and face the same potential loss of \$280. They also have the same vNM utility-of-money function $U(m) = ln(m)$. They differ, however, in the probability of loss, which is $p_S = \frac{1}{2}$ for Sara and $p_M = \frac{1}{5}$ for Mary.

(a) Calculate the slope of Sara's reservation indifference curve at the no-insurance point.

(b) Calculate the slope of Mary's reservation indifference curve at the no-insurance point.

(c) Find the maximum premium that Sara would be willing to pay for full insurance and calculate the insurance company's expected profit from selling that full-insurance contract to Sara.

(d) Find the maximum premium that Mary would be willing to pay for full insurance and calculate the insurance company's expected profit from selling that full-insurance contract to Mary.

Exercise 7.2 Diana and Fran have the same initial wealth of \$4,096 and face the same potential loss of \$2,800. They also have the same vNM utility-of-money function $U(m) = \sqrt{m}$. They differ, however, in the probability of loss, which is $p_D = \frac{1}{4}$ for Diana and $p_F = \frac{1}{16}$ for Fran.

Consider a monopolist seller of insurance who knows all of the above information about Diana and Fran.

(a) What insurance contract would the monopolist offer to Diana?

(b) What insurance contract would the monopolist offer to Fran?

(c) Assume that, when indifferent between not insuring and insuring, both Diana and Fran will choose to insure. Calculate the monopolist's expected profit from selling insurance to Diana and Fran.

7.5.2   **Exercises for Section 7.3: The monopolist under asymmetric information**

Exercise 7.3 There are 16,000 individuals, all identical in terms of initial wealth $W_0 = \$4,000$, potential loss $\ell = \$2,500$ and vNM utility-of-money function $U(m) = 10\ln\left(\frac{m}{1,000}\right)$. Of these individuals, 12,000 have a high probability of loss $p_H = \frac{1}{5}$ and 4,000 have a low probability of loss $p_L = \frac{1}{15}$. A monopolist seller of insurance is considering using Option 1 (Section 7.3.1). What will its expected total profits be? [As usual, assume that – if indifferent between insuring and not insuring – individuals will choose to insure.]

Exercise 7.4 Consider again the case described in Exercise 7.3: there are 16,000 individuals, all identical in terms of initial wealth $W_0 = \$4,000$, potential loss $\ell = \$2,500$ and vNM utility-of-money function $U(m) = 10\ln\left(\frac{m}{1,000}\right)$; of these individuals, 12,000 have a high probability of loss $p_H = \frac{1}{5}$ and 4,000 have a low probability of loss $p_L = \frac{1}{15}$.

(a) Show that, for a monopolist seller of insurance, Option 2 (Section 7.3.2) is not profitable.

(b) Calculate what the monopolist's total expected profits would be if it offered a full-insurance contract that makes the L-type indifference between insuring and not insuring. [As usual, assume that – if indifferent between insuring and not insuring – individuals will choose to insure.]

Exercise 7.5 Consider again the case described in Exercise 7.3, but reduce the number of high-risk individuals from 12,000 to 6,000; thus there are 10,000 individuals, all identical in terms of initial wealth $W_0 = \$4,000$, potential loss $\ell = \$2,500$ and vNM utility-of-money function $U(m) = 10\ln\left(\frac{m}{1,000}\right)$; of these individuals, 6,000 have a high probability of loss $p_H = \frac{1}{5}$ and 4,000 have a low probability of loss $p_L = \frac{1}{15}$.

(a) Show that, for a monopolist seller of insurance, Option 2 (Section 7.3.2) is profitable, by calculating the slopes of the relevant curves at the no-insurance point.

(b) Write two equations, whose solution gives the contract that maximizes the monopolist's profits under Option 2. If you are able to, compute the solution and determine the monopolist's expected total profits if it offers that contract. [As usual, assume that – if indifferent between insuring and not insuring – individuals will choose to insure.]

Exercise 7.6 There are 6,000 individuals, all with the same initial wealth $W_0 = 16,000$, facing the same potential loss $\ell = 7,000$ and with the same vNM utility-of-money function $U(m) = \sqrt{m}$. Of these 6,000 individuals, 1,000 are high-risk with a probability of loss $p_H = \frac{2}{10}$ while the remaining 5,000 are low-risk with a probability of loss $p_L = \frac{1}{10}$.

(a) Calculate the monopolist's total expected profits if it decides to pursue Option 1.

(b) Calculate the average probability of loss $\bar{p}$.

(c) Write two equations whose solution gives the profit-maximizing contract under Option 2.

(d) Suppose that, under Option 3, the monopolist decides to offer a full-insurance contract with premium \$1,400. Write a pair of equations whose solution gives the other contract that the monopolist will offer.

(e) The solution of the pair of equations in Part (d) is the following contract, expressed in term of wealth levels: $C = (10169.41, 15832.48)$. Calculate the monopolist's profits if it offers the two contracts of Part (d).

Exercise 7.7 There are 8,000 individuals, all with the same initial wealth $W_0 = 10,000$, facing the same potential loss $\ell = 6,000$ and with the same vNM utility-of-money function $U(m) = \ln(m)$. Of these 8,000 individuals, 1,500 are high-risk with a probability of loss $p_H = \frac{1}{4}$ while the remaining 6,500 are low-risk with a probability of loss $p_L = \frac{1}{16}$.

(a) Calculate the monopolist's total expected profits if it decides to pursue Option 1.

(b) Calculate the average probability of loss $\bar{p}$.

(c) Write two equations whose solution gives the profit-maximizing contract under Option 2.

(d) Suppose that, under Option 3, the monopolist decides to offer a full-insurance contract with premium \$2,000. Write a pair of equations whose solution gives the other contract that the monopolist will offer.

(e) The solution of the pair of equations in Part (d) is the following contract, expressed in term of wealth levels: $C = (4120.36, 9980.26)$. Calculate the monopolist's profits if it offers the two contracts of Part (d).

7.5.3   Exercises for Section 7.4: A perfectly competitive insurance industry

Exercise 7.8 Consider again the information given in Exercise 7.6: there are 6,000 individuals, all with the same initial wealth $W_0 = 16,000$, facing the same potential loss $\ell = 7,000$ and with the same vNM utility-of-money function $U(m) = \sqrt{m}$; of these 6,000 individuals, 1,000 are high-risk with probability of loss $p_H = \frac{2}{10}$ while the remaining 5,000 are low-risk with probability of loss $p_L = \frac{1}{10}$.

(a) Find the pair of contracts that is the only candidate for a free-entry perfectly competitive equilibrium.

(b) Calculate the average probability of loss $\bar{p}$.

(c) Write a pair of equations such that: (1) if it has a solution then the pair of contracts of Part (a) is **not** a free-entry perfectly competitive equilibrium and (2) if it does not have a solution then the pair of contracts of Part (a) **is** a free-entry perfectly competitive equilibrium.

Exercise 7.9 Consider again the information given in Exercise 7.7: there are 8,000 individuals, all with the same initial wealth $W_0 = 10,000$, facing the same potential loss $\ell = 6,000$ and with the same vNM utility-of-money function $U(m) = \ln(m)$; of these 8,000 individuals, 1,500 are high-risk with probability of loss $p_H = \frac{1}{4}$ while the remaining 6,500 are low-risk with probability of loss $p_L = \frac{1}{16}$.

(a) Find the pair of contracts that is the only candidate for a free-entry perfectly competitive equilibrium.

(b) Calculate the average probability of loss $\bar{p}$.

(c) Write a pair of equations such that: (1) if it has a solution then the pair of contracts of Part (a) is **not** a free-entry perfectly competitive equilibrium and (2) if it does not have a solution then the pair of contracts of Part (a) **is** a free-entry perfectly competitive equilibrium.

7.6 Solutions to Exercises

Solution to Exercise 7.1

(a) The slope of Sara's reservation indifference curve at $NI = (120, 400)$ is

$$-\frac{p_S}{1 - p_S}\left(\frac{U'(120)}{U'(400)}\right) = -\frac{\frac{1}{2}}{1 - \frac{1}{2}}\left(\frac{\frac{1}{120}}{\frac{1}{400}}\right) = -\frac{10}{3} = -3.33.$$

(b) The slope of Mary's reservation indifference curve at $NI = (120, 400)$ is

$$-\frac{p_M}{1 - p_M}\left(\frac{U'(120)}{U'(400)}\right) = -\frac{\frac{1}{5}}{1 - \frac{1}{5}}\left(\frac{\frac{1}{120}}{\frac{1}{400}}\right) = -\frac{5}{6} = -0.83.$$

(c) To find the full-insurance contract that makes Sara indifferent between insuring and not insuring we need to solve the equation $\ln(W) = \frac{1}{2}\ln(120) + \frac{1}{2}\ln(400)$. The solution is $W = 219.09$, so that the maximum premium that Sara is willing to pay for full insurance is $400 - 219.09 = \$180.91$. If Sara purchases this full-insurance contract then the insurance company's expected profit is $180.91 - \frac{1}{2}(280) = \$40.91$.

(d) To find the full-insurance contract that makes Mary indifferent between insuring and not insuring we need to solve the equation $\ln(W) = \frac{1}{5}\ln(120) + \frac{4}{5}\ln(400)$. The solution is $W = 314.40$, so that the maximum premium that Mary is willing to pay for full insurance is $400 - 314.40 = \$85.60$. If Mary purchases this full-insurance contract then the insurance company's expected profit is $85.60 - \frac{1}{5}(280) = \$29.60$.

$\square$

Solution to Exercise 7.2

(a) The monopolist will offer Diana the full-insurance contract that makes her indifferent between insuring and not insuring, which is determined by the solution to $\sqrt{W} = \frac{1}{4}\sqrt{1,296} + \frac{3}{4}\sqrt{4,096}$. The solution is $W = 3,249$, so that the premium of the full-insurance contract is $4,096 - 3,249 = \$847$. If Diana purchases this full-insurance contract then the insurance company's expected profit from this contract is $847 - \frac{1}{4}(2,800) = \$147$.

(b) The monopolist will offer Fran the full-insurance contract that makes her indifferent between insuring and not insuring, which is determined by the solution to $\sqrt{W} = \frac{1}{16}\sqrt{1,296} + \frac{15}{16}\sqrt{4,096}$. The solution is $W = 3,875.06$, so that the premium of the full-insurance contract is $4,096 - 3,875.06 = \$220.94$. If Fran purchases this full-insurance contract then the insurance company's expected profit is $220.94 - \frac{1}{16}(2,800) = \$45.94$.

(c) The monopolist's expected profit from insuring Diana and Fran is $147 + 45.94 = \$192.94$.

$\square$

Solution to Exercise 7.3

The monopolist would offer the full-insurance contract that makes the H-types indifferent between insuring and not insuring. To find that contract, solve the equation $U(W) = p_H U(W_0 - \ell) + (1 - p_H)U(W_0)$, that is,

$$10\ln\left(\frac{W}{1,000}\right) = \frac{1}{5}10\ln(1.5) + \frac{4}{5}10\ln(4).$$

The solution is $W = 3,287.50$. Thus the offered full-insurance contract has a premium of $4,000 - 3,287.50 = \$712.50$. This contract will be purchased only by the H-types (the L-types are better off without insurance). Thus the monopolist's expected total profits are

$$12,000\left[712.50 - \frac{1}{5}(2,500)\right] = \$2,549,956.09.$$

□

Solution to Exercise 7.4

(a) We need to show that the L-type reservation indifference curve is less steep at the no-insurance point, than the average isoprofit line, that is,

$$\frac{p_L}{1 - p_L}\left(\frac{U'(W_0 - \ell)}{U'(W_0)}\right) \leq \frac{\bar{p}}{1 - \bar{p}} \tag{7.26}$$

First we compute the average probability of loss $\bar{p}$. Since $q_H = \frac{12,000}{16,000} = \frac{3}{4}$,

$$\bar{p} = \frac{3}{4}\left(\frac{1}{5}\right) + \frac{1}{4}\left(\frac{1}{15}\right) = \frac{1}{6}.$$

Thus

$$\frac{\bar{p}}{1 - \bar{p}} = \frac{1}{5} = 0.2.$$

On the other hand,

$$\frac{p_L}{1 - p_L}\left(\frac{U'(W_0 - \ell)}{U'(W_0)}\right) = \frac{1}{14}\frac{\frac{10}{1,500}}{\frac{10}{4,000}} = \frac{4}{21} = 0.1905.$$

Thus inequality (7.26) is indeed satisfied.

(b) To find that contract, solve the equation $U(W) = p_L U(W_0 - \ell) + (1 - p_L)U(W_0)$, that is,

$$10\ln\left(\frac{W}{1,000}\right) = \frac{1}{15}10\ln(1.5) + \frac{14}{15}10\ln(4).$$

The solution is $W = 3,746.81$. Thus the offered full-insurance contract has a premium of $4,000 - 3,746.81 = \$253.19$. This contract would be purchased by both types. Thus the monopolist's expected total profits would be $N(253.19 - \bar{p}\ell)$:

$$16,000\left[253.19 - \frac{1}{6}(2,500)\right] = \$-2,615,626.67,$$

that is, a loss.

□

Solution to Exercise 7.5

(a) We need to show that the L-type reservation indifference curve is steeper, at the no-insurance point, than the average isoprofit line, that is,

$$\frac{p_L}{1-p_L}\left(\frac{U'(W_0-\ell)}{U'(W_0)}\right) > \frac{\bar{p}}{1-\bar{p}} \tag{7.27}$$

First we compute the average probability of loss $\bar{p}$. Since $q_H = \frac{6{,}000}{10{,}000} = \frac{3}{5}$,

$$\bar{p} = \frac{3}{5}\left(\frac{1}{5}\right) + \frac{2}{5}\left(\frac{1}{15}\right) = \frac{11}{75}.$$

Thus

$$\frac{\bar{p}}{1-\bar{p}} = \frac{11}{64} = 0.1719.$$

On the other hand,

$$\frac{p_L}{1-p_L}\left(\frac{U'(W_0-\ell)}{U'(W_0)}\right) = \frac{1}{14}\frac{\frac{10}{1{,}500}}{\frac{10}{4{,}000}} = \frac{4}{21} = 0.1905.$$

Thus inequality (7.27) is indeed satisfied.

(b) The equations are as follows (see (7.9) and (7.10) on page 190):

$$p_L U(W_1) + (1-p_L) U(W_2) = p_L U(W_0 - \ell) + (1-p_L) U(W_0)$$

$$\frac{p_L}{1-p_L}\left(\frac{U'(W_1)}{U'(W_2)}\right) = \frac{\bar{p}}{1-\bar{p}}.$$

that is,

$$\frac{1}{15}10\ln\left(\frac{W_1}{1{,}000}\right) + \frac{14}{15}10\ln\left(\frac{W_1}{1{,}000}\right) = \frac{1}{15}10\ln(1.5) + \frac{14}{15}10\ln(4)$$

$$\frac{\frac{1}{15}}{\frac{14}{15}}\left(\frac{\frac{10}{W_1}}{\frac{10}{W_2}}\right) = \frac{\frac{11}{75}}{\frac{64}{75}}.$$

The solution is $W_1 = 1{,}650.99$ and $W_2 = 3{,}972.69$. Thus the premium of the offered contract is $4{,}000 - 3{,}972.69 = \$27.31$ and the deductible is $3{,}972.69 - 1{,}650.99 = \$2{,}321.70$. Both types purchase this contract. Thus the monopolist's expected total profits are:

$$10{,}000\left[27.31 - \frac{11}{75}(2{,}500 - 2{,}321.70)\right] = \$11{,}593.33.$$

□

Solution to Exercise 7.6

(a) First calculate the maximum premium that the H-types are willing to pay for full insurance by solving

$$\frac{2}{10}\sqrt{9,000} + \frac{8}{10}\sqrt{16,000} = \sqrt{16,000 - h}.$$

The solution is $h_{max}^H = \$1,560$. Thus under Option 1 the monopolist would only offer full insurance at a premium of $1,560, attracting only the H-types; its total expected profits would be

$$1,000\left(1,560 - \frac{2}{10}7,000\right) = \$160,000.$$

(b) The average probability of loss is

$$\bar{p} = q_H p_H + (1 - q_H) p_L = \frac{1}{6}\left(\frac{2}{10}\right) + \frac{5}{6}\left(\frac{1}{10}\right) = \frac{7}{60}.$$

(c) The equations whose solution gives the profit-maximizing contract under Option 2 are:

$$p_L U(W_0 - \ell) + (1 - p_L) U(W_0) = p_L U(W_0 - h - d) + (1 - p_L) U(W_0 - h)$$

$$\frac{p_L}{1 - p_L}\left(\frac{U'(W_0 - h - d)}{U'(W_0 - h)}\right) = \frac{\bar{p}}{1 - \bar{p}}, \qquad \text{that is,}$$

$$\frac{1}{10}\sqrt{9,000} + \frac{9}{10}\sqrt{16,000} = \frac{1}{10}\sqrt{16,000 - h - d} + \frac{9}{10}\sqrt{16,000 - h}$$

$$\frac{\frac{1}{10}}{\frac{9}{10}}\left(\frac{\frac{1}{2\sqrt{16,000 - h - d}}}{\frac{1}{2\sqrt{16,000 - h}}}\right) = \frac{\frac{7}{60}}{\frac{53}{60}}.$$

(d) The assumption is that $C_H = (h_H = 1400, d_H = 0)$. To find contract $C_L = (h_L, d_L)$ solve the following equations:

$$\frac{2}{10}\sqrt{16,000 - h - d} + \frac{8}{10}\sqrt{16,000 - h} = \sqrt{16,000 - 1,400}$$

$$\frac{1}{10}\sqrt{16,000 - h - d} + \frac{9}{10}\sqrt{16,000 - h} = \frac{1}{10}\sqrt{9,000} + \frac{9}{10}\sqrt{16,000}$$

(e) The two contracts are: $C_H = (h_H = 1400, d_H = 0)$, which will be bought by the H-types, and $C_L = (h_L = 167.52, d_L = 5663.07)$, which will be bought by the L-types.[14] Thus the monopolist's expected total profits will be

$$1,000\left(1,400 - \frac{2}{10}7,000\right) + 5,000\left[167.52 - \frac{2}{10}(7,000 - 5,663.07)\right] = \$169,135. \ \square$$

---

[14]The contract was given in terms of wealth levels as $(10169.41, 15832.48)$, from which we obtain the premium as $16,000 - 15,832.48 = 167.52$ and the deductible as $15,832.48 - 10,169.41 = 5,663.07$.

Solution to Exercise 7.5

(a) We need to show that the L-type reservation indifference curve is steeper, at the no-insurance point, than the average isoprofit line, that is,

$$\frac{p_L}{1-p_L}\left(\frac{U'(W_0-\ell)}{U'(W_0)}\right) > \frac{\bar{p}}{1-\bar{p}} \qquad (7.27)$$

First we compute the average probability of loss $\bar{p}$. Since $q_H = \frac{6,000}{10,000} = \frac{3}{5}$,

$$\bar{p} = \frac{3}{5}\left(\frac{1}{5}\right) + \frac{2}{5}\left(\frac{1}{15}\right) = \frac{11}{75}.$$

Thus

$$\frac{\bar{p}}{1-\bar{p}} = \frac{11}{64} = 0.1719.$$

On the other hand,

$$\frac{p_L}{1-p_L}\left(\frac{U'(W_0-\ell)}{U'(W_0)}\right) = \frac{1}{14}\frac{\frac{10}{1,500}}{\frac{10}{4,000}} = \frac{4}{21} = 0.1905.$$

Thus inequality (7.27) is indeed satisfied.

(b) The equations are as follows (see (7.9) and (7.10) on page 190):

$$p_L U(W_1) + (1-p_L)U(W_2) = p_L U(W_0-\ell) + (1-p_L)U(W_0)$$

$$\frac{p_L}{1-p_L}\left(\frac{U'(W_1)}{U'(W_2)}\right) = \frac{\bar{p}}{1-\bar{p}}.$$

that is,

$$\frac{1}{15}10\ln\left(\frac{W_1}{1,000}\right) + \frac{14}{15}10\ln\left(\frac{W_1}{1,000}\right) = \frac{1}{15}10\ln(1.5) + \frac{14}{15}10\ln(4)$$

$$\frac{\frac{1}{15}}{\frac{14}{15}}\left(\frac{\frac{10}{W_1}}{\frac{10}{W_2}}\right) = \frac{\frac{11}{75}}{\frac{64}{75}}.$$

The solution is $W_1 = 1,650.99$ and $W_2 = 3,972.69$. Thus the premium of the offered contract is $4,000 - 3,972.69 = \$27.31$ and the deductible is $3,972.69 - 1,650.99 = \$2,321.70$. Both types purchase this contract. Thus the monopolist's expected total profits are:

$$10,000\left[27.31 - \frac{11}{75}(2,500 - 2,321.70)\right] = \$11,593.33.$$

□

Solution to Exercise 7.6

(a) First calculate the maximum premium that the H-types are willing to pay for full insurance by solving

$$\frac{2}{10}\sqrt{9,000} + \frac{8}{10}\sqrt{16,000} = \sqrt{16,000 - h}.$$

The solution is $h^H_{max} = \$1,560$. Thus under Option 1 the monopolist would only offer full insurance at a premium of $1,560, attracting only the H-types; its total expected profits would be

$$1,000\left(1,560 - \frac{2}{10}7,000\right) = \$160,000.$$

(b) The average probability of loss is

$$\bar{p} = q_H p_H + (1 - q_H)p_L = \frac{1}{6}\left(\frac{2}{10}\right) + \frac{5}{6}\left(\frac{1}{10}\right) = \frac{7}{60}.$$

(c) The equations whose solution gives the profit-maximizing contract under Option 2 are:

$$p_L U(W_0 - \ell) + (1 - p_L)U(W_0) = p_L U(W_0 - h - d) + (1 - p_L)U(W_0 - h)$$

$$\frac{p_L}{1 - p_L}\left(\frac{U'(W_0 - h - d)}{U'(W_0 - h)}\right) = \frac{\bar{p}}{1 - \bar{p}}, \qquad \text{that is,}$$

$$\frac{1}{10}\sqrt{9,000} + \frac{9}{10}\sqrt{16,000} = \frac{1}{10}\sqrt{16,000 - h - d} + \frac{9}{10}\sqrt{16,000 - h}$$

$$\frac{\frac{1}{10}\left(\frac{1}{2\sqrt{16,000 - h - d}}\right)}{\frac{9}{10}\left(\frac{1}{2\sqrt{16,000 - h}}\right)} = \frac{\frac{7}{60}}{\frac{53}{60}}.$$

(d) The assumption is that $C_H = (h_H = 1400, d_H = 0)$. To find contract $C_L = (h_L, d_L)$ solve the following equations:

$$\frac{2}{10}\sqrt{16,000 - h - d} + \frac{8}{10}\sqrt{16,000 - h} = \sqrt{16,000 - 1,400}$$

$$\frac{1}{10}\sqrt{16,000 - h - d} + \frac{9}{10}\sqrt{16,000 - h} = \frac{1}{10}\sqrt{9,000} + \frac{9}{10}\sqrt{16,000}$$

(e) The two contracts are: $C_H = (h_H = 1400, d_H = 0)$, which will be bought by the H-types, and $C_L = (h_L = 167.52, d_L = 5663.07)$, which will be bought by the L-types.[14] Thus the monopolist's expected total profits will be

$$1,000\left(1,400 - \frac{2}{10}7,000\right) + 5,000\left[167.52 - \frac{2}{10}(7,000 - 5,663.07)\right] = \$169,135. \ \square$$

---

[14] The contract was given in terms of wealth levels as $(10169.41, 15832.48)$, from which we obtain the premium as $16,000 - 15,832.48 = 167.52$ and the deductible as $15,832.48 - 10,169.41 = 5,663.07$.

Solution to Exercise 7.7

(a) First calculate the maximum premium that the H-types are willing to pay for full insurance by solving

$$\frac{1}{4}\ln(4,000) + \frac{3}{4}\ln(10,000) = \ln(10,000 - h).$$

The solution is $h_{max}^H = \$2,047.29$. Thus under Option 1 the monopolist would only offer full insurance at a premium of $2,047.29, attracting only the H-types; its total expected profits would be

$$1,500\left(2,047.29 - \frac{1}{4}(6,000)\right) = \$820,935.$$

(b) The average probability of loss is

$$\bar{p} = q_H p_H + (1 - q_H)p_L = \frac{3}{16}\left(\frac{1}{4}\right) + \frac{13}{16}\left(\frac{1}{16}\right) = \frac{25}{256}.$$

(c) The equations whose solution gives the profit-maximizing contract under Option 2 are:

$$p_L U(W_0 - \ell) + (1 - p_L)U(W_0) = p_L U(W_0 - h - d) + (1 - p_L)U(W_0 - h)$$

$$\frac{p_L}{1 - p_L}\left(\frac{U'(W_0 - h - d)}{U'(W_0 - h)}\right) = \frac{\bar{p}}{1 - \bar{p}}$$

that is,

$$\frac{1}{16}\ln(4,000) + \frac{15}{16}\ln(10,000) = \frac{1}{16}\ln(10,000 - h - d) + \frac{15}{16}\ln(10,000 - h)$$

$$\frac{\frac{1}{16}}{\frac{15}{16}}\left(\frac{\frac{1}{10,000 - h - d}}{\frac{1}{10,000 - h}}\right) = \frac{\frac{25}{256}}{\frac{231}{256}}.$$

(d) The assumption is that $C_H = (h_H = 2000, d_H = 0)$. To find contract $C_L = (h_L, d_L)$ solve the following equations:

$$\frac{1}{4}\ln(10,000 - h - d) + \frac{3}{4}\ln(10,000 - h) = \ln(10,000 - 2,000)$$

$$\frac{1}{16}\ln(10,000 - h - d) + \frac{15}{16}\ln(10,000 - h) = \frac{1}{16}\ln(4,000) + \frac{15}{16}\ln(10,000)$$

(e) The two contracts are: $C_H = (h_H = 2000, d_H = 0)$, which will be bought by the H-types, and $C_L = (h_L = 19.74, d_L = 5859.9)$, which will be bought by the L-types.[15] Thus the monopolist's expected total profits will be

$$1,500\left(2,000 - \frac{1}{4}6,000\right) + 6,500\left[19.74 - \frac{1}{16}(6,000 - 5,859.9)\right] = \$821,394.38. \square$$

[15]The contract was given in terms of wealth levels as $(4120.36, 9980.26)$, from which we obtain the premium as $10,000 - 9,980.26 = 19.74$ and the deductible as $9,980.26 - 4,120.36 = 5,859.9$.

Solution to Exercise 7.8

(a) Contract C_H is the full-insurance contract that yields zero profits if bought only by the H-types. Thus its premium is given by the solution to $h_H - p_H \ell = 0$, that is, $h_H = \frac{2}{10}(7,000) = \$1,400$. Contract C_L is given by the intersection of the H-type indifference curve through C_H and the low-risk zero-profit line; thus it is given by the solution to

$$\sqrt{16,000 - 1,400} = \frac{2}{10}\sqrt{16,000 - h - d} + \frac{8}{10}\sqrt{16,000 - h}$$

$$h - \frac{1}{10}(7,000 - d) = 0$$

which is $C_L = (h_L = 109.32, d_L = 5906.81)$.

(b) The average probability of loss is

$$\bar{p} = q_H p_H + (1 - q_H) p_L = \frac{1}{6}\left(\frac{2}{10}\right) + \frac{5}{6}\left(\frac{1}{10}\right) = \frac{7}{60}.$$

(c) We need to express the fact that there is a contract at which the average zero-profit line intersects the L-type indifference curve through contract $C_L = (h_L = 109.32, d_L = 5906.81)$:

$$h - \frac{7}{60}(7,000 - d) = 0$$

$$\frac{1}{10}\sqrt{16,000 - 109.32 - 5,906.81} + \frac{9}{10}\sqrt{16,000 - 109.32}$$

$$= \frac{1}{10}\sqrt{16,000 - h - d} + \frac{9}{10}\sqrt{16,000 - h}.$$

$\square$

Solution to Exercise 7.9

(a) Contract C_H is the full-insurance contract that yields zero profits if bought only by the H-types. Thus its premium is given by the solution to $h_H - p_H \ell = 0$, that is, $h_H = \frac{1}{4}(6,000) = \$1,500$. Contract C_L is given by the intersection of the H-type indifference curve through C_H and the low-risk zero-profit line; thus it is given by the solution to

$$\ln(10,000 - 1,500) = \frac{1}{4}\ln(10,000 - h - d) + \frac{3}{4}\ln(10,000 - h)$$

$$h - \frac{1}{16}(6,000 - d) = 0$$

which is $C_L = (h_L = 90.98, d_L = 4544.31)$.

(b) The average probability of loss is

$$\bar{p} = q_H p_H + (1 - q_H) p_L = \frac{3}{16}\left(\frac{1}{4}\right) + \frac{13}{16}\left(\frac{1}{16}\right) = \frac{25}{256}.$$

(c) We need to express the fact that there is a contract at which the average zero-profit line intersects the L-type indifference curve through contract $C_L = (h_L = 90.98, d_L = 4544.31)$:

$$h - \frac{25}{256}(6,000 - d) = 0$$

$$\frac{1}{16}\ln(10,000 - 90.98 - 4,544.31) + \frac{15}{16}\ln(10,000 - 90.98)$$

$$= \frac{1}{16}\ln(10,000 - h - d) + \frac{15}{16}\ln(10,000 - h).$$

□

Index

Index